BOOKS THAT
CHANGED
THE WORLD

BOOKS THAT
CHANGED
THE WORLD

ROBERT B. DOWNS

AMERICAN LIBRARY ASSOCIATION
CHICAGO, 1956

ACKNOWLEDGMENTS

The author wishes to thank the following publishers and authorized representatives for their kind permission to reprint from the books and periodicals indicated below:

BRITISH PERIODICALS LIMITED: An article by Julian Huxley in *Contemporary Review*.

THE CLARENDON PRESS: *The Prince* by Niccolò Machiavelli, translated by Vivian Hill Thomson.

GOODSELL OBSERVATORY, CARLETON COLLEGE: "Copernicus, the Founder of Modern Astronomy" by Curvin H. Ginrich and "Copernicus and Science" by Harlan T. Stetson in *Popular Astronomy*.

HARCOURT, BRACE AND COMPANY, INC. (New York) and VICTOR GOLLANCZ LTD. (London): *War Without Violence* by Krishnalal Shridharani.

HOUGHTON MIFFLIN COMPANY (New York) and HURST AND BLACKETT LTD. (London): *Mein Kampf* by Adolf Hitler, translated by Ralph Manheim.

THE KOSCIUSZKO FOUNDATION: *Nicholas Copernicus, 1543-1943* and *Nicholas Copernicus: A Tribute of Nations*, edited by S. P. Mizwa.

LITTLE, BROWN & COMPANY: *The Influence of Sea Power Upon History* by Alfred T. Mahan.

THE MACMILLAN COMPANY (New York) and ERNEST BENN LTD. (London): Works by Sigmund Freud, translated by A. A. Brill.

ROYAL GEOGRAPHICAL SOCIETY: "The Geographical Pivot of History" by Sir Halford J. Mackinder in *Geographical Journal*.

THE SATURDAY REVIEW: An article by Paul Oehser.

THE SCIENTIFIC AMERICAN: "The Influence of Albert Einstein" by Banesh Hoffman.

WILLIAM SLOAN ASSOCIATES, INC. *The Universe and Dr. Einstein* by Lincoln Barnett, Copyright, 1948, by Harper & Brothers, Copyright, 1948, by Lincoln Barnett.

THE STACKPOLE COMPANY: A selection by Ludwig Lore.

CHARLES C. THOMAS, Publisher, and DR. CHAUNCEY D. LEAKE: *Anatomical Studies on the Motion of the Heart and Blood* by William Harvey, translated by Dr. Leake.

UNIVERSITY OF CALIFORNIA PRESS: *Mathematical Principles* by Isaac Newton, translated by Andrew Motte and revised by Florian Cajori.

UNIVERSITY OF GLASGOW: *The Origins of the General Theory of Relativity* by Albert Einstein.

Contents

Introduction

A popular delusion widely prevalent holds that books are inanimate, ineffective, peaceful objects, belonging to the cloistered shades and academic quiet of monasteries, universities, and other retreats from a materialistic, evil world. According to this curious misconception, books are full of impractical theory, and of slight significance for the hardheaded man of affairs.

A more realistic understanding is given to the jungle savage, as he bows down before the printed page, with its apparently supernatural power to convey messages. Throughout history, the evidence is piled high that books, rather than being futile, harmless, and innocent, are frequently dynamic, vital things, capable of changing the entire direction of events—sometimes for good, sometimes for ill.

In the dictators of every era is found a shrewd insight into the potentialities of books. Whenever and wherever tryants and authoritarian regimes have wanted to suppress opposition and to kill ideas, their first thought, almost invariably, has been to destroy books of contrary view, and oftentimes their authors. Conversely, they have cunningly turned to their own advantage, to bolster their grip on the people, certain other books, e g , Hitler's *Mein Kampf*, Karl Marx's *Das Kapital*, and the voluminous writings of Lenin and Stalin. No one realizes better than the despot the enormous explosive forces pent up in books.

Occasionally the same point is forcefully brought home to democratic nations. An instance is the widespread sense of shock and incredulity among the American people and their friends abroad a few years ago at the news that the U.S. State Department, in its information libraries abroad, was engaged in a widespread program of book censorship and—in several localities—actual book-burnings. So violent was the reaction that President Eisenhower himself took a hand, trying to clear the name of the American government, by delivering his famous "Don't Join the Book Burners" speech. Instinctively, people everywhere perceived that books are as basic to modern culture and civilization as they have been in past centuries.

The purpose of the present work is to demonstrate, through consideration of certain specific examples, the immense power wielded by books. At the outset, it should be stressed that

7

there is no intention of offering a list of "best books," or "great books." The making of such lists is a favorite pastime of literary critics, authors, editors, educators, and librarians, whose recommendations run predominantly to belles-lettres. Instead, the aim here is to discover those books which have exerted the most profound influence on history, economics, culture, civilization, and scientific thought, from, roughly, the Renaissance down to the mid-twentieth century.

The critical problem in such a project is, of course, selection. A handful of titles comes automatically to mind. After these, individual choices vary widely. A majority are eliminated by application of the number one criterion: the book must have had a great and continuing impact on human thought and action, not for a single nation, but for a major segment of the world. When exposed to this acid test, one suggested title after another dropped out.

For practical reasons, it was arbitrarily decided to restrict the discussion to books in science and the social sciences, omitting such vastly important fields as religion, philosophy, and literature. It may well be that the total impression of religious and literary masterpieces far exceeds that of books in all other categories combined. Yet, how can one determine the intangible influence of, say, the King James version of the Bible? Application of any objective, noncontroversial standards to that stupendous work, or to the writings of Shakespeare and Milton, offers almost insuperable obstacles. Their stamp on society has been so all-pervasive—on language, literature, philosophy, modes of thought, ethics, and every other facet of life—as to be virtually immeasurable.

Assuming, though, that religion and philosophy, ancient and modern, were to be included, a mighty company would enter: The Bible (King James and Douay versions), the *Talmud,* the *Koran,* the sacred Buddhist and Hindu writings, Confucius, the Greek philosophers, St. Augustine, St. Thomas Aquinas, Martin Luther, Immanuel Kant, and a host of others. Viewed in the light of influence, two works of American vintage, Mary Baker Eddy's *Science and Health,* and Joseph Smith's *Book of Mormon,* would also have to be accorded consideration.

Even more difficult, perhaps, would be the choice of the greatest literary monuments—fiction, drama, poetry, essays—that have moved and inspired the world. Such names come readily to mind as the Greek and Roman classical writers, Dante, Chaucer, Rabelais, Cervantes, Molière, Shakespeare, Milton, Goethe, Heine, Dostoevsky, and scores of others possibly lower in stature.

More measurable in their effect are the celebrated travel narratives, which since the time of Marco Polo have broadened man's horizon and expanded his world. The incomparable traveler of the Middle Ages, Marco Polo, in the thirteenth century opened up to Europe the practically unknown Orient, and left a fascinating account of his adventures and discoveries. Christopher Columbus' "Letter" of 1493, reporting his first voyage to America, was promptly reprinted in various languages and countries of Europe, naturally creating tremendous excitement and interest. There followed shortly the more questionable letters of Amerigo Vespucci, printed in 1507 by Martin Waldseemüller in his *Cosmographiae Introductio,* a work which led to the New World being called America. The ensuing century, the most notable era of exploration and discovery in recorded history, saw a flood of printed travel literature, much of which was collected by Richard Hakluyt, late in the sixteenth century, for his *Principall Navigations, Voiages, Traffiques and Discoveries of the English Nation,* and Samuel Purchas' *Pilgrimes.*

In the realm of travel, too, one should not overlook such a purely fictional book as Jules Verne's *Around the World in Eighty Days* (1872), which stirred imaginations in a way that perhaps no nonfictional work could have done. More recently, Wendell Willkie's *One World* (1943) contributed immensely toward giving his fellow-countrymen an international outlook, and doubtless played a part in the idea of an organization of the United Nations.

It is of interest to note and to compare previous attempts to name the books of greatest influence. One such list was prepared for the *Publishers' Weekly* by Edward Weeks, John Dewey, and Charles A. Beard, in 1935. Each selected the twenty-five books issued since 1885 which, in his opinion, had been most influential. The poll resulted in a final list of fifty titles, only four of which (Marx's *Das Kapital,* Bellamy's *Looking Backward,* Frazer's *Golden Bough,* and Spengler's *Decline of the West*) were unanimous choices, while twenty-nine titles received but a single vote. Of the books discussed in the present work, for the period covered by them, only Mackinder is altogether omitted by Weeks, Dewey, and Beard, though Hitler received no vote except Beard's, and on Marx's name alone was there unanimity. In the perspective of twenty years, the distinguished jury would doubtless make drastic changes, if it were able to revise its ratings today.

A similar approach was used by Malcolm Cowley and Bernard Smith a few years later (1939) in their *Books That Changed Our Minds.* On the basis of a poll of American educators, historians, critics, lecturers, and publicists, a dozen titles came to the top as having had most weight, in the judgment of this group, in shaping the contemporary American mind; but a total of 134 different books were recommended by the various individuals consulted. The final selections were:

Freud, *The Interpretation of Dreams*
Adams, *The Education of Henry Adams*
Turner, *The Frontier in American History*
Sumner, *Folkways*
Veblen, *Business Enterprise*
Dewey, *Studies in Logical Theory*
Boas, *The Mind of Primitive Man*
Beard, *Ecônomic Interpretation of the Constitution*
Richards, *The Principles of Literary Criticism*
Parrington, *Main Currents in American Thought*
Lenin, *The State and Revolution*
Spengler, *The Decline of the West*

Of these twelve works, Weeks, Dewey, and Beard had seen fit to include only Freud, Adams, Turner, and Spengler.

Still another essay toward determining the most influential books was made by an English writer, Horace Shipp, in his little volume, *Books That Moved the World* (1945). Without any restrictions as to time, or place, or subjects, Shipp settled upon ten titles:

The Bible
Plato, *The Republic*
St. Augustine, *The City of God*
The Koran
Dante, *The Divine Comedy*
Shakespeare, *Plays*
Bunyan, *The Pilgrim's Progress*
Milton, *Areopagitica*
Darwin, *The Origin of Species*
Marx, *Das Kapital*

The limitations imposed on the present study would eliminate all except the last three of the ten. Actually, only the final two are included.

From the foregoing illustrations, it is clear that a unanimous verdict is exceedingly difficult to achieve on any given book. Selection, inevitably, is highly personal and subjective. Complete agreement is improbable on a majority of the chosen titles, though it is hoped that a strong case has been made for every one of the sixteen authors and their books. It may be of interest to mention some of the works that received careful consideration, and then, for one reason or another, were rejected.

For example, among classics in science Andreas Vesalius' *De Corporis Humani Fabrica* (1543) may deserve a place in the history of medicine on a par with Harvey's *De Motu Cordis*, and Leibniz's writings in mathematics and physics rank with Newton's *Principia Mathematica*. In the social sciences, Frederick Jackson Turner's *The Frontier in American History*, while a brilliant pioneer work, is of less world-wide significance in its field than Mackinder's *The Geographic Pivot of History*. Marx and Engels' *The Communist Manifesto* has been a dynamic force for social change for more than a century, but is a less mature, less carefully documented, and probably in the long run less influential work than Marx's *Das Kapital*. Some critics would prefer Thoreau's *Walden* to his *Civil Disobedience;* the former, however, is more imponderable in its influence. Among other "also-rans" were Parson Mason Locke Weems' *Life of Washington* (1800), which for six generations has helped to direct American thought and tradition (notably in the case of Abraham Lincoln); Richard Henry Dana's *Two Years Before the Mast* (1840), an epic that did much to improve conditions at sea for American sailors; and Upton Sinclair's *The Jungle* (1906), exposing deplorable conditions in the Chicago stockyards and leading to drastic reforms. All the latter three were judged to be too limited in scope and breadth of influence to justify inclusion.

Facetiously perhaps, though the suggestions are certainly not without merit, recommendations were received for bringing in Fannie Farmer's *Boston Cooking School Cook Book,* Emily Post's *Etiquette,* and Dr. Alfred Kinsey's *Sexual Behavior in the Human Male and Female.*

Of the sixteen works in the final list, six classify in the sciences, dating from 1543 to 1915, and ten in the social sciences, broadly speaking, from 1523 to 1927. Such a classification is doubtless without meaning, however, for the social impact of the scientific volumes has been fully as profound as those defined in the social sciences proper. Mrs. Stowe's *Uncle Tom's Cabin,* despite its fictional form, qualifies in every way as a sociological document.

As one reviews these sixteen dynamite-laden books, there is always a question present: Did the times make the book, or vice versa, i.e. was a particular book influential chiefly because the period was ripe for it? Would the book have been equally significant in another era, or could it even have been written at any other date? It is impossible to escape the conclusion that the times produced the book in nearly every instance. In some other historical epoch, the work would either not have been produced at all, or if it had appeared would have attracted little attention.

Examples are on every hand. Machiavelli's *The Prince* was written for the express purpose of freeing his beloved Italy from foreign aggression. England was ready for a vast expansion of her commercial and industrial economy when Adam Smith was writing his *Wealth of Nations*. Thomas Paine's *Common Sense* triggered the American Revolution, already primed for explosion; and Harriet Beecher Stowe's *Uncle Tom's Cabin* did likewise for the Civil War. Except for dreadful conditions prevailing in European industry, especially the English factory system, in the mid-nineteenth century, Karl Marx would have lacked ammunition for *Das Kapital.* Inauguration of a naval race among world powers after 1890 was inspired by Admiral Mahan's *Influence of Sea Power Upon History,* but the pressure for expansion and imperialistic adventure already existed. Adolf Hitler might well have remained an unknown Austrian house painter except for the chaos in Germany following World War I.

On the other hand, like slow fuses, there are books which did not make their full impact until years after their initial publication. Adam Smith and Karl Marx, to illustrate, were dead when the importance of their books was perceived. Thoreau had been gone half a century when his doctrine of civil disobedience was applied by Mahatma Gandhi in India and South Africa. Not until the rise of the German school of geopoliticians under Haushofer's direction did Mackinder's theories, formulated several decades earlier, receive the notice they deserved. These are among the names of pioneering thinkers who knew the disappointment of having their first editions go begging.

Also a recurring question in the back of one's mind, while pondering the select roll, is this: how can influence be measured? As has been said, in each case the aim has been to choose books whose effects can be judged in terms of concrete results or actions. That is, they must have demonstrated a direct connection with certain courses of events. Frequently, a book has attempted to find a solution to problems in a limited field at some particular period. Dealing as they do, therefore, with timely and topical matters, such books inevitably tend to date more rapidly than the great works of religion, philosophy, or literature.

A well-nigh infallible index to the extent of influence is the strength of contemporary sentiment, pro and con. If a book stirs up violent opposition and equally partisan feeling in support of its point of view, the probabilities are that it has deeply affected the thinking of the people. Official censorship and other efforts at suppression also are indicative of its reception. Insight into these attitudes is provided by such sources as contemporary newspapers, controversial pamphlet literature, accounts of historians, and biographical studies. The crucial test is whether or not the theories, programs, or ideas advocated eventually win acceptance, cross international borders, are translated into other languages, cause disciples, imitators, and rivals to rise, and are gradually incorporated into the lives and thoughts of peoples and nations.

A curious manifestation of fame is the creation of adjectives and nouns drawn from an individual to describe a particular concept or pattern of thought. Thus there have been added to everyday vocabulary such terms as Machiavellian, Copernican, Malthusian, Newtonian, Freudian, Darwinism, Marxism, and Hitlerism, each connoting a definite set of ideas, and attesting to the fame or infamy—depending upon the point of view—of its prototype.

In view of the extreme difficulty as to readability of perhaps a majority of titles on the select list, this question may reasonably be asked: How could these works exert influence on any except a narrow band of specialists? Certainly few laymen could comprehend and follow with ease the original Latin texts of Copernicus, Harvey, and Newton, or Einstein's theories in any language. Only the trained social scientist will be able to appreciate fully the often tortuous reasoning of an Adam Smith, a Malthus, or a Marx, while a biological background enriches the understanding of a Harvey, Darwin, or Freud. The answer to the question is that the mass of people obtain ideas second-hand, predigested, by way of a filtering-down process, through such media as popularizations in book form, magazines and newspapers, classroom lessons, public lectures, and, more recently, radio, television, and motion pictures. Except for *Common Sense, Uncle Tom's Cabin,* and *Mein Kampf,* none of the sixteen select titles was a best seller in it own time. Their influence, accordingly, has resulted from interpretation by experts. Oftentimes, applications to daily living are made without the conscious knowledge of people generally, as, for example, the mechanistic discoveries of Newton, or Einstein's theories in relation to nuclear fission and atomic energy.

As one reviews the sixteen books chronologically one is struck by the continuity of knowledge—the connecting threads which tie them together. Truly, as Hutchins phrased it, there is in progress here "The Great Conversation." Copernicus received inspiration from the ancient Greek philosophers. Newton, in turn, "stood on the shoulders of giants"— Copernicus, Galileo, Kepler, and others. Without them, an Einstein might never have existed. Darwin freely acknowledged his debt to a host of preceding biologists, geographers, and geologists, on whose work he built in developing the theory of the origin of species. The experimental laboratory approach to science, as opposed to the strictly philosophical, may be said to have begun with Copernicus and to have been practiced by all his great successors, including Harvey, Newton, Darwin, and Freud.

The passion for freedom, conceivably an age-old obsession with man, is exemplified by the stirring pleas of Machiavelli, Adam Smith, Paine, Thoreau, and Stowe. Karl Marx drew heavily on classical English economists, especially Adam Smith, Malthus, and Ricardo, and tried to pattern his work on Darwin's. Mahan's *Influence of Sea Power Upon History* was essentially a secondary work, utilizing as sources the writings of earlier naval, military, and general historians.

While not accepting some of Mahan's conclusions, Mackinder and later geopoliticians found his ideas provocative and stimulating. Consciously or unconsciously, Hitler's *Mein Kampf* derived much from Machiavelli, Darwin, Marx, Mahan, Mackinder, and Freud.

Certain additional comments might be made on the present selection of books and authors. Has the natural tendency, for example, to emphasize one's own country or language been avoided? Probably not. The list includes four Americans— Paine, Thoreau, Stowe, and Mahan—and six British representatives—Harvey, Newton, Smith, Malthus, Darwin, and Mackinder. There are also three Germans (Marx, Einstein, Hitler), an Italian (Machiavelli), a Pole (Copernicus), and an Austrian (Freud). Of the six continental Europeans, three are Jews. If a Chinese, a Frenchman, or a Russian were making the list, no doubt there would be biases in other directions.

Another point open to criticism is the definition of a book. What is a book? Should it be judged by size alone? The thought is preposterous. Nevertheless, strictly defined, Paine's *Common Sense*, Thoreau's *Civil Disobedience*, Mackinder's *Geographic Pivot of History*, and the original statement of Einstein's *Special Theory of Relativity* are no more than pamphlets. The last three, in fact, first appeared as periodical articles. What a contrast these offer to heavy tomes like the *Principia Mathematica, The Wealth of Nations*, later editions of Malthus on population, *Das Kapital*, and *Mein Kampf*. Voltaire is quoted as having said that the big books are never the ones to set a nation on fire; "it is always the little books, packed with emotions, aflame with passion, that do the business"—a quotation that would apply to Paine and Thoreau, but not Mackinder and Einstein. Actually, for the present list, size is virtually without significance.

A related consideration is the length of time spent in writing. The record, apparently, was established by Copernicus, whose *De Revolutionibus* was more than thirty years in the making, though the author was certainly not continuously engaged in its production. Who would be willing to say that the Copernican treatise is a more profound work than Newton's *Principia Mathematica*, which was completed in an eighteen-month period? By a curious coincidence, Adam Smith's *Wealth of Nations*, Darwin's *Origin of Species*, and Marx's *Das Kapital* were each seventeen years in the writing. At the other end of the scale, Machiavelli's *The Prince* was turned out in six months, and Paine's *Common Sense* in perhaps three or four months.

The wide variations in writing periods may be attributed to several factors. Individual personalities account for some of the differences. Scientists like Copernicus, Newton, Harvey, and Darwin refused to rush into print until their findings had been thoroughly verified and subjected to stringent tests. Even after the most careful checking, they hesitated to publish, because of fear of controversy, potential censorship, their desire for absolute perfection, possible criticism by fellow-scientists, dislike of publicity, or like reasons. The economic treatises of Smith and Marx involved the time-consuming assembling of an enormous mass of data and extensive revisions. On the other hand, such impetuous fellows as Machiavelli, young Malthus, Paine, and Thoreau had urgent messages to deliver without delay.

A majority of the sixteen selected authors are known principally for a single book. With few exceptions, the fame of each rests upon one title and all else is forgotten. Harvey, Newton, Smith, Malthus, Marx, Stowe, Mahan, and Einstein wrote further books—in some cases were prolific authors—but who save a few specialists could name them? Paine, Thoreau, Darwin, and Freud are exceptions to the rule, for their fertile pens produced other books that are in some ways as celebrated as those here listed.

A few biographical notes may reveal other aspects of the authors' characters and personalities. Does marital status, for example, have an important bearing on the creation of a masterpiece? Copernicus was a monk. Also unmarried were

Newton, Smith, Thoreau, and Hitler. Harvey, Mahan, Mackinder, and Paine were married but childless, and Paine's two marriages turned out disastrously. Malthus had three children and Einstein had two; Malthus was married once and Einstein twice. Several others—Machiavelli, Darwin, Stowe, Marx, and Freud—were not only devoted spouses but producers of large families. Again, one would hesitate to draw any inferences from these facts.

It might be supposed that age and maturity would be essential to the author of a great book. What import did they actually have for the select sixteen? When their first editions came from the presses, the oldest of the lot, Copernicus, was 70, and the most youthful, Einstein, was about 26. Malthus and Thoreau were in their early thirties, and Paine and Hitler in their late thirties. The ten-year period from age 44 to 54 was most fruitful of all, for coming within that range were, from youngest to oldest, Machiavelli, Freud, Newton, Marx, Mahan, Darwin, Harvey, and Smith. Stowe and Mackinder were in their early forties.

By way of summary, certain characteristics shared by a majority of the authors stand out. Omitting the scientists in the group, for whom the comments are less pertinent, the books included were written by nonconformists, radicals, fanatics, revolutionists, and agitators. Often, they are badly written books, lacking in literary style. The secret of their success, to repeat, was that the times were ready for them. The books carried messages, frequently of a highly emotional nature, appealing to millions of people. Sometimes the influence was beneficent and sometimes evil; clearly, books can be forces for both good and bad. The intention here, in any case, is not to measure moral values, but instead to demonstrate that books are dynamic and powerful instruments, tools, or weapons.

The World of Man

1 | ANATOMY OF POWER POLITICS

NICCOLÒ MACHIAVELLI: *The Prince*

For over four centuries, "Machiavellian" has been synonomous in the world's mind with something diabolical, treacherous, villainous, cruel, and vicious. The term's progenitor, Niccolò Machiavelli, is a popular symbol for the scheming, crafty, hypocritical, immoral, completely unprincipled, and unscrupulous politician whose whole philosophy is that the end justifies the means. The highest law to Machiavelli, it is universally believed, was political expediency. In seventeenth-century England, "Old Nick" was an interchangeable epithet for Machiavelli and Satan. Is there any defense for the accused, or were there any extenuating circumstances?

Machiavelli's sinister reputation rests almost entirely upon a single book, *The Prince*, written in 1513, but unpublished until 1532, five years after the author's death. No book can be dissociated from the period in which it was created, a fact that has never been more aptly illustrated than by *The Prince*. And yet, like every great book, it contains lessons for all times.

Little is known of Machiavelli's life prior to 1498, when, at the age of twenty-nine, he became secretary of the Florentine republic. For eighteen years he served the city-state. Diplomatic missions took him to Tuscany, then across the Apennines to Rome, and later beyond the Alps. He became acquainted with Countess Caterina Sforza; Pandolfo Petrucci, tyrant of Siena; Ferdinand of Aragon, Louis XII of France, the Emperor Maximilian, Pope Alexander VI, Pope Julius II, and Cesare Borgia. Diplomatic conflict between Florence and the other city-states of Venice, Pisa, Milan, and Naples was unceasing. The politics of the era were unbelievably corrupt. Machiavelli, a shrewd student of human nature, was in his

17

element, and on numerous occasions displayed ability and skill in carrying on difficult negotiations. His later realism or cynicism toward political affairs was doubtless based upon experience, for he learned to discount all motives except greed and selfishness.

A turn in the wheel of fortune came for Machiavelli. With Spain's assistance, the Medicis overthrew the republic and restored their rule in Florence. Machiavelli was discharged, imprisoned, tortured, and finally banished to his small country estate near San Casciano. There, except for brief periods, he remained in retirement until his death in 1527. His principal pastime during those, to him, long dull years was writing: *The Prince, The Discourses, The Art of War*, and the *History of Florence*—all primarily concerned with politics, ancient and contemporary.

Any sentiment in Machiavelli's nature in relation to public affairs is hard to detect, but on one matter he felt deeply. He was a genuine patriot with an ardent longing for a strong, united Italy. He might be a cold, skeptical observer, a cynical man of pure intellect, until he discussed Italian unity, and then he became inspired with passion, eloquence, warmth, and life. Italy's condition in the early sixteenth century was sad enough to make any patriot weep.

A tremendous political, economic, and theological upheaval was under way in Machiavelli's Italy. Elsewhere, in England, France, and Spain, after lengthy struggles, national unification had been substantially achieved. In Italy, on the other hand, the conception of a national or federal organization was unknown. There were five major political units governing the country: Milan, Florence, Venice, the Church State, and Naples. Largest and strongest was Venice. The numerous political divisions were a constant source of weakness for Italy, and practically invited foreign intrigue and intervention. Invasions had started with Charles VIII of France in 1494. Within a few years after his retreat, Louis XII and Ferdinand of Aragon agreed to divide the Kingdom of Naples between them. The Emperor Maximilian sent his troops in to conquer Venice. Armies from Germany, Switzerland, France, and Spain were marching and fighting on Italian soil.

Meanwhile, among the Italians themselves, private quarrels, public feuds, robbery, and murder were rife. Republic warred with republic, each jealous of the other's power, and completely unable to form a common front against foreign foes. The Church, at the most degraded period of its history, and dreading the rise of a rival to its temporal power, preferred disunion to union for Italy.

Machiavelli recognized, perhaps more clearly than any man of his time, the dangers threatening Italy. Meditating, in his forced retirement, upon the evils which had befallen his beloved country, he became convinced that the only hope of salvation lay in the rise of a great leader—a leader strong and ruthless enough to force his authority on the petty Italian states, merging them into a single nation capable of defending itself and of driving the hated foreigners from the land. Where to find such a ruler? *The Prince* was Machiavelli's conception of the kind of leader required, and a detailed blueprint of the path he must follow to gain success.

Though *The Prince* is dedicated to Lorenzo de' Medici, new ruler of Florence, the hero of the book is Cesare Borgia, son of Pope Alexander VI, a cardinal at seventeen, able military leader, conqueror of Romagna, and a cruel, pitiless dictator. In 1502, Machiavelli had been sent as an envoy to his court, and, as Nevins commented, "saw with admiration how skillfully Borgia alternated the use of caution and audacity, of kindly words and bloody deeds; how coolly he employed perfidy and hypocrisy; how savagely he used terrorism to hold those whom he conquered in subjection; and how tyrannically effective was his grip on a captured state." By his use of duplicity, cruelty, and bad faith, Cesare attained brilliant, but temporary, success. Machiavelli was a firm partisan of a republican form of government, but when he examined the desperate and deplorable condition of Italy, he was persuaded that a Cesare Borgia would be an ideal leader to end the state of chaos.

And so, with patriotic fervor inspired by his vision of a united nation, aware of the critical needs of the hour, and conscious of the golden opportunity open to the new ruler, Machiavelli turned all his pent-up energy and enthusiasm to the composition of *The Prince*. The work was written in the last six months of 1513, and sometime thereafter delivered to Lorenzo's court, with the author's dedicatory statement, "seeing that it is not possible to make a better gift than to offer the opportunity of understanding in the shortest time all that I have learnt in so many years, and with so many troubles and dangers."

The essential argument of *The Prince* is that the welfare of the state justifies everything and there are different standards of morals in public life and private life. It is proper, according to this doctrine, for a statesman to commit in the public interest acts of violence and deceit that would be thoroughly reprehensible and even criminal in private transactions. In effect, Machiavelli separated ethics from politics.

The Prince is a guidebook for princes (or, as some have said, a manual for tyrants) to instruct them in how to gain and to hold power—power not for the ruler's sake, however, but for the good of the people, in order to provide them with a stable government, secure against revolution or invasion. By what means are stability and security to be won?

Hereditary monarchies are dismissed briefly, for, assuming that the ruler has ordinary acumen and intelligence, he will be able to maintain his control of the government. On the other hand, the problems of a new monarchy are far more complex. If recently conquered territories are of the same nationality and language as the state to which they are annexed, control is relatively easy, especially if two principles are followed: "the one, that the blood of the ancient line of princes be destroyed; second, that no change be made in respect of laws or taxes.

"But when states are acquired in a country differing in language, usages, and laws, difficulties multiply, and great good fortune, as well as address, is needed to overcome them." Possible means for their control, Machiavelli goes on to suggest, are for the ruler to go and reside in the area personally, to send colonies (cheaper than maintaining occupying armies), to make friends of feebler neighbors and to endeavor to weaken stronger ones. By disregarding these basic rules, Louis XII of France had suffered defeat and loss of his conquests.

In a consideration of "How Provinces Are To Be Governed," Machiavelli offers three methods by which a state accustomed "to live under its own laws and in freedom . . . may be held. The first is to destroy it; the second, to go and reside there in person; the third, to suffer it to live on under its own laws, subjecting it to tribute, and entrusting its government to a few of the inhabitants who will keep the rest your friends." Of the several choices, either of the first two is recommended as safest.

If, however, the newly acquired city or province has been accustomed to live under a prince, and his line is extinguished, it will be impossible for the citizens, used on the one hand, to obey, and deprived, on the other, of their old ruler, to agree to choose a leader from among themselves; and as they know not how to live as freemen, and are therefore slow to take up arms, a stranger may readily gain them over and attach them to his cause.

In further discussion "Of New Princedoms," Machiavelli warned "it should be kept in mind that the temper of the mul-

titude is fickle, and that while it is easy to persuade them of
a thing, it is hard to fix them in that persuasion. Wherefore,
matters should be so ordered that when men no longer believe
of their own accord, they may be compelled to believe by
force."

The author then proceeds to extol and glorify the career
of Cesare Borgia, as the strong leader par excellence, apologiz-
ing for treason and assassination.

> When all the actions of the duke are recalled, I do not
> know how to blame him, but rather it appears to me . . .
> that I ought to offer him for imitation to all those who,
> by the fortune or the aims of others, are raised to govern-
> ment. Because he, having a lofty spirit and far-reaching
> aims, could not have regulated his conduct otherwise. . . .
> Therefore, he who considers it necessary to secure himself
> in his new principality, to win friends, to overcome either
> by force or fraud, to make himself beloved and feared
> by the people, to be followed and revered by the soldiers,
> to exterminate those who had power or reason to hurt
> him, to change the old order of things for new, to be
> severe and gracious, magnanimous and liberal, to destroy
> a disloyal soldiery, and to create new, to maintain friend-
> ship with kings and princes in such a way that they must
> help him with zeal and offend with caution, cannot find
> a more lively example than the actions of this man.

A usurper who has seized a state "should make haste to
inflict what injuries he must, at a stroke, that he may not
have to renew them daily, but be enabled by their discon-
tinuance to reassure men's minds, and afterwards win them
over by benefits. . . . Benefits should be conferred little by
little, so that they may be more fully enjoyed."

Fear of punishment is but one of the means to be used by
a wise sovereign in controlling his subjects:

> It is essential for a prince to be on a friendly footing
> with his people, since, otherwise, he will have no resource
> in adversity. . . . Let no one quote against me the old
> proverb, "He who builds on the people builds on sand,"
> for that may be true of a private citizen who presumes
> on his favor with the people, and counts on being rescued
> by them when overpowered by his enemies or by the mag-
> istrates. But a prince who is a man of courage and is
> able to command, who knows how to preserve order in
> his state, need never regret having founded his security
> on the affection of the people.

For treating of ecclesiastical princedoms, that is those under direct Church government, Machiavelli reserved some of his most scathing and satirical remarks.

They are acquired by merit or good fortune, but are maintained without either; being upheld by the venerable ordinances of religion, which are all of such a nature and efficacy that they secure the authority of their princes in whatever way they may act or live. These princes alone have territories which they do not defend, and subjects whom they do not govern.

Here and elsewhere in his writings, Machiavelli's bitter charge against the Roman Church at the beginning of the sixteenth century was that it had not united Italy against the foreigner. His plea was for strict separation of church and state.

Because a strong government requires a good army, Machiavelli considered military affairs of the highest importance, and devoted considerable space to the subject. Most of the Italian states of his time were accustomed to employ hired mercenaries, largely foreigners, to defend them. Such troops, argued Machiavelli, are "useless and dangerous," and a national army composed of citizens would be far more effective and reliable. Inasmuch as national survival may depend on armed might, a ruling prince should regard military matters as his principal study and occupation.

Several chapters are devoted by Machiavelli to the conduct of princes—their proper behavior under various conditions.

There is the greatest difference between the way in which men live and that in which they ought to live. . . . It is essential for a prince who desires to maintain his position, to have learned how to be other than good, and to use or not to use his goodness as necessity requires. . . . Everyone, I know, will admit that it would be laudable for a prince to be endowed with all of the qualities that are reckoned good; but since it is impossible for him to possess or constantly practice them all . . . he must be discreet enough to know how to avoid the infamy of those vices that would deprive him of his government.

A prince should be unconcerned about gaining a reputation for miserliness, as he "spends either what belongs to himself and his subjects, or what belongs to others. . . . Of what does not belong to you or to your subjects you should be a lavish giver . . . for to be liberal with the property of others [acquired by military conquest] does not take from your reputation but adds to it. What injures you is to give away what is your own. And there is no quality so self-destructive as liberality; for while you practice it you lose the means whereby it can be practiced, and become poor and despised, or else, to avoid poverty, you become rapacious and hated."

Cruelty ought to be regarded by the prince as one of the weapons to keep his subjects united and obedient, "For he who quells disorder by a very few signal examples will in the end be more merciful than he who from too great leniency permits things to take their course and so to result in rapine and bloodshed; for these injure the whole state, whereas the severities of the prince injure individuals."

Machiavelli says in a famous passage:

> From this arises the question whether it is better to be loved rather than feared, or feared rather than loved. It might perhaps be answered that we should wish to be both: but since love and fear can hardly exist together, if we must choose between them, it is far safer to be feared than loved. For of men it may generally be affirmed that they are thankless, fickle, false, studious to avoid danger, greedy of gain, devoted to you while you are able to confer benefits upon them, and ready, while danger is distant, to shed their blood, and sacrifice their property, their lives, and their children for you; but in the hour of need they turn against you.

Here is utter cynicism, though Machiavelli concludes his weighing of love versus fear by advising the prince that "he must do his utmost to escape hatred."

No part of *The Prince* has been more generally denounced and condemned than chapter eighteen on "How Princes Should Keep Faith." The evil connotations of the term "Machiavellian" are traceable more to this section than to all the remainder of the book. Here the author agrees that keeping faith is praiseworthy, but that deceit, hypocrisy, and perjury are necessary and excusable for the sake of maintaining political power.

> There are two ways of contending, one in accordance with the laws, the other by force; the first of which is proper to men, the second to beasts. But since the first method is often ineffectual, it becomes necessary to resort to the second. A prince should, therefore, understand how to use well both the man and the beast. . . . But since a prince should know how to use the beast's nature wisely,

he ought of beasts to choose both the lion and the fox; for the lion cannot protect himself from traps and the fox cannot defend himself from wolves . . . a prudent prince neither can nor ought to keep his word when to keep it is hurtful to him and if the causes which led him to pledge it are removed. If all men were good, this would not be good advice, but since they are dishonest and do not keep faith with you, you, in return, need not keep faith with them; and no prince was ever at a loss for plausible reasons to cloak a breach of faith. . . . But men remain so simple, and governed so absolutely by their present needs, that he who wishes to deceive them will never fail in finding willing dupes. . . . Thus, it is well to seem merciful, faithful, humane, religious, and upright, and also to be so; but the mind should remain so balanced that were it needful not to be so, you should be able and know how to change to the contrary. . . . Everyone sees what you seem, but few know what you are.

It is essential, counseled Machiavelli, for a prince to avoid being hated or despised. The two principal ways in which he is likely to incur hatred are "by being rapacious and by interfering with the property and with the women of his subjects. . . . A prince is despised when he is seen to be fickle, frivolous, effeminate, pusillanimous, or irresolute." Furthermore, rulers should make themselves popular by distributing all favors in person, "and leave to the magistrates responsibility for inflicting punishment, and, indeed, the general disposal of all things which are likely to arouse discontent." Not even fortresses will save the prince, if the people hate him.

Instructing the prince on "How he should bear himself," Machiavelli urged that—

. . . a prince should show himself a patron of merit, and should honor those who excel in every art. He ought accordingly to encourage his subjects by enabling them to pursue their callings, whether mercantile, agricultural, or any other, in security, so that this man shall not be deterred from beautifying his possessions from the apprehension that they may be taken from him, or that other refrain from opening a trade through fear of taxes.

Reminiscent of ancient Rome, so greatly admired by Machiavelli, is the advice to the prince, "at suitable seasons of the year to entertain the people with festivals and shows."

Machiavelli was a firm believer in fortune or destiny, perhaps a reflection of the attitude in his time toward astrology.

"I think it may be the case," he wrote, "that fortune is the mistress of one half our actions, and yet leaves the control of the other half, or a little less, to ourselves." His point of view was only moderately fatalistic, however, for he was convinced that man could exercise some control over his fate, and "that it is better to be impetuous than cautious. For fortune is a woman who to be kept under must be beaten and roughly handled; and we see that she suffers herself to be more readily mastered by those who so treat her than by those who are more timid in their approaches. And always, like a woman, she favors the young, because they are less scrupulous and fiercer, and command her with greater audacity."

The Prince is concluded with "An Exhortation to Liberate Italy," a ringing appeal to patriotism. The time had arrived for a new prince, "some Italian hero" to come forward, for Italy in "her present abject condition" was "more a slave than the Hebrew, more oppressed than the Persian, more disunited than the Athenian, without a leader, without order, beaten, spoiled, torn in pieces, over-run and abandoned to destruction in every shape. . . . We see how she prays God to send someone to rescue her from these barbarous cruelties and oppressions. We see too how ready and eager she is to follow any standard were there only some one to raise it."

Machiavelli ends his eloquent plea with these words:

> This opportunity then, for Italy at last to look on her deliverer, ought not to be allowed to pass away. With what love he [the new prince] would be received in all those provinces which have suffered from the foreign inundation, with what thirst for vengeance, with what fixed fidelity, with what devotion, and what tears, no words of mine can declare. What gates would be closed against him? What people would refuse him obedience? What jealousy would stand in his way? What Italian but would yield him homage? This barbarous tyranny stinks in every nostril.

Over three and a half centuries were to elapse before Machiavelli's dream of a united Italy, free of foreign occupation and domination, was to be realized.

Manuscript copies of *The Prince* were circulated during the author's lifetime and for several years afterwards. Its publication in 1532 was approved by Pope Clement VII, cousin of the prince to whom it was dedicated. In the next twenty years, there were twenty-five editions. Then a storm began to gather. The Council of Trent ordered the destruction of Machiavelli's works. He was denounced as an atheist in Rome, and his writings were banned there and elsewhere in Europe. The Jesuits burned him in effigy in Germany. Both Catholics and Protestants joined in the clamor against him. In 1559 all of Machiavelli's works were placed on the Index of Prohibited Books.

Not until the nineteenth century did Machiavelli's reputation win some measure of exoneration and vindication. Revolutionary movements in America, France, Germany, and elsewhere, caused an irresistible trend toward secularization of government, toward separation of church and state. The Italian crusade for freedom, which reached a successful climax in 1870, drew inspiration from the great patriot Machiavelli. In a most perceptive essay, H. Douglas Gregory demonstrated that by following the Machiavellian precepts, the Italian leader, Count Cavour, was able to unite Italy and drive out her invaders, while to have followed any other course would have brought disaster and failure.

That dictators and tyrants of every era have found much useful advice in *The Prince* is undeniable. The list of avid readers is impressive: Emperor Charles V and Catherine de Medici admired the work; Oliver Cromwell procured a manuscript copy, and adapted its principles to the Commonwealth government in England; Henry III and Henry IV of France were carrying copies when they were murdered; it helped Frederick the Great to shape Prussian policy; Louis XIV used the book as his "favorite nightcap"; an annotated copy was found in Napoleon Bonaparte's coach at Waterloo; Napoleon III's ideas on government were chiefly derived from it; and Bismarck was a devoted disciple. More recently, Adolf Hitler, according to his own word, kept *The Prince* by his bedside, where it served as a constant source of inspiration; and Benito Mussolini stated, "I believe Machiavelli's *Prince* to be the statesman's supreme guide. His doctrine is alive today because in the course of four hundred years no deep changes have occurred in the minds of men or in the actions of nations." (Later, Mussolini changed his mind, for in 1939, on the list of authors, ancient and modern, placed on the fascist index of books which Roman librarians must not circulate appeared the name of Machiavelli.)

On the other hand, keen analysts of historical events have made it clear that such tyrants as Hitler and Mussolini generally came to bad ends because they disregarded or misinterpreted certain fundamental principles enunciated by Machiavelli.

Students of Machiavelli are agreed that no full understanding of his ideas is possible without reading both his *Discourses* and *The Prince.* The *Discourses,* written over a five-year period, and first published in the same year as *The Prince,* is a considerably larger work. One distinction between them, it has been suggested, is that the *Discourses* deal with "what should be" and *The Prince* with "what is." *The Prince* is concerned entirely with principalities, that is with states ruled by single monarchs. The *Discourses* deal with principles to be followed by republics.

From a comparative reading of the two books, one must come to the startling conclusion that Machiavelli was a convinced republican. He had no liking for despotism, and considered a combination of popular and monarchical government best. No ruler was safe without the favor of his people. The most stable states are those ruled by princes checked by constitutional limitations. The judgment of the people is sound, in Machiavelli's view, as may be noted in his attack on the ancient proverb, "To build on the people is to build on sand." His ideal government was the old Roman republic, and he constantly harked back to it in the *Discourses.*

Why, then, did Machiavelli, valuing above all things a republican government for a free people, produce *The Prince?* The book was written for a specific time and for a specific set of conditions. Machiavelli doubtless realized that it would be impossible to establish a successful republic in sixteenth-century Italy. *The Prince* was written for the sole purpose of enlisting the aid of a strong man to rescue the Italian people from their desperate plight and state of political corruption. Confronted by an acute crisis, Italy could not be too discriminating over the weapons for her salavation.

Widely disparate opinions concerning Machiavelli are still held, despite efforts made to rehabilitate his name. The situation described some years ago by Giuseppe Prezzolini continues to prevail:

> We now have the Jesuits' Machiavelli, an enemy of the Church; the patriots' Machiavelli, the messiah of a unified Italy and the House of Savoy; the militarists' Machiavelli, a precursor of national armies; the philosophers' Machiavelli, who invented a new way of thought—the practical spirit; and the Machiavelli of the writers, who admire his virile style and audacious syntax. And all these Machiavellis are legitimate.

It is hardly disputable that no man previous to Karl Marx has had as revolutionary an impact on political thought as Machiavelli. He has a legitimate claim to the title of "Founder of the Science of Politics."

2 | AMERICAN FIREBRAND

THOMAS PAINE: *Common Sense*

No rational person would have predicted a brilliant future for Thomas Paine when he arrived in America at the age of thirty-seven. His entire career up to that point had been a succession of failures and frustrations. Every enterprise to which he had set his hand had come to a dismal conclusion. What reason was there to suppose that within a period of a few years the recently arrived immigrant to the New World would emerge as one of the greatest pamphleteers in the English language, one of the most controversial figures in American history, a political agitator and revolutionist whose name was known, feared and hated, or applauded and extolled, throughout the British American colonies, Great Britain, and Western Europe? It appeared as though the ocean voyage had affected a startling metamorphosis in his personality and character, changing him almost overnight from mediocrity to genius.

And yet an examination of Paine's earlier years would give evidence that they had not been lost and, in fact, were a kind of preparation for his new life. Born at Thetford, county of Norfolk, in eastern England, on January 29, 1737, son of a Quaker father and an Anglican mother, he had from the beginning experienced extreme poverty, privation, and drudgery. Until he reached thirteen, he attended grammar school, where, in his own words, he acquired "an exceedingly good moral education and a tolerable stock of useful learning." His flair for science and invention—for the practical as opposed to the theoretical—came to the surface even then and remained with him throughout a busy life.

After this brief formal education, Paine was apprenticed to learn his father's trade of corset-maker. Three years of this work, and then the glamor of the sea and boredom with a monotonous job caused him to run away from home to enlist on the privateer *Terrible,* under a captain bearing the formidable name of Death. Rescued by his father, he resumed stay-making until age nineteen, when he again had a brief fling at privateering, on the *King of Prussia.* Now cured of his romantic conception of a sailor's life, he settled down once again to his trade, but in London rather than Thetford, laboring in a staymaker's shop near Drury Lane. His leisure was spent attending lectures on astronomy.

There followed years of troubled and indecisive wandering. At Sandwich, he married an orphan servant girl, who died within a year. Her father had been an exciseman; and drawn to the profession because it promised to give him leisure for other interests, Paine obtained an appointment as an excise officer. No surer way could have been found to lose friends and alienate people, for his job was to catch smugglers, and the hands of rich and poor were against him. Discharged from his post for lack of conscientiousness in enforcing the rules, Paine returned briefly to staymaking, then starved as a teacher on £25 a year at Kensington. Reinstated in the excise service, he remarried in 1771, and joined his wife and her mother at Lewes in operating a tobacco and grocery shop, to supplement his income.

During these latter years, Paine spent much of his time in the White Hart Tavern, in meetings of a social club which he had joined. For the edification of the members, he composed humorous verses and patriotic songs, as well as occasional papers on more serious subjects, and frequently engaged in warm arguments on issues of the day. His proficiency in debate led his fellow-excisemen to select him to act as their spokesman in a plea for higher wages and improved working conditions. Many weeks were subsequently spent by Paine in the preparation of a paper entitled "The Case of the Salary of the Officers of Excise and Thoughts on the Corruption Arising from the Poverty of Excise Officers." In the winter of 1772-73, he went to London to present his appeal to members of Parliament and other officials.

Not only was Paine's petition for the excisemen rejected, but he was discharged for neglect of duties, the tobacco shop went into bankruptcy, Paine's furniture and personal belongings had to be sold to save him from debtor's prison, and he was separated from his wife. Thus, approaching middle age, he was left alone and penniless.

Fortunately, during his London sojourn, Paine had met Benjamin Franklin, sent there as commissioner of the colonies, and Franklin, perhaps perceiving his genius, persuaded Paine to try his luck in America. A letter of introduction from Franklin to his son-in-law, Richard Bache, in Philadelphia, characterized Paine as "an ingenious, worthy young man," and recommended his employment as a clerk, assistant tutor in a school, or assistant surveyor. The Franklin letter was Paine's chief asset when he landed in Philadelphia in early December 1774.

However, Paine brought with him an invaluable asset of another kind—his background of experience. He had observed the primitive brutality with which justice was administered in England, he had known abject poverty, he had heard and read much about man's natural rights, he had seen the vast chasm separating the millions of ordinary folk from the few thousand members of the royalty and nobility in Britain, and he knew of the rotten-borough scheme of choosing the House of Commons, and of the corruption and stupidity of the royal family. Having thought deeply on these matters, Paine was possessed with a profound compassion for humanity, a love of democracy, and an urge for universal social and political reform.

Soon after his arrival in Philadelphia, Paine was employed as editor of the *Pennsylvania Magazine,* a newly established journal, and he continued in that position for most of the eighteen months of its existence. Almost immediately his long career as a crusader began, with publication of an essay condemning Negro slavery and strongly advocating emancipation. Five weeks later, the first American antislavery society was formed in Philadelphia. There followed contributions advocating equal rights for women, proposing international copyright laws, denouncing cruelty to animals, ridiculing the custom of dueling, and asking for the abolition of war for the settlement of disputes between nations.

Even as he wrote, however, an international war, in which Paine himself was to play a major role, was rapidly developing. In the spring of 1775 came the battles of Concord, Lexington, and Bunker Hill. After "the massacre at Lexington" in April, Paine wrote to Benjamin Franklin, "I thought it very hard to have the country set on fire about my ears almost the moment I got into it."

Sentiment in the colonies was seriously divided on the proper course to be followed, ranging from such extremists as Samuel Adams and John Hancock, who were strong for war, to the Tories, ever loyal to the King. George Washington, Benjamin Franklin, and Thomas Jefferson were among the leaders who protested their loyalty to Britain and viewed askance the thought of separation and independence. Both the first and second Continental Congresses adopted resolutions affirming their allegiance to the Crown, petitioning only for a just settlement of their grievances.

In the midst of the confused thinking, the conflicting opinions and impulses, the pulling and hauling, one man saw clearly the trend of events and their probable outcome. From the beginning, Thomas Paine viewed separation from England as inevitable. He spent the entire fall of 1775 setting down his ideas. Before publication, the work was shown to several friends, one of whom, Dr. Benjamin Rush, suggested the title *Common Sense* and helped Paine to find a publisher, Robert Bell, a Scotch bookseller and printer in Philadelphia.

Common Sense made its appearance on January 10, 1776, "Written by an Englishman," a pamphlet of forty-seven pages, priced at two shillings. In three months, 120,000 copies had been bought, and estimates of total sales have ranged up to half a million, the equivalent in proportion to population of a sale of 30,000,000 copies in the United States today. Virtually every literate person in the thirteen colonies is believed to have read it. Despite the enormous sales, Paine elected to receive not a penny of royalties.

Nothing comparable to *Common Sense* in its immediate impact is to be found in the history of literature. It was a clarion call to the American colonists to fight for their independence—without compromise or vacillation. Revolution was pointed out to them as the only solution of their conflict with Great Britain and George III. "Since nothing but blows will do," declared Paine, "for God's sake let us come to a final separation. Dearly, dearly do we pay for the repeal of the acts, if that is all we fight for . . . it is as great a folly to pay a Bunker-hill price for law as for land. . . . 'Tis not the affair of a city, a county, a province or a kingdom, but of a *continent*. . . . 'Tis not the concern of a day, a year or an age; posterity are involved in the contest. . . . Now is the seed-time of continental union, faith and honor. . . . The Continental Belt is too loosely buckled . . . independence is the only *bond* that tie and keep us together."

A relatively mild and disarming paragraph introduces *Common Sense:*

> Perhaps the sentiments contained in the following pages, are not *yet* sufficiently fashionable to procure them general favor; a long habit of not thinking a thing *wrong,* gives it a superficial appearance of being *right,* and raises at first a formidable outcry in defense of custom. But the tumult soon subsides. Time makes more converts than reason.

The first portion of the pamphlet deals with the origin and nature of government, with particular application to the English constitution. The author's philosophy of government is contained in such sentences as:

Government, even in its best state, is but a necessary evil; in its worst state an intolerable one. . . . Government, like dress, is the badge of lost innocence; the palaces of kings are built upon the ruins of bowers of paradise. . . . The more perfect civilization is, the less occasion has it for government.

The origin and rise of government, Paine argues, was "rendered necessary by the inability of moral virtue to govern the world; here too is the design and end of government, viz., freedom and security."

A sharp distinction is drawn between society and government. Men are attracted into society because through social co-operation certain wants can be satisfied. In this state, man possesses certain natural rights, such as liberty and equality. Ideally, man should be able to live in peace and happiness without government, if the "impulses of conscience" were "clear, uniform and irresistibly obeyed." Since mankind is naturally weak and imperfect morally, some restraining power is required, and this is provided by government. Upon society rather than government, however, depend the security, progress, and comfort of the people. More influential than any political institutions are social usage and custom, the mutual relations and mutual interests of men.

Paine then proceeds to "offer a few remarks on the so much boasted constitution of England," commenting, "That it was noble for the dark and slavish time in which it was erected, is granted. When the world was overrun with tyranny the least remove therefrom was a glorious rescue. But that it is imperfect, subject to convulsions, and incapable of producing what it seems to promise is easily demonstrated." What should be one of the major attributes of government—responsibility —he considered completely lacking in the British constitution. It was so complex that it was impossible to determine who was accountable for anything. The only commendable part of the constitution was the people's right, theoretically at least, to elect members of the House of Commons. Paine proposed a single democratically elected legislative chamber for the colonies, a president and a cabinet, with the executive branch responsible to the congress.

But it was for the institution of hereditary monarchy that Paine reserved his harshest words and most scathing contempt. He attacked the whole principle of monarchy, and the English form in particular.

Government by kings was first introduced into the world by the heathens, from whom the children of Israel copied the custom. It was the most prosperous invention the devil ever set on foot for the promotion of idolatry. The heathens paid divine honors to their deceased kings, and the Christian world has improved on the plan by doing the same to their living ones. . . . To the evil of monarchy we have added that of hereditary succession; and as the first is a degradation and lessening of ourselves, so the second, claimed as a matter of right, is an insult and imposition on posterity. . . . One of the strongest *natural* proofs of the folly of hereditary rights in kings is that nature disproves it, otherwise she would not so frequently turn it into ridicule by giving mankind an Ass for a Lion.

The legitimacy of the English succession as far back as the Conquest was dubious, in Paine's eyes. As he puts it, "A French bastard landing with an armed banditti, and establishing himself King of England against the consent of the natives, is in plain terms a very paltry rascally original.—It certainly has no divinity in it." If the monarchy insured a race of good and wise men, it would not be objectionable, but "it opens a door to the *foolish,* the *wicked,* and the *improper.* . . . Men who look upon themselves born to reign, and others to obey, soon grow insolent; selected from the rest of mankind their minds are early poisoned by importance . . . when they succeed to the government are often the most ignorant and unfit of any throughout the dominions." Permitting underage and overage kings to sit on the throne also produces a train of evils: in the one case the actual administration of the country is in the hands of a regent, and in the other it is subject to the whims of a senile, worn-out monarch.

To the argument that hereditary succession prevents civil wars, Paine pointed out that since the Conquest, England had suffered "no less than eight civil wars and nineteen rebellions." His conclusion is:

In England a king has little more to do than to make war and give away places; which, in plain terms, is to impoverish the nation and set it together by the ears. A pretty business indeed for a man to be allowed eight hundred thousand sterling a year for, and worshipped into the bargain! Of more worth is one honest man to society, and in the sight of God, than all the crowned ruffians who ever lived.

In several passages Paine paid his respects to George III. After the massacre at Lexington, he wrote, "I rejected the hardened, sullen-tempered Pharoah of England for ever; and disdain the wretch, that with the pretended title of *Father of his people,* can unfeelingly hear of their slaughter, and composedly sleep with their blood upon his soul." In a later paragraph he adds: "But where, say some, is the King of America? I'll tell you, friend, he reigns above, and doth not make havoc of mankind like the royal brute of Britain."

Having exploded popular ideas of monarchical government Paine proceeded to "Some thoughts on the present state of the American affairs." Economic arguments for separation from Britain were stressed. To the Tories' contention that America had flourished because of her connection with England, Paine rejoined:

America would have flourished as much, and probably much more, had no European power had any thing to do with her. The articles of commerce, by which she has enriched herself, are the necessaries of life, and will always have a market while eating is the custom of Europe. . . . Our corn will fetch its price in any market in Europe, and our imported goods must be paid for, buy them where we will.

The fact that Britain had protected the colonies against the Spanish, French, and Indians, Paine dismissed with the comment: "She would have defended Turkey from the same motives, *viz.* for the sake of trade and dominion," and, in any case, the defense was "at our expense as well as her own."

One of the strongest ties holding the colonies against separation, Paine recognized, was a sentimental conception of Britain as the mother country. If this were true, "Then the more shame upon her conduct. Even brutes do not devour their young, nor savages make war upon their families. . . . The phrase *parent* or *mother* country has been jesuitically adopted by the king and his parasites, with a low papistical design of gaining an unfair bias on the credulous weakness of our minds. Europe, and not England, is the parent country of America." The New World, he pointed out, had been "the asylum for the persecuted lovers of civil and religious liberty from *every* part of Europe. . . . Not one third of the inhabitants, even of this province, are of English descent. Wherefore, I reprobate the phrase of parent or mother country applied to England only, as being false, selfish, narrow and ungenerous."

Foreshadowing George Washington's later warning "to steer

clear of permanent alliances with any portion of the foreign world," and Thomas Jefferson's policy of "Peace, commerce, and honest friendship with all nations—entangling alliances with none," Paine suggested there would be numerous disadvantages to continued connection with Britain:

> . . . because, any submission to or dependance on Great Britain, tends directly to involve this continent in European wars and quarrels; and sets us at variance with nations, who would otherwise seek our friendship, and against whom, we have neither anger nor complaint. As Europe is our market for trade, we ought to form no partial connexion with any part of it. It is the true interest of America to steer clear of European contentions, which she never can do while, by her dependance on Britain, she is made the make-weight in the scale of British politics. Europe is too thickly planted with kingdoms to be long at peace, and whenever a war breaks out between England and any foreign power, the trade of America goes to ruin, *because of her connexion with Britain.*

The manifold inconveniences of British government were reviewed, and Paine concluded:

> . . . it is not in the power of Britain to do this continent justice; the business of it will soon be too weighty and intricate to be managed with any tolerable degree of convenience, by a power so distant from us, and so very ignorant of us; for if they cannot conquer us, they cannot govern us. To be always running three or four thousand miles with a tale or a petition, waiting four or five months for an answer, which, when obtained, requires five or six more to explain it in, will in a few years be looked upon as folly and childishness. . . . There is something absurd, in supposing a continent to be perpetually governed by an island. In no instance has nature made the satellite larger than its primary planet.

To the doubters and faint of heart who still believed harmony and reconciliation possible, Paine delivered an impassioned plea:

> Can ye restore to us the time that is past? Can ye give to prostitution its former innocence? Neither can you reconcile Britain and America. The last cord now is broken, the people of England are presenting addresses

against us. There are injuries which nature cannot forgive; she would cease to be nature if she did. As well can the lover forgive the ravisher of his mistress, as the continent forgive the murders of Britain.

While the rest of the world was burdened with oppression, America should open her doors wide to freedom, and prepare an asylum for persecuted mankind.

Paine devoted his final chapter to some very practical considerations on "the present ability of America," designed to build up the self-confidence of the Americans and to convince them that they had the manpower, manufacturing experience, and natural resources, not only to wage war successfully with Britain, but, if necessary, to win against a hostile world. The colonies already possessed a large body of armed and disciplined men. A navy comparable to Britain's could be constructed in a brief time, for tar, timber, iron, and cordage were available in quantity, and "Ship building is America's greatest pride, and in which she will, in time, excel the whole world." A fleet was needed, in any case, for defense and protection, because the English navy "three or four thousand miles off can be of little use, and on sudden emergencies, none at all."

In the light of the religious controversies in which he subsequently became involved, it is of interest to note Paine's religious views at this stage in his career:

As to religion, I hold it to be the indispensable duty of all governments, to protect all conscientious professors thereof, and I know of no other business which government has to do therewith [an argument apparently against an established church and for separation of church and state]. . . . For myself, I fully and conscientiously believe, that it is the will of the Almighty, that there should be a diversity of religious opinions among us: it affords a larger field for our Christian kindness. Were we all of one way of thinking, our religious dispositions would want matter for probation; and on this liberal principle, I look on the various denominations among us, to be like children of the same family, differing only in what is called their Christian names.

Summarizing the reasons for his conviction that "nothing can settle our affairs so expeditiously as an open and determined declaration for independence," Paine concluded *Common Sense* with the enumeration of four factors: (1) as long as America was regarded as a subject of Britain, no other nation would attempt to mediate the differences between them; (2) no aid could be expected from France or Spain in repairing the breach and strengthening the connection between Britain and America, because such a step would be to their disadvantage; (3) while the Americans professed to be subjects of Britain, they would, in the eyes of foreign nations, be considered rebels, and therefore would win little sympathy; (4) if the Americans would prepare a manifesto setting forth their grievances against Britain, and their intention of breaking off all connections with her, sending copies of the declaration to other countries, expressing their peaceable disposition toward them and their desire to establish trade relations, the results would be highly favorable.

Closing his case, Paine maintained:

. . . until an independence is declared, the continent will feel itself like a man who continues putting off some unpleasant business from day to day, yet knows it must be done, hates to set about it, wishes it over, and is continually haunted with the thoughts of its necessity.

Wherefore, instead of gazing at each other, with suspicious or doubtful curiosity, let each of us hold out to his neighbor the hearty hand of friendship, and unite in drawing a line, which, like an act of oblivion, shall bury in forgetfulness every former dissention. Let the name of whig and tory be extinct; and let none other be heard among us, than those of *a good citizen; an open and resolute friend; and a virtuous supporter of the* RIGHTS OF MANKIND, *and of the* FREE AND INDEPENDENT STATES OF AMERICA.

This was the revolutionary message communicated to the American people by *Common Sense,* running the gamut from down-to-earth, realistic, practical arguments to emotion-charged, violently partisan, and biased appeals of the born agitator.

The immediate and cataclysmic effects of *Common Sense* may be illustrated by quotations from some contemporary leaders. George Washington's doubts evaporated as he wrote to Joseph Reed at Norfolk: "A few more of such flaming arguments as were exhibited at Falmouth and Norfolk, added to the sound doctrine and unanswerable reasoning contained in the pamphlet *Common Sense,* will not leave numbers at a loss to decide upon the propriety of separation"; and a few weeks later, also to Reed, "By private letters which I have lately received from Virginia, I find Paine's *Common Sense* is working a wonderful change there in the minds of many men." John Adams, writing to his wife, "I sent you a pamphlet entitled *Common Sense,* written in vindication of doctrines, which there is reason to expect, that the further encroachments of tyranny and depredations of oppression will soon make the common faith," to which, after reading, Abigail replied, *"Common Sense,* like a ray of revelation, has come in season to clear our doubts and fix our choice." Benjamin Rush said of Paine's writings, "They burst from the press with an effect that has rarely been produced by type and paper in any age or country"; General Charles Lee added, "I own it has convinced me"; Franklin noted, "It has had a prodigious effect"; and William Henry Drayton reported that "This declaration came like an explosion of thunder upon the members" of the Continental Congress.

In his *History of the American Revolution,* Sir George Trevelyan commented:

> It would be difficult to name any human composition which has had an effect at once so instant, so extended, and so lasting. . . . It was pirated, parodied and imitated, and translated into the language of every country where the new republic had well wishers. . . . According to contemporary newspapers *Common Sense* turned thousands to independence who before could not endure the thought. It worked nothing short of miracles and turned Tories into Whigs.

Within a few months after the appearance of *Common Sense,* most of the states had instructed their delegates to vote for independence, only Maryland hesitating and New York opposed. On July 4, 1776, less than six months from the date when Paine's famous pamphlet came off the press, the Continental Congress, meeting in the State House at Philadelphia, proclaimed the independence of the United States of America. Though Paine did not write the Declaration, he was closely associated with Thomas Jefferson while it was being composed, and except for the omission of an antislavery clause which Paine advocated, the principles for which he stood were incorporated in the celebrated manifesto.

An account of Paine's subsequent career is only indirectly relevant to the story of *Common Sense.* The highlights may be sketched briefly. He enlisted in the Revolutionary army soon after the Declaration of Independence. As a prolific spokesman for the American cause he contributed tremendously to national unity and spirit through a series of pamphlets, each entitled *The Crisis.* The first of these begins with the much quoted lines: "These are the times that try men's souls. The summer soldier and the sunshine patriot will, in this crisis, shrink from the service of their country; but he that stands it now deserves the love and thanks of man and woman." After a few months, recognizing his value as a propagandist and morale builder, Congress took Paine out of the army and appointed him Secretary to the Committee of Foreign Affairs—in effect our first Secretary of State. Controversies forced his resignation from this post, following which he was appointed Clerk of the Pennsylvania Assembly. In 1781 he was sent to France with John Laurens, to get financial assistance for the hard-pressed American government; he returned the same year with money and supplies.

The Revolution over, in 1783, Paine turned to mechanical inventions, designing the first iron suspension bridge, and experimenting with steam power. The decision was made to consult engineers in France and England on some of the technical problems, and in 1787 Paine went to Europe, where he remained for fifteen years.

Soon after his arrival abroad, the French Revolution erupted, an event which Paine enthusiastically supported as further vindication of his democratic ideas. In defense of the Revolution, replying to Edmund Burke's attacks, he produced his famed *The Rights of Man.* Forced hurriedly to leave England to avoid arrest for treason, as a result of the doctrines expressed therein, he fled to France, where he had been elected to the Convention as a member representing Calais. In an attempt to save Louis XVI from execution, Paine broke with such extremists as Robespierre and Marat. When these elements took over the government, Paine was arrested, deprived of his honorary French citizenship, imprisoned for ten months, and narrowly escaped the guillotine. Released from prison through the intercession of the American ambassador James Monroe, he was nursed back to health in Monroe's home.

The great work of this period was *The Age of Reason,* sometimes referred to as the "atheist's bible." Actually, Paine was a pious deist, believing in one God and a hereafter, and *The Age of Reason,* though highly critical of the Old Testament, had been written to stem the strong tide of atheism sweeping France in the Revolutionary era. Nevertheless, theologians and orthodox religious groups bitterly condemned Paine as a dangerous radical and unbeliever.

When Paine returned to America in 1802, he found himself received not as a Revolutionary hero, but virtually ostracized by political leaders and churchgoers, because of his authorship of *The Age of Reason* and his radical political theories. In New Rochelle, New York, where he settled, he was denied the right to vote on the ground that he was not an American citizen. An attempt was even made to murder him. After seven incredible years of abuse, hatred, neglect, poverty, and ill health, he died in 1809, at the age of 72. He was denied burial in a Quaker cemetery.

The bitterness, falsehoods, and violent prejudices of Paine's last years have persisted to recent times. Theodore Roosevelt referred to him as "a filthy little atheist," though, like the Holy Roman Empire, which was neither holy, Roman, nor an empire, Paine was neither filthy, little, nor an atheist. As late as 1933, a radio program about Paine was banned from a New York City station. Not until 1945, forty-five years after its establishment, was he elected to the Hall of Fame of Great Americans. In the same year, the city of New Rochelle got around to restoring to the Revolutionary hero the rights of citizenship which he lost in 1806.

This was the man who perhaps more than any other deserves the title "Founder of American Independence," who first used the phrase "The United States of America," who foresaw that "The United States of America will sound as pompously in history as the Kingdom of Great Britain," and who proclaimed, "The cause of America is, in a great measure, the cause of all mankind." No better index to Paine's character can be found than his reply to Franklin's remark, "Where liberty is, there is my country." "Where liberty is not," said Paine, "there is mine."

Even in his own time, the hymn of hate and misrepresentation was not universal. Andrew Jackson dared to say, "Thomas Paine needs no monument made by hands; he has erected a monument in the hearts of all lovers of liberty."

3 | PATRON SAINT OF FREE ENTERPRISE

ADAM SMITH: *Wealth of Nations*

Within two months after Tom Paine's *Common Sense* had helped precipitate the Declaration of Independence and other momentous events of the American Revolution, a book destined to bring profound repercussions in a different sphere of human activity appeared in London. Unlike Paine's fiery tract, Adam Smith's ponderous, two-volume treatise, *An Inquiry Into the Nature and Causes of the Wealth of Nations,* was a delayed action bomb, attracting slight notice at first. Not until the century following the author's death, in fact, did his work reach its full impact.

The year 1776 may logically be regarded as the close of one epoch and the beginning of another. The American Revolution had started, the French Revolution was brewing, and the Industrial Revolution, sparked by the discovery of steam power, was gathering speed. One commentator has characterized the preceding era as "the dark ages of modern time." In England virtually every aspect of economic life was under strict governmental control. Prices were stabilized, wages and hours of labor fixed, production regulated, and foreign trade, both imports and exports, completely dominated by the state. War was almost always present. National policy dictated a strong army and navy, a large population, grabbing of colonies throughout the world, and weakening, by fair means or foul, of rival countries, such as France. Any suggestion of an equitable distribution of wealth was violently opposed by the ruling classes. Education was reserved for the privileged few, criminal laws were extremely severe, and political rights for the masses existed largely in theory rather than in practice.

As it had done for generations, the landed aristocracy still held the reins of government; but a new and powerful class of merchants and industrialists had risen, demanding and receiving special privileges for themselves. In the view of this group, exports were blessings, imports calamities; money should not be permitted to leave the country; a "favorable" balance of trade should always be maintained; wages for labor should be low and hours long; high tariffs must protect home industries; a strong merchant marine was essential; and any measures which aided the mercantilists *ipso facto* were assumed to benefit the nation as a whole. Under highly vocal pressure, Parliament had enacted most of these concepts into law.

Then came Adam Smith, intent on exploding what he considered erroneous and harmful ideas. Smith's adult life up to this point may be regarded as preparation for the monumental task to which he now set himself. A native of Scotland, he matriculated at age fourteen (1737) at the University of Glasgow. There he came under the influence of a great teacher, Francis Hutcheson, whose frequently reiterated belief in "the greatest happiness of the greatest number" became Smith's permanent ruling philosophy. Proceeding next to Oxford University, where he remained for six years, Smith devoted most of his time to extensive reading over a wide range of literature. Upon returning to Scotland, he gave public lectures in Edinburgh until 1751, when he was appointed first to the chair of logic and metaphysics and shortly thereafter to the chair of moral philosophy at the University of Glasgow. For twelve years he served as a gifted and popular lecturer, adding to his reputation by publication of a best seller, *Theory of Moral Sentiments*—a work regarded by his contemporaries as superior to the *Wealth of Nations*. Tempted by generous financial rewards, Smith resigned his professorship to accompany a young nobleman, as companion and tutor, on a three-year tour of the Continent. There he became acquainted with the leading economists, philosophers, and political thinkers of the time, particularly in France.

As early as 1759, a draft of what subsequently developed into the *Wealth of Nations* existed in Smith's notes, but the work was slow in coming to fruition. Years of meditation, study and reading, first-hand observations, conversations with people in many walks of life, and endless revision were to pass before Smith was ready to turn his magnum opus over to the printer. The three years before publication were mostly spent in London, where he discussed his book with Benjamin Franklin, American colonial agent. Not until March 9, 1776, did the work come from the press. Since that date, it has gone through innumerable editions, and has been translated into most of the world's living languages.

The encyclopedic scope of the *Wealth of Nations* makes it far more than a mere economic treatise. One critic has called it "a history and criticism of all European civilization." Commencing with a discussion of the division of labor, Smith diverges into considerations of the origin and use of money, prices of commodities, wages of labor, profits of stock, rent of land, value of silver, and distinctions between productive and unproductive labor. There follow an account of the economic development of Europe since the fall of the Roman Empire, extended analyses and criticisms of the commercial and colonial policies of European nations, the revenue of the sovereign, different methods of defense and administration of justice in primitive societies, the origin and growth of standing armies in Europe, a history of education in the Middle Ages and a criticism of the universities of Smith's time, a history of the temporal power of the church, the growth of public debts, and, in conclusion, an examination of principles of taxation and systems of public revenue.

Smith's general thesis, on which the *Wealth of Nations* is based, might have been propounded by Niccolò Machiavelli, to wit: every human being is motivated primarily by self-interest. A desire for wealth is only one of the manifestations. Selfish impulses and incentives are the background of all mankind's activities. Furthermore, rather than finding this aspect of human behavior objectionable and undesirable, Smith believed that the selfishness of the individual is conducive to society's welfare. A nation's prosperity can best be provided, he suggested, by allowing the "uniform, constant, and uninterruped effort of every man to better his condition. . . . It is not from the benevolence of the butcher, the brewer, or the baker that we expect our dinner, but from their regard to their own interest. We address ourselves, not to their humanity, but to their self-love, and never talk to them of our own necessities, but of their advantages." It was because of such passages as these that Ruskin referred to Smith as "the half-breed and half-witted Scotchman who taught the deliberate blasphemy: 'Thou shalt hate the Lord, thy God, damn his law, and covet thy neighbor's goods.' "

Modern industry, Smith contended, is made possible by the division of labor and the accumulation of capital—both of which are explained by self-interest, or the "natural order," as it was referred to by eighteenth-century philosophers. Unconsciously, a "divine hand" leads man so that, in working for his own gain, he is contributing to the good of the whole. It naturally followed that there should be a minimum of government interference with the economic order—the best government, as Tom Paine argued in another connection, is the government that governs least.

A graphic illustration, pinmaking, is used by Smith to demonstrate the advantages of division of labor: "A workman not educated in this business . . . nor acquainted with the use of the machinery employed in it . . . could scarce, perhaps, with his utmost industry, make one pin a day, and certainly could not make twenty." By breaking the manufacturing process down "into eighteen distinct operations, which, in some manufactories, are all performed by distinct hands . . . I have seen a small manufactory of this kind where ten men only were employed . . . make among them upwards of forty-eight thousand pins in a day." This was a "consequence of a proper division and combination of their difficult operations."

The division of labor, Smith continued, had its origin among primitive peoples.

In a tribe of hunters or shepherds a particular person makes bows and arrows, for example, with more readiness and dexterity than any other. He frequently exchanges them for cattle or for venison with his companions; and he finds at last that he can in this manner get more cattle and venison, than if he himself went to the field to catch them. From a regard to his own interest, therefore, the making of bows and arrows grows to be his chief business. . . .

Another excels in making the frames and covers of their little huts or moveable houses. . . .

In the same manner a third becomes a smith or a brazier; a fourth a tanner or dresser of hides or skins . . . and thus the certainty of being able to exchange all that surplus part of the produce of his own labour, which is over and above his own consumption, for such parts of the produce of other men's labour as he may have occasion for, encourages every man to apply himself to a particular occupation, and to cultivate and bring to perfection whatever talent or genius he may possess for that particular species of business.

Proceeding next to a consideration of money and commodity prices, Smith states a principle generally condemned as erroneous by orthodox economists, but widely adopted as a rallying cry of socialist thinkers of later eras. "Labour alone," he says, "never varying in its own value, is alone the ultimate and real standard by which the value of all commodities can at all times and places be estimated and compared. It is their real price; money is their nominal price only."

Nowhere in the *Wealth of Nations* is Smith more outspoken, and occasionally indignant, than in his comments on the disparities in bargaining power between employers and workers, and in his opposition to the mercantilist notion that low wages would force laborers to work more and thereby increase England's prosperity. On the first point, he remarks, "The workmen desire to get as much, the masters to give as little as possible. The former are disposed to combine in order to raise, the latter in order to lower the wages of labour."

He continues:

It is not, however, difficult to foresee which of the two parties must, upon all ordinary occasions, have the advantage in the dispute; and force the other into a compliance with their terms. The masters, being fewer in number, can combine much more easily; and the law, besides, authorizes, or at least does not prohibit their combinations, while it prohibits those of the workmen. We have no acts of parliament against combining to lower the price of work; but many against combining to raise it. In all such disputes the masters can hold out much longer. A landlord, a farmer, a master manufacturer, or merchant, though they did not employ a single workman, could generally live a year or two upon the stocks which they have already acquired. Many workmen could not subsist a week, few could subsist a month, and scarce any a year without employment. In the long-run the workman may be as necessary to his master as his master is to him, but the necessity is not so immediate.

Smith's obvious sympathy with the lowly workmen is shown in such passages as these:

Servants, labourers and workmen of different kinds, make up the far greater part of every great political society. But what improves the circumstances of the greater part can never be regarded as an inconveniency to the whole. No society can surely be flourishing and happy, of which the far greater part of the members are poor and miserable. It is but equity, besides, that they who feed, cloath and lodge the whole body of the people, should have such a share of the produce of their own labour as to be themselves tolerably well fed, cloathed and lodged: . . . The liberal reward of labour . . . increases the industry of the common people. The wages of labour are the encouragement of industry, which like every other human quality, improves in proportion to the encouragement it receives. . . . Where wages are high, accordingly, we shall always find the workmen more active, diligent and expeditious, than where they are low.

And again:

Our merchants and master-manufacturers complain much of the bad effects of high wages in raising the price, and thereby lessening the sale of their goods both at home and abroad. They say nothing about the effects of high profits. They are silent with regard to the pernicious effects of their own gains. They complain only of those of other people.

Twenty-two years before publication of the *Principles of Population,* Malthusian theories were forecast by Smith:

> Every species of animals naturally multiplies in proportion to their means of subsistence, and no species can ever multiply beyond it. But in civilized society it is only among the inferior ranks of people that the scantiness of subsistence can set limits to the further multiplication of the human species; and it can do so in no other way than by destroying a great part of the children which their fruitful marriages produce.

In view of the gains of labor in modern times, the feudal restraints and restrictions which prevailed in Adam Smith's century are hardly credible. The ban on any form of labor organization was only one of the severe handicaps imposed on workmen. Even more burdensome were apprenticeship laws and the law of settlements.

The apprenticeship statute dated back to Queen Elizabeth's reign. As described by Smith, it provided "that no person should for the future exercise any trade, craft, or mystery at that time exercised in England, unless he had previously served to it an apprenticeship of seven years at least." During these seven years, the employer furnished only subsistence. Unscrupulous employers naturally used the device to exploit their workers, taking much and giving little, while the apprentices were in a virtual state of bondage. In denouncing the practice, Smith maintained that long apprenticeships were unnecessary, for most trades could be learned in a few weeks. Further, apprenticeship regulations were an unfair interference with the workman's right to contract for his own services, to choose his own occupation, and to transfer from a low-wage to a high-wage job.

Equally onerous was the law of settlements. "There is scarce a poor man in England at forty years of age, I will venture to say," wrote Smith, "who has not in some part of his life felt himself most cruelly oppressed by this ill-contrived law of settlements." Like the apprenticeship act, the law of settlements was promulgated in the Elizabethan era. Its original purpose was to establish order in the distribution of poor relief. Each parish was made responsible for the care of its indigent members. To prevent the number of the community's poor from increasing, newcomers were not permitted to take up residence unless they were persons of substantial means. In its application to laborers, the law's practical effect was to create a class of prisoners for life in the town of their birth, placing nearly insuperable obstacles in the way of a workman who wished to move from one locality to another. Here again was an example, in Adam Smith's estimation, of the iniquities of government interference with the rights of man and with the natural workings of the economic system.

An attempt was made by Smith to distinguish between "productive" and "unproductive" labor.

> Great nations are never impoverished by private, though they sometimes are by public prodigality and misconduct. The whole, or almost the whole public revenue, is in most countries employed in maintaining unproductive hands. Such are the people who compose a numerous and splendid court, a great ecclesiastical establishment, great fleets and armies, who in time of peace produce nothing which can compensate the expence of maintaining them, even while the war lasts. Such people, as they themselves produce nothing, are all maintained by the produce of other men's labour. When multiplied therefore, to an unnecessary number, they may in a particular year consume so great a share of this produce, as not to leave a sufficiency for maintaining the productive labourers.

Sound advice, unfortunately not heeded by the American colonies, was also offered on slave labor.

> The experience of all ages and nations, I believe, demonstrates that the work done by slaves, though it appears to cost only their maintenance, is in the end the dearest of any. A person who can acquire no property, can have no other interest but to eat as much, and to labour as little as possible. Whatever work he does beyond what is sufficient to purchase his own maintenance, can be squeezed out of him by violence only, and not by any interest of his own.

From the problems of labor, Smith turned next to the advocacy of land reforms. There, too, he thought unwise governmental regulations and outmoded laws were standing in the path of progress. Much of the land in eighteenth-century Britain was under entail; an owner could thereby establish rules concerning the division and sale of his land binding upon his heirs for centuries after his demise. Another ancient custom was primogeniture, a feudal practice to prevent the breakup of large estates. Under the law of primogeniture, the eldest son was the sole heir. "Nothing," remarked Adam Smith, "can be more contrary to the real interest of a numerous family, than a right which in order to enrich one, beggars all the rest of the children." He urged free trade in land, through the repeal of laws establishing entails, primogenitures, and other restrictions on the free transfer of land by gift, devise, or sale.

A famous chapter in the *Wealth of Nations* deals with colonies. One authority has asserted that it "remains the best summary of colonial policy ever written." The discussion is divided in three parts: (1) "Of the motives for establishing new colonies," in which are reviewed the colonial enterprises of Greece, Rome, Venice, Portugal, and Spain; (2) "Causes of the prosperity of new colonies," enumerating such factors as plentiful and cheap land, high wages, rapid growth of population, and the colonists' knowledge of agriculture and other arts (the comparatively enlightened colonial policies of England are contrasted with the narrow and restrictive policies of Portugal and Spain); (3) "Of the advantages which Europe has derived from the discovery of America, and from that of a passage to the East Indies by the Cape of Good Hope," discoveries ranked by Smith as "the two greatest and most important events recorded in the history of mankind."

Restrictions placed on colonies in order to achieve monopolies of their trade were condemned by Smith as violations of the colonies' "natural rights." The mercantile system applied to the colonies was as absurd and costly as it was to the mother country. Also, there would be a continual financial drain on the colonizing power, for the colonies would never willingly tax themselves sufficiently to pay the expense of their own defense.

Smith was able to view the rebellious American colonists with far more objectivity than were most of his fellow-countrymen. A proper solution to the controversy, he believed, was to represent the American colonists in the British parliament—union rather than separation, with representation based on tax revenues. If eventually, as was not unlikely, the American exceeded the British taxes, the capital might be moved across the Atlantic, "to that part of the Empire which contributed most to the general defense and support of the whole." This would have constituted an effective answer to Tom Paine's assertion that "there is something absurd in supposing a continent to be perpetually governed by an island," for the roles would then have been reversed.

If the differences between England and her American colonies could not be reconciled peaceably, Smith urged independence for the colonies, though he realistically recognized that "to propose that Great Britain should voluntarily give up all authority over her colonies, and leave them to elect their own magistrates, to enact their own laws, and to make peace and war as they might think proper, would be to propose such a measure as never was, and never will be adopted by any nation in the world . . . how troublesome soever it might be to govern it, and how small the revenue which it afforded might be in proportion to the expense which it occasioned."

Smith's clear mind and prescience are revealed in this prophetic passage on America's future:

> From shopkeepers, tradesmen, and attornies, they [the American colonists] are become statesmen and legislators, and are employed in contriving a new form of government for an extensive empire, which, they flatter themselves, will become, and which, indeed, seems very likely to become, one of the greatest and most formidable that ever was in the world.

The most celebrated and, undoubtedly, the key division of the *Wealth of Nations* is "Book IV," entitled "Of Systems of Political Economy." Here are considered two different systems: the system of commerce, and the system of agriculture, though the space devoted to commerce is eight times as great as that given to agriculture. Therein Smith developed the laissez-faire principles ever since associated with his name. All conclusions concerning labor, land, commodities, money, prices, agriculture, stock, and taxes come to a focus in the argument for free trade, internal and external. Only through unrestricted domestic and foreign commerce could the nation achieve full development and prosperity. Abolish, pleaded Smith, the duties, bounties, and prohibitions of the mercantilist regime and the trading monopolies of the chartered companies, all of which hamstring the natural growth of industry and trade, and the free flow of goods to consumers. Discard the fallacious doctrine of "balance of trade," so revered by the mercantilists. Money is only a tool, and "there is no certain criterion by which we can determine on which side what is called the balance between any two countries lies, or which of them exports to the greatest value. . . . Wealth does not consist in money, or in gold and silver, but in what money purchases, and is valuable only for purchasing."

A division of labor between nations is as desirable and as logical as between individuals.

The natural advantages which one country has over another in producing particular commodities are sometimes so great, that it is acknowledged by all the world to be in vain to struggle with them. By means of glasses, hotbeds, and hotwalls, very good grapes can be raised in Scotland, and very good wine too can be made of them at about thirty times the expense for which at least equally good can be brought from foreign countries. Would it be a reasonable law to prohibit the importation of all foreign wines, merely to encourage the making of claret and burgundy in Scotland?

The economic advantages of free trade are summarized by Smith in these statements:

It is the maxim of every prudent master of a family, never to attempt to make at home what it will cost him more to make than to buy. . . . What is prudence in the conduct of every private family can scarce be folly in that of a great kingdom. If a foreign country can supply us with a commodity cheaper than we ourselves can make it, better buy it of them with some sort of the produce of our own industry, employed in a way in which we have some advantage.

The mutual benefits of foreign trade were stressed by Smith:

Between whatever places foreign trade is carried on, they all of them derive two distinct benefits from it. It carries out that surplus part of the produce of their land and labor for which there is no demand among them, and brings back in return for it something else for which there is a demand. . . . By means of it, the narrowness of the home market does not hinder the division of labor in any particular branch of art or manufacture from being carried to the highest perfection. By opening a more extensive market for whatever part of the produce of their labor may exceed the home consumption, it encourages them to improve its productive powers, and to augment its annual produce to the utmost, and thereby to increase the real revenue and wealth of the society.

That Smith was not absolutely dogmatic in his insistence upon free trade, however, is shown by certain exceptions or limitations he was willing to concede in application of the principle. In a few cases, he pointed out, "it will generally be advantageous to lay some burden upon foreign, for the encouragement of domestic industry. The first is, when some particular sort of industry is necessary for the defence of the country," even though on purely economic grounds it could not be justified, for "defence is more important than opulence." Living in a warring world, Smith granted that rich nations, with which it was profitable to trade in times of peace, might be more dangerous enemies in wartime than poor nations. Also, he agreed that some tariff protection for "infant industries" would enable them to develop more rapidly, perhaps to a point where they could be economically defensible. Further, Smith recommended that all tariff reductions be made "slowly, gradually, and after a very long warning," in order to protect plant investments in industries not capable of meeting foreign competition, and to provide time for workers to seek new jobs. These were realistic concessions to the arguments of free-trade opponents.

If government kept hands off business, industry, agriculture, and most other day-to-day activities of the nation, as Smith advocated, what did he regard as suitable functions for government? The range of responsibilities would be narrow. Essentially, the state should be limited to warding off foreign attack and administering justice. Smith was also willing to have it engage in "erecting and maintaining certain public works and certain public institutions, which it can never be for the interest of any individual, or small number of individuals, to erect and maintain; because the profit could never repay the expense to any individual or small number of individuals, though it may frequently do much more than repay it to a great society." In Smith's brief list of functions properly assignable to the state were included upkeep of the highways, lighting the streets of cities, and water supplies. Thus, Adam Smith saw little excuse for the existence of what he termed that "insidious and crafty animal vulgarly called the statesman or politician" outside of maintaining external peace and internal order.

In one of his exceptions, however, he was far ahead of his time—participation by the government in the general education of the people. In support of his arguments for public education, Smith comments:

A man without the proper use of the intellectual
faculties of a man, is, if possible, more contemptible
than even a coward, and seems to be mutilated and de-
formed in a still more essential part of the character of
human nature. Though the state was to derive no advantage from the instruction of the inferior ranks of people,
it would still deserve its attention that they should not be
altogether uninstructed. The state, however, derives no
inconsiderable advantage from their instruction. The
more they are instructed, the less liable they are to the
delusions of enthusiasm and superstition, which, among
ignorant nations, frequently occasion the most dreadful
disorders. An instructed and intelligent people besides,
are always more decent and orderly than an ignorant
and stupid one. They feel themselves, each individually
more respectable, and more likely to obtain the respect
of their lawful superiors, and they are therefore more
disposed to respect those superiors. . . . In free countries, where the safety of government depends very much
upon the favourable judgment which the people may
form of its conduct, it must surely be of the highest importance that they should not be disposed to judge rashly
or capriciously concerning it.

An unbiased, impartial estimation of Adam Smith and his
work is complex even after nearly two hundred years. There
is, for example, the view of Buckle in his *History of Civilization:* "*The Wealth of Nations* is . . . probably the most important book which has ever been written, whether we consider the amount of original thought which it contains, or its
practical influence." A writer less sympathetic to Smith's
ideas, Max Lerner, nevertheless acknowledged that the
Wealth of Nations "has done as much perhaps as any modern book thus far to shape the whole landscape of life as we
live it today." Lerner observed discerningly that, "those who
read it were chiefly those who stood to profit from its view
of the world—the rising class of businessmen, their political
executive committees in the parliaments of the world, and
their intellectual executive committees in the academies.
Through them it has had an enormous influence upon the
underlying population of the world, although generally unknown to them, and through them also it has had an enormous
influence upon economic opinion and national policy."
The judgment of these two authorities is confirmed by the
well-known English political economist, J. A. R. Marriott, who

remarked that: "There is probably no single work in the language which has in its day exercised an influence so profound alike upon scientific economic thought and upon administrative action. There is every reason why it should exercise it still." Another economist, W. R. Scott, added: "Intellectually, he [Smith] was pre-eminently a master in seeing economic life steadily and whole."

On the other hand, many liberal and radical thinkers have found it difficult to forgive Smith for the excesses of laissez faire practiced by businessmen and industrialists, who appropriated Smith's writings as their gospel. Doctrines which he had advocated for the protection of the workman, the farmer, the consumer, and society at large, subsequently were twisted by unprincipled interests to mean unbridled license for themselves, free of all government control or interference.

There is also the old argument about the priority of the chicken or the egg. Would Smith's principles have been followed in the development of commerce and industry if he had never written a word, or did the *Wealth of Nations* precipitate the vast changes which followed its publication, furnishing a philosophy and plan for the new movement? Perhaps the truth lies somewhere midway.

Admittedly, Adam Smith picked the right time to be born. Standing on the threshold between two historical eras, he spoke for the new economic liberalism, and a receptive world listened and used his precepts to effect a great economic transformation. British businessmen, as the Industrial Revolution progressed, recognized the validity of Smith's doctrines, discarded mercantilist restrictions and privileges, and in the nineteenth century developed Britain into the world's wealthiest nation. The impact of Smith's ideas was scarcely less striking on other leading trading countries. Few would deny that Adam Smith richly deserves the title of "Father of Modern Economics."

4 TOO MANY MOUTHS

THOMAS MALTHUS:
Essay on the Principle of Population

A favorite amusement of the late eighteenth century was dreaming up utopias. The idealism associated with revolutionary movements in America and France inspired visionaries to conclude that the perfection of man was just over the horizon, and the creation of an earthly paradise was imminent.

Among the dreamers, two, William Godwin in England, and the Marquis de Condorcet in France, had the most devoted followings, voicing for the multitudes the aspirations and visions of a new day. Typical of the incorrigible optimists are views expressed by Godwin in his *Political Justice*. The time would come, he believed, when we would be so full of life that we need not sleep, so full of living that we need not die, and the need of marriage would be superseded by emphasis on developing the intellect; in short, men would be as angels. "Other improvements," he rhapsodized, "may be expected to keep pace with those of health and longevity. There will be no war, no crimes, no administration of justice, as it is called, and no government. Besides this, there will be neither disease, anguish, melancholy nor resentment. Every man will seek with ineffable ardour the good of all."

To dispel the fear of too many people and too little food, Godwin wrote, "Myriads of centuries of still increasing population may pass away and the earth be still found sufficient for the subsistence of its inhabitants." Eventually, he thought, the sexual passion might abate; and Condorcet suggested that it might be gratified without a high rate of reproduction.

These beautiful bubbles invited pricking, and the needle was furnished by an impertinent young cleric, Thomas Robert Malthus, a thirty-two-year-old Fellow of Jesus College, Cambridge. His answer to the social perfectionists, *An Essay on the Principle of Population,* 1798, became one of the great classics of political economy.

A contemporary of Adam Smith and Thomas Paine, though considerably their junior, Malthus was the second son of

54

Daniel Malthus. The father, a country gentleman in easy circumstances, a friend of Rousseau and executor of his estate, was one of Godwin's warmest admirers. Both father and son were fond of debate, and Thomas attacked while Daniel defended utopian views. Finally, at the father's urging, Thomas decided to state his opinions in writing. The celebrated *Essay* was the result, a book which during the past 156 years has had a profound influence on human thought and human practice, and perhaps at no period more pronounced than in the present era. What Adam Smith had done twenty-two years earlier in his inquiry into the nature and causes of wealth, Malthus complemented with his searching analysis of the nature and causes of poverty.

An Essay on the Principle of Population as It Affects the Future Improvement of Society, with Remarks on the Speculations of Mr. Godwin, M. Condorcet, and Other Writers, published anonymously, was little more than a pamphlet (50,000 words) in the 1798 version, and was evidently issued in a small edition, for copies are now exceedingly rare. "It was written," the author later reported, "on the spur of the occasion, and from the few materials which were then within my reach in a country situation." The theme of the *Essay* was not new, for various eighteenth-century writers, including Benjamin Franklin, had discussed the problem of population growth, but none had presented it so forcefully, with so much fervor, or with such clear discernment as did Malthus.

Two basic assumptions are stated by Malthus at the outset:

First, that food is necessary to the existence of man;
Secondly, that the passion between the sexes is necessary, and will remain nearly in its present state.

Not even the utopians had supposed that man would ultimately be able to live without food.

But Mr. Godwin has conjectured that the passion between the sexes may in time be extinguished. . . . The best arguments for the perfectibility of man are drawn from a contemplation of the great progress that he has already made from the savage state. . . . But towards the extinction of the passion between the sexes, no progress whatever has hitherto been made. It appears to exist in as much force at present as it did two thousand, or four thousand years ago.

Assuming then that his "postulata" were irrefutable, Malthus proceeded to lay down his famous principle:

. . . that the power of population is indefinitely greater than the power in the earth to produce subsistence for man. Population, when unchecked, increases in a geometrical ratio. Subsistence increases only in an arithmetical ratio. A slight acquaintance with numbers will show the immensity of the first power in comparison to the second.

Elaborating the proposition further, Malthus buttressed his case in this way:

Through the animal and vegetable kingdoms, nature has scattered the seeds of life abroad with the most profuse and liberal hand. She has been comparatively sparing in the room, and the nourishment necessary to rear them. . . . The race of plants, and race of animals shrink under this great restrictive law. And the race of man cannot, by any efforts of reason, escape from it. Among plants and animals its effects are waste of seed, sickness, and premature death. Among mankind, misery and vice.

These hard but realistic facts, in Malthus' estimation, placed insurmountable difficulties in the way of the perfectibility of society. No possible reform could remove the pressure of natural laws, obstacles which prevent the "existence of a society, all the members of which, should live in ease, happiness, and comparative leisure; and feel no anxiety about providing the means of subsistence for themselves and families."

Choosing as an illustration of the workings of his geometrical ratio, the growth of population in the United States, "where the means of subsistence have been more ample, the manners of the people more pure, and consequently the checks to early marriage fewer," Malthus found the population, exclusive of immigration, had doubled in twenty-five years. From this evidence he deduced that where checks and balances are lacking and no restrictions placed on nature, the rate of increase in any country would double the population every generation. His critics have frequently called attention to flaws in Malthus' rule, for the situation which prevailed in the United States during the era cited was atypical of conditions in any other period of American history or of the history of any other nation.

Applying his yardstick of natural population growth to England, that is, a potential doubling every twenty-five years, Malthus turned to the question of subsistence. His conclusion is "that by the best possible policy, by breaking up more land, and by great encouragements to agriculture, the produce of this Island may be doubled in the first twenty-five years."

Troubles would start to accumulate, however, in the next generation. While the population would be doubling again, that is quadrupling in the fifty-year span, "It is impossible to suppose that the produce could be quadrupled." The best that could be hoped for would be an increase in the food supply triple the beginning rate. Expressed numerically, the Malthus formula would run, for population: 1, 2, 4, 8, 16, 32, 64, etc., and for subsistence: 1, 2, 3, 4, 5, 6, 7, etc.

A logical sequence of Malthus' line of reasoning is that there must be constant checks upon the growth of population. The most drastic check of all is the scarcity of food. A series of "immediate checks" falls into a "positive" group, including unwholesome occupations, severe labor, extreme poverty, diseases, bad nursing of children, great cities, plagues, and famine; and a "preventive" group, namely, moral restraint and vice.

Certain inevitable practical conclusions followed, in Malthus' view. If human beings were to enjoy the greatest possible happiness, they should not assume family obligations unless they could afford them. Those without adequate means to support a family should remain celibate. Furthermore, public policy, such as the poor laws, should avoid encouraging the laboring class and others to bring into the world children whom they could not support.

A man who is born into a world already possessed, if he cannot get subsistence from his parents, on whom he has a just demand, and if the society do not want his labour, has no *claim* of right to the smallest portion of food, and, in fact, has no business to be where he is.

This was written in reply to Paine's *Rights of Man.*

Charity, private or governmental, was undesirable because it gave money to the poor without increasing the amount of food available, thereby raising prices and creating shortages. Also objectionable were public housing schemes, for they had the effect of stimulating early marriages, and consequently of causing a rapid increase in population. Higher wages had a similar catastrophic effect. The sole means of escape from

this grim dilemma was delayed marriage with "moral restraint," i.e., continence.

Actually, in Malthus' eyes, any project to better society
and alleviate want was likely to end by merely aggravating
the evils it sought to cure. This tough-minded, apparently
antisocial attitude of the young clergyman alienated humanitarians of his own and succeeding generations. The Malthus
doctrines were received enthusiastically, however, by the
wealthy and power-holding classes of his time. Mass poverty
and other social maladjustments could now be blamed on
early marriages and too many children—rather than on mal-
distribution of wealth.

The Malthus attitude toward government relief programs
may be illustrated by this quotation:

> The poor-laws of England tend to depress the general
> condition of the poor in these two ways. This first obvious
> tendency is to increase population without increasing the
> food for its support. A poor man may marry with little
> or no prospect of being able to support a family in inde-
> pendence. They may be said therefore in some measure
> to create the poor which they maintain; and as the pro-
> visions of the country must, in consequence of the in-
> creased population, be distributed to every man in smaller
> proportions, it is evident that the labour of those who
> are not supported by parish assistance will purchase a
> smaller quantity of provisions than before, and conse-
> quently, more of them must be driven to ask for support.
> Secondly, the quantity of provisions consumed in work-
> houses upon a part of the society, that cannot in gen-
> eral be considered the most valuable part, diminishes the
> shares that would otherwise belong to more worthy mem-
> bers; and thus in the same manner forces more to be-
> come dependent.

There is a summary view of Malthus' theories near the end
of his essay:

> Other circumstances being the same, it may be
> affirmed that countries are populous according to the
> quantity of human food which they produce or can ac-
> quire, and happy according to the liberality with which
> this food is divided, or the quantity which a day's labour
> will purchase. Corn countries are more populous than
> pasture countries, and rice countries more populous than
> corn countries. But their happiness does not depend upon

their being thinly or fully inhabited, upon their poverty or their richness, their youth or their age, but on the proportion which the population and the food bear to each other.

The appearance of Malthus' essay loosed a storm of criticism, protest, and vituperation, chiefly from two sources: the theological conservatives and the social radicals. "For thirty years," says his chief biographer, Bonar, "it rained refutations." Malthus was the most abused man of the age, put down as "a man who defended smallpox, slavery and child murder, who denounced soup kitchens, early marriage and parish allowances; who had the impudence to marry after preaching against the evils of a family; who thought the world so badly governed that the best actions do the most harm; who, in short, took all romance out of life."

A few critics dismissed the whole Malthus thesis lightly. Hazlitt "did not see what there was to discover after reading the tables of Noah's descendants, and knowing that the world is round." Coleridge remarked, "Are we now to have a quarto to teach us that great misery and great vice arise from poverty, and that there must be poverty in its worst shape wherever there are more mouths than loaves and more Heads than Brains?"

Other commentators were bitter: William Thompson, leader of early English socialism, wrote:

> Insult not the suffering, the great majority of mankind, with the glaring falsehood, that by means of limited population or not eating potatoes their own happiness is in their own hands, whilst the causes are left which render it morally and physically impossible for them to live without potatoes and improvident breeding.

Another violent expression came from William Cobbett: "How can Malthus and his nasty and silly disciples, how can those who want to abolish the Poor Rates, to prevent the poor from marrying; how can this at once stupid and conceited tribe look the labouring man in the face, while they call on him to take up arms, to risk his life in defense of the land."

It was Cobbett, incidentally, who invented the nickname "Parson" for Malthus. Cobbett is addressing a young farmer:

> "Why," said I, "how many children do you reckon to have had at last?"

"I do not care how many," said the man, "God never sends mouths without sending meat."

"Did you never hear," said I, "of one Parson Malthus?"

"No sir."

"If he were to hear of your words, he would be out-raged, for he wants an Act of Parliament to prevent poor people from marrying young, and from having such lots of children."

"Oh, the brute," exclaimed the wife, while the husband laughed, thinking I was joking.

An objection frequently brought against the Malthusian doctrine when it first appeared was that it was inconsistent with the benevolence of the Creator. Malthus was accused of having published an irreligious book—a damaging accusation against a clergyman of the established church. Because of this criticism, Malthus in the second edition of his *Essay* stressed "moral restraint," a device which would keep the population within bounds, while eliminating misery and vice, and thereby remove "all apparent imputation on the goodness of the Deity."

In a program commemorating the centenary of Malthus' death, in 1935, Bonar came to his defense against those who, he believed, had misrepresented, misread, misquoted, and misunderstood Malthus. In his view, Malthus had been af-firmative, not negative, in his approach. Bonar suggested that Malthus' "heart's desire for the human race" included:

1. A lower death rate for all.
2. A higher standard of life and livelihood for the poor.
3. An end of the waste of young human lives.

Malthus saw quite clearly that the prevention of a rapid birth rate was practiced increasingly by nations as they became more civilized and better educated, and as they acquired higher living standards. Consequently, his views on the future of human society were guardedly optimistic. In England, itself, Malthus observed that "the most cursory view of society must convince us, that throughout all ranks the preventive check to population prevails in a considerable degree." Realistically, he treated the various social classes—gentlemen, tradesmen and farmers, laborers and domestic servants—separately, be-cause of their different economic circumstances. An anxiety to maintain a certain social position, he thought, would pre-vent hasty marriages. For example:

A man of liberal education, but with an income only just sufficient to enable him to associate in the rank of gentlemen, must feel absolutely certain, that if he marries and has a family, he shall be obliged, if he mixes at all in society, to rank himself with moderate farmers, and the lower class of tradesmen. Two or three steps of descent in society, particularly at this round of the ladder, where education ends, and ignorance begins, will not be considered by the generality of people, as a fancied and chimerical, but a real and essential evil.

As can be inferred from the contemporary quotations, Malthus was far from ignored in his own lifetime. The impression made by the first edition of the *Essay* caused the English government to take a census of population in 1801, the first of any consequence since the coming of the Armada. Earlier proposals for a census had been opposed as anti-Scriptural and un-English. Another aftermath of the *Essay* was the modification of the government's Poor Laws to avoid some of the mistakes pointed out by Malthus.

The impact of Malthusian ideas on natural science was fully as powerful as on the social sciences. Both Charles Darwin and Alfred Russel Wallace freely acknowledged their indebtedness to Malthus in the development of the theory of evolution by natural selection. Darwin wrote:

In October 1838, that is fifteen months after I had begun my systematic enquiry, I happened to read for amusement Malthus' *Population,* and being well prepared to appreciate the struggle for existence [a phrase used by Malthus] which everywhere goes on from long-continued observation of animals and plants, it at once struck me that under these circumstances favourable variations would tend to be preserved and unfavourable ones to be destroyed. The result of this would be a new species. Here then I had at last got hold of a theory by which to work.

In similar vein, Wallace wrote:

It was the first work I had yet read treating any of the problems of philosophical biology, and its main principles remained with me as a permanent possession, and twenty years later gave me the long-sought clue to the effective agent in the evolution of organic species.

The angry protests of the clergy and social rebels, with which the 1798 edition of the *Essay* was received, left Malthus undisturbed; he had become fascinated with the subject and was determined to pursue it further. To reinforce his arguments, he toured Europe, in 1799, in search of materials, "through Sweden, Norway, Finland, and a part of Russia, these being the only countries at the time open to English travellers"; and he made another tour in France and Switzerland during the short peace of 1802. During this period he published a pamphlet entitled *An Investigation of the Cause of the Present High Price of Provisions,* taking the point of view that prices and profits are primarily determined by what he called "effective demand."

Five years after the appearance of the first edition of the *Essay,* a considerably enlarged second version came off the press—a quarto volume of 610 pages. It lacked the verve, sprightly style, and youthful cocksureness of the earlier work, and now assumed the form of a scholarly economic treatise, heavily documented and footnoted, though, except for the development of the idea of "moral restraint," the basic principles were unchanged. Four more editions were brought out in the author's lifetime. By its fifth edition the *Essay* had reached three volumes, totaling about 1,000 pages. The only other major work produced by Malthus, so occupied was he with the successive revisions of the *Essay,* was *The Principles of Political Economy Considered with a View to Their Practical Applications,* published in 1820.

Malthus' personal career was relatively quiet and peaceful. He had been free to pursue his economic studies and writing, with little other responsibility, until 1804, when he married, at the age of thirty-eight. The following year he was appointed professor of modern history and political economy at the newly established East India Company's college at Haileybury, for the general education of civil servants of the East India Company. This was the earliest chair of political economy to be established in an English college or university. Malthus remained at Haileybury for thirty years, until his death in 1834. He had three children, of whom two, a son and a daughter, grew to maturity.

The fires stirred up by Malthus have never died down. The controversies, pro and con, still continue to rage. Such recent titles supporting the Malthusian thesis as the *Challenge of Man's Future,* the *Road to Survival, Limits of the Earth,* and *Our Plundered Planet* draw retorts in articles entitled "The Malthusian Scarecrow," "Eat Hearty," "The Malthusian

Mischief," and "Mankind Need Not Starve." What is a balanced point of view on the Malthusian theories today?

A major factor in the population problem since the mid-nineteenth century has been the increasing acceptance of contraceptive techniques, bringing about planned limitations of families except among those lacking knowledge or who are deterred by religious scruples. This movement, known variously as Neo-Malthusianism, birth control, or planned parenthood, has been called "the most significant demographic movement in the modern world." Malthus specifically rejected and condemned contraception, however, and the practice in his time was regarded as something "foul, strange, and unnatural." Nevertheless, it has become one of the principal population checks of modern society, adding a fourth to Malthus' trio of "vice, misery, and moral restraint."

In 1800, when Malthus was writing, the world's population was estimated at one billion. In the past 150 years it has grown to two and a half billions. A high proportion of the expansion resulted from an increase in the length of life rather than from any phenomenal rise in the birth rate. In the advanced nations of the world, innumerable lives have been saved by changes in medical, sanitary, and social practices. The Industrial Revolution brought England an immense increase in the production of manufactured goods, and these were exchanged for food and raw materials from unindustrialized countries. All forms of transportation were improved to give added mobility. Surplus population was siphoned off by emigration to newly developed continents. The dire predictions of Malthus, therefore, were at least delayed in coming to pass, and perhaps have been postponed indefinitely, insofar as the Western world is concerned.

There remain, however, critical areas of the globe which serve as perfect illustrations of Malthusian theories. The Near East, most of Asia, and a majority of Central and South American countries are characterized by high fertility, and a correspondingly high death rate. In those areas, lives saved by medicine and sanitation are likely to be lost by poverty and famine.

As the antithesis of that situation, some of the most highly civilized and cultured nations of the earth have entered a period of stabilization or falling population, notably France, Sweden, Iceland, Austria, England, Wales, and Ireland. Stabilization has come about through low fertility, a reduction in the number of young people, and the increased length of life.

The production of food has been increased immensely since Malthus' time, and authorities agree it would be possible to make further substantial gains, through more efficient methods of production, irrigation and reclamation of marginal land, substitution of vegetable foods for animal foods, and by better control over insect pests. The crop surpluses prevailing in the United States and Canada could be cited as evidence of an error in the Malthusian principle. But notwithstanding our vast production of food, there remain hundreds of millions of people in the Orient and elsewhere who exist on a near-starvation or bare subsistence level. Thus the spectacle of perhaps two-thirds of the world's population enduring malnutrition, famine, ill-health, and disease would appear to make the issues raised by Malthus a century and a half ago as real and vital today as they were then.

Even those critics who contend that the Malthusian thesis has been invalidated in certain respects by developments which were not, or could not have been foreseen by Malthus, concede that major consequences have flowed from his ideas. As Hobhouse acutely observed, "The Malthusian theory was one cause of the defeat of its own prophecies. It was the belief that population was growing too fast that operated indirectly to check it."

Of many commentators who have written on Malthus' *Essay on the Principle of Population,* perhaps none has given a fairer or more discerning appraisal than John Maynard Keynes, who believed that:

> The book can claim a place amongst those which have had great influence on the progress of thought. It is profoundly in the English tradition of humane science—in that tradition of Scotch and English thought, in which there has been, I think, an extraordinary continuity of *feeling,* if I may so express it, from the eighteenth century to the present time—the tradition which is suggested by the names of Locke, Hume, Adam Smith, Paley, Bentham, Darwin, and Mill, a tradition marked by a love of truth and a most noble lucidity, by a prosaic sanity free from sentiment or metaphysic, and by an immense disinterestedness and public spirit. There is a continuity in those writings, not only of feeling, but of actual matter. It is in this company that Malthus belongs.

5 INDIVIDUAL VERSUS STATE

HENRY DAVID THOREAU:
"Civil Disobedience"

The name of Henry David Thoreau conjures up in the imagination a keen observer of nature, a lover of solitude and the outdoors, an exponent of the simple life, a poet and mystic, a master of English prose style.

Much less frequently is Thoreau remembered as the author of some of the most extreme radical manifestoes in American history, a spokesman, as described by one of his biographers, for "the most outspoken doctrines of resistance ever penned on this continent." Going far beyond Thomas Jefferson's "That government is best which governs least," Thoreau concluded that "That government is best which governs not at all."

These words introduce Thoreau's celebrated essay "Civil Disobedience," which first appeared in an obscure, short-lived periodical—Elizabeth Peabody's *Aesthetic Papers*—in May 1849. Originally called "Resistance to Civil Government," the title was later changed to "On the Duty of Civil Disobedience," or merely "Civil Disobedience." When first published, the work attracted slight attention and few readers. During the next hundred years, it was read by thousands and affected the lives of millions.

Was Thoreau a philosophical anarchist in his beliefs? An analysis of "Civil Disobedience," its setting and background, may provide an answer to that complex question.

As for Thoreau himself, little in his beginnings was calculated to produce a social rebel. Born of French and Scottish stock at Concord, Massachusetts, in 1817, he grew up in a conservative environment of genteel poverty. Four years at Harvard were undistinguished, though there is a glimpse of the future nonconformist in the fact that he wore a green coat to chapel, "because the rules required black." Much time was spent in the college library, and young Thoreau's interest in writing was stimulated by two excellent teachers: Edward T. Channing and Jones Very.

Happy to return to the green fields and woods of Concord, Thoreau never left them thereafter except for short visits. He turned his hand to a variety of occupations. After a brief, inauspicious fling at public school teaching, three years were spent in partnership with his brother John operating a private school. There followed intermittent periods of assisting his father in the family business of making lead pencils, serving as general handy man for the community, acting as town surveyor, giving occasional lectures, and attempting to become a professional author.

For two brief periods Thoreau lived in the home of Ralph Waldo Emerson. There he became acquainted with members of the Transcendental Club, and participated actively in the discussions of this noted group of New England writers and thinkers. Emerson's influence on his intellectual development was strong, including furnishing some of the ideas for "Civil Disobedience."

Thoreau had no ambition to accumulate wealth, or to perform any work other than enough to provide him the minimum essentials for living. His consuming passion, always, was to achieve leisure time for the fundamentally important matters, as he saw them, of rambling in the Concord fields, studying nature at first hand, meditating, reading, writing—to do the things he wanted to do. His simple needs could be met without engaging in a life of drudgery, such as he observed his neighbors leading. Instead of the Biblical formula of six days of work and one day of rest, Thoreau preferred to reverse the ratios—devoting only the seventh day to labor. In short, everything he stood for was the antithesis of the teachings of Adam Smith, the maxims of Franklin's Poor Richard, and the traditional American ideals of hard work and quick riches.

To exemplify his conception of the simple life, shed of all superfluities, Thoreau spent two years at Walden Pond near Concord. There he built a hut, planted beans and potatoes, ate the plainest food (mainly rice, corn meal, potatoes, and molasses), and lived alone, withdrawn from society. It was a time of concentrated thinking and writing, out of which grew one of the greatest books in American literature: *Walden, or Life in the Woods* (1854).

Ostensibly, *Walden* is a record of Thoreau's life in his rural retreat, and is full of memorable descriptions of the seasons, the scenery, and the animal life about him. But *Walden* is far more than the observations of a naturalist, as Izaak Walton's *Compleat Angler* is more than a manual on fishing. Its comments on the superficialities and limitations of society and government have universal significance. Over the years, the social criticism has drawn as many readers as the portions dealing with natural history. In its way, *Walden* is as radical a document as the earlier published "Civil Disobedience," to which it bears a close kinship.

While visiting in Concord in 1843, soon after he began his sojourn at Walden Pond, Thoreau was arrested and jailed for nonpayment of poll tax. In his refusal to pay the tax, he was following the example of Bronson Alcott, father of the "Little Women," who had been arrested two years earlier for the same offense. Both were using this means to protest against the state's support of slavery. Thoreau was imprisoned for only one night, for an aunt, contrary to his wishes, stepped in and paid the tax.

Not until several years later did Thoreau tell the story, in "Civil Disobedience," of his brush with the law over the poll tax violation. Originally written as a lecture in 1848, the printed version came off the press the following year. The Mexican War of 1846-47 had but recently been concluded and slavery was a burning issue. The Fugitive Slave Law, which was to arouse Thoreau's special indignation, was soon to be enacted. These matters, plus his poll tax battle, were the inspiration for "Civil Disobedience."

Any war was repugnant to Thoreau's ideals, but the Mexican War particularly so, for its only purpose, he believed, was to extend the hated institution of Negro slavery into new territory. Why, he asked, should he be required to provide financial support for a government guilty of such injustices and stupidity? Here was the birth of his doctrine of civil disobedience. Anything except a politician at heart, Thoreau decided the time had come to examine the nature of the state and its government. What should be the relation of the individual to the state, and of the state to the individual? From a consideration of these questions emerged Thoreau's philosophy of personal integrity and of man's place in society.

"Government," wrote Thoreau, "is at best but an expedient; but most governments are sometimes inexpedient. The objections that have been brought against a standing army, and they are many and weighty, and deserve to prevail, may also at last be brought against a standing government."

Thoreau acknowledged that the American government was a relatively excellent one.

> Yet, this government never of itself furthered any enterprise, but by the alacrity with which it got out of its way. *It* does not keep the country free. *It* does not

settle the West. *It* does not educate. The character inherent in the American people has done all that has been accomplished; and it would have done somewhat more, if the government had not sometimes got in its way. For government is an expedient by which men would fain succeed in letting one another alone; and, as has been said, when it is most expedient the governed are most let alone by it.

Almost immediately after presenting the case for no government, Thoreau recognized that man had not yet reached a state of perfectibility where a complete lack of government was feasible, and began to modify his stand.

To speak practically and as a citizen, unlike those who call themselves no-government men, I ask for, not at once no government, but *at once* a better government. Let every man make known what kind of government would command his respect, and that will be one step toward obtaining it.

The rights of minorities and the fallacies of majority rule were emphatically stated by Thoreau. A majority rules, he argued, "not because they are most likely to be in the right, nor because this seems fairest to the minority, but because they are physically the strongest. But a government in which the majority rule in all cases cannot be based on justice, even as far as men understand it." Never, he believed, should the citizen "resign his conscience to the legislator. . . . We should be men first and subjects afterward. It is not desirable to cultivate a respect for the law, so much as for the right."

Politicians, as a class, Thoreau held in low esteem. "Most legislators, politicians, lawyers, ministers, and office holders," he remarked, "serve the state chiefly with their heads; and as they rarely make any moral distinctions, they are as likely to serve the Devil, without *intending* it, as God. A very few, as heroes, patriots, martyrs, reformers in the great sense, and *men*, serve the state with their consciences also, and so necessarily resist it for the most part; and they are commonly treated as enemies by it."

Thoreau then proceeded to attack the American government of his day. "I cannot for an instant," he declared, "recognize that political organization as *my* government which is the *slave's* government also." It was the duty of citizens to resist evil in the state even to the point of open and deliberate disobedience to its laws.

When a sixth of the population of a nation which has undertaken to be the refuge of liberty are slaves . . . I think it is not too soon for honest men to rebel and revolutionize. . . . This people must cease to hold slaves and to make war on Mexico, though it cost them their existence as a people.

Likewise deplored by Thoreau was the citizen who felt that he had done his full duty merely by casting a ballot.

All voting is a sort of gaming, like checkers or backgammon, with a slight moral tinge to it, a playing with right and wrong, with moral questions, and betting naturally accompanies it. The character of the voters is not staked. . . . Even voting *for the right* is *doing* nothing for it. It is only expressing to men feebly your desire that it should prevail. . . . There is but little virtue in the actions of masses of men.

The proper attitude of the citizen toward unjust laws was debated by Thoreau. Was it better to wait for majority action to change the laws, or to refuse at once to obey the laws? Thoreau's unequivocal answer was, that if the government "requires you to be the agent of injustice to another, then, I say, break the law. . . . What I have to do is to see, at any rate, that I do not lend myself to the wrong which I condemn."

It is of the very nature of government, Thoreau suggested, to oppose changes and reforms, and to mistreat its critics. "Why," he asked, "does it always crucify Christ, and excommunicate Copernicus and Luther, and pronounce Washington and Franklin rebels?"

Those who opposed slavery, Thoreau urged, "should at once effectually withdraw their support, both in person and property, from the government of Massachusetts, and not wait until they constitute a majority of one, before they suffer the right to prevail through them. I think that it is enough if they have God on their side, without waiting for that other one. Moreover, any man more right than his neighbors constitutes a majority of one already."

As a symbol of civil disobedience, a method open to every citizen, Thoreau advocated refusal to pay taxes. If a thousand or even fewer men would express their disapproval of the government in that fashion, Thoreau thought, reform would inevitably follow. Even if resistance to authority meant punishment, "Under a government which imprisons any unjustly, the true place for a just man is also a prison. . . . If the alternative is to keep all just men in prison, or give up war and slavery, the state will not hesitate which to choose." By paying taxes to an unjust government, the citizen condones wrongs committed by the state.

Thoreau saw, however, that the propertied class had too much at stake to rebel, for "the rich man—not to make any invidious comparisons—is always sold to the institution which makes him rich. Absolutely speaking, the more money, the less virtue, for money comes between a man and his objects, and obtains them for him." Not suffering the handicap of wealth, Thoreau could afford to resist. "It costs me less in every sense to incur the penalty of disobedience to the State than it would to obey. I should feel as if I were worth less in that case."

Thoreau was realistic also in seeing the weight of economic objections which held the state of Massachusetts from taking action against slavery.

> Practically speaking, the opponents to a reform in Massachusetts are not a hundred thousand politicians at the South, but a hundred thousand merchants and farmers here who are more interested in commerce and agriculture than they are in humanity, and are not prepared to do justice to slave and to Mexico, *cost what it may*.

For six years, adhering to his principles, Thoreau reported that he paid no poll tax. His short prison term left him unshaken in his convictions, but with less regard for the state.

> I saw that the State was half-witted, that it was timid as a lone woman with her silver spoons, and that it did not know its friends from its foes, and I lost all my remaining respect for it, and pitied it. Thus the State never intentionally confronts a man's sense, intellectual or moral, but only his body, his senses. It is not armed with superior wit or honesty, but with superior physical strength. I was not born to be forced. I will breathe after my own fashion.

Thoreau differentiated between taxes. He states that he "never declined paying the highway tax," nor the school tax, "because I am as desirous of being a good neighbor as I am of being a bad subject." Where he drew the line was in paying general taxes to support slavery and war. "I simply wish to refuse allegiance to the State, to withdraw and stand aloof from it effectually," in these matters.

There was no desire, either, on Thoreau's part to pose as a martyr or saint.

I do not wish to quarrel with any man or nation. I do not wish to split hairs, to make fine distinctions, or set myself up as better than my neighbors. I seek rather, I may say, even an excuse for conforming to the laws of the land. I am but too ready to conform to them. Indeed, I have reason to suspect myself on this head; and each year as the tax-gathering comes round, I find myself disposed to review the acts and position of the general and State governments, and the spirit of the people, to discover a pretext for conformity.

Furthermore, Thoreau again admitted that, though they fell far below his ideals, "The Constitution, with all its faults is very good; the law and the courts are very respectable; even this State and this American government are, in many respects, very admirable, and rare things, to be thankful for."

Despite his strictures on majority rule, too, Thoreau had some faith in popular judgment. In his view, legislators lacked ability to deal effectively with the "comparatively humble questions of taxation and finance, commerce and manufactures and agriculture. If we were left solely to the wordy wit of legislators in Congress for our guidance, uncorrected by the seasonable experience and the effectual complaints of the people, America would not long retain her rank among the nations."

Thoreau concludes "Civil Disobedience" with a statement of his concept of perfect government, and a resounding reaffirmation of his belief in the dignity and worth of the individual.

To be strictly just, the authority of government . . . must have the sanction and consent of the governed. It can have no pure right over my person and property but what I concede to it. The progress from an absolute to a limited monarchy, from a limited monarchy to a democracy, is a progress toward a true respect for the individual. . . . Is a democracy, such as we know it, the last improvement possible in government? Is it not possible to take a step further towards recognizing and organizing the rights of man? There will never be a really free and enlightened State until the State comes to recognize the individual as a higher and independent power, from which all its own power and authority are derived, and treats him accordingly. I please myself with imagining a State at last which can afford to be just to all men, and to treat the individual with respect as a neighbor; which even would not think it inconsistent with its own repose if a few were to live aloof from it, not meddling with it, nor embraced by it, who fulfilled all the duties of neighbors and fellow-men. A State which bore this kind of fruit, and suffered it to drop off as fast as it ripened, would prepare the way for a still more perfect and glorious State, which also I have imagined, but not yet anywhere seen.

In essence, Thoreau's basic contention in "Civil Disobedience" was that the state exists for individuals, not individuals for the state. A minority should refuse to yield to a majority if moral principles must be compromised in order to do so. Further, the state has no right to offend moral liberty by forcing the citizen to support injustices. Man's conscience should always be his supreme guiding spirit.

The impact of "Civil Disobedience" on Thoreau's own time was negligible. References to the work in the writings of his contemporaries are almost nonexistent. With the Civil War little more than a decade ahead, it might be assumed that the essay would have struck a popular chord. Apparently it was buried under an avalanche of Abolitionist literature, and remained obscure and largely forgotten until the following century.

Now, the scene shifts to South Africa and India. In 1907, a copy of "Civil Disobedience" fell into the hands of a Hindu lawyer in Africa, Mohandas Karamchand Gandhi, who was already meditating upon the merits of passive resistance as a defense for his people. Here is an account of the incident, as recollected by the Mahatma, twenty-two years later, to Henry Salt, one of Thoreau's earliest biographers:

> My first introduction to Thoreau's writings was, I think, in 1907, or later, when I was in the thick of the passive resistance struggle. A friend sent me the essay on "Civil Disobedience." It left a deep impression upon me. I translated a portion for the readers of "Indian Opinion in South Africa," which I was then editing, and I made copious extracts for the English part of that paper. The essay seemed to be so convincing and truthful that I felt the need of knowing more of Thoreau, and I came across your Life of him, his *Walden*, and other shorter essays, all of which I read with great pleasure and equal profit.

A slightly different version is recounted by one of Gandhi's closest associates in South Africa, Henry Polak:

I cannot now recall, [in 1931] whether, early in 1907, Gandhi or I first came across the volume of Thoreau's Essays (published I believe in Scott's Library), but we were both of us enormously impressed by the confirmation of the rightness of the principle of passive resistance and civil disobedience . . . contained in the essay "On the Duty of Civil Disobedience." After consultation with Mr. Gandhi, I reproduced the essay in the columns of *Indian Opinion* and it was translated into the Gujarati language, in which, as well as in English, the paper was published, and the essay was subsequently circulated in pamphlet form. Later in the same year, *Indian Opinion* organized an essay competition on "The Ethics of Passive Resistance," with special reference to Thoreau's essay and Socrates's writings that had already come to Mr. Gandhi's attention.

Gandhi, who had been dissatisfied with the term "passive resistance," but had found no suitable substitute, at once adopted "civil disobedience" to describe his movement. Here was a statement of principle, he decided, that meant firmness without violence, and a devotion to truth and justice—a political policy completely in accord with Gandhi's philosophy. "Civil Disobedience" in the hands of Mahatma Gandhi became a bible of nonresistance. For his Hindu followers, Gandhi coined an equivalent, *Satyagraha,* a combination of two Sanskrit words, translated as "soul force" or "the force which is born of truth and love or nonviolence."

Thoreau's fight against slavery in the United States, says Gandhi's biographer, Krishnalal Shridharani, "imbued Gandhi with the faith that it is not the number of the resisters that counts in a Satyagraha, but the purity of the sacrificial suffering." Gandhi declared:

Writs are impossible when they are confined to a few recalcitrants. They are troublesome when they have to be executed against many high-souled persons who have done no wrong and who refuse payment to vindicate a principle. They may not attract much notice when isolated individuals resort to this method of protest. But clean examples have a curious method of multiplying themselves. They bear publicity and the sufferers instead of incurring odium receive congratulations. Men like Thoreau brought about the abolition of slavery by their personal examples.

In this statement, Gandhi was echoing Thoreau's words on the power of a small but determined minority. Thereby, as Shridharani commented, Thoreau "not only propounded the weapon of civil disobedience which constitutes one important stratagem in Gandhi's Satyagraha, but he also pointed out the potentiality of non-co-operation, which Gandhi enlarged upon afterwards as a means to destroy a corrupt state."

Gandhi remained in South Africa through 1914, carrying on a running battle with government forces led by General Jan Smuts. The campaign was marked by persecution, violence of many descriptions, imprisonments, and all the other tools available to a powerful government attempting to suppress an unpopular minority. Gandhi's techniques of non-co-operation, nonresistance, civil disobedience, or *Satyagraha,* paid off, however, in the end, Prime Minister Smuts and his government granted every important demand of the Indians, including abolition of fingerprint legislation, repeal of a three-pound head tax, validation of Hindu and Moslem marriages, removal of restrictions on the immigration of educated Indians, and a promise to protect the legal rights of the Indian citizens.

Andrews, another Gandhi biographer, concluded that the South African campaign must stand "not only as the first but as the classic example of the use of nonresistance by organized masses of men for the redress of grievances."

According to Shridharani, Gandhi's interpretation of civil disobedience was that:

Only those who are otherwise willing to obey the law . . . could have a right to practice civil disobedience against unjust laws. It was quite different from the behavior of outlaws, for it was to be practiced openly and after ample notice. It was not likely, therefore, to foster a habit of lawbreaking or to create an atmosphere of anarchy. And it was to be resorted to only when all other peaceful means, such as petitions and negotiations and arbitration, had failed to redress the wrong.

Early in 1915, Gandhi returned to India. There, until his death at the hands of a Hindu assassin in 1948, he led the forces that eventually won freedom for India and Pakistan. Again there were rioting, massacres, long prison terms, suppression of civil liberties, and unjust laws with which to contend. Civil disobedience was frequently used during these years and was sharpened by Gandhi into a weapon of remarkable effectiveness. The first steps were agitation, demonstrations, negotiations, and, if possible, arbitration. If these did not produce results, such economic sanctions were resorted to as strikes, picketing, general strikes, commercial boycott, and sit-down strikes. Another tactic was nonpayment of taxes.

In August, 1947, dominion status was granted by Britain to Hindu India and Moslem Pakistan.

Undoubtedly, the future will witness further use of the principles of civil disobedience, as conceived by Thoreau and perfected by Gandhi. The power of oppressed peoples everywhere, even in the ruthless dictatorships of modern times, can make itself felt through these means. A current example is the fight of the colored races of South Africa against the Strijdom government—a renewal of Gandhi's crusade.

"Even the most despotic government," said Gandhi, "cannot stand except for the consent of the governed which consent is often forcibly procured by the despot. Immediately the subject ceases to fear the despotic force, his power is gone."

Thoreau rejected authoritarianism and totalitarianism in any form. His doctrines run absolutely counter to socialism and communism, or· to any other ideology that would place the state above individual rights. It must be conceded that trends of government in the mid-twentieth century show Thoreau's ideas fighting a losing battle. Nevertheless, in the world at large the problem of the citizen's relation to his government—the nature and extent of his obedience to the state—has never been more urgent.

"In Thoreau," wrote Parrington, "the eighteenth-century philosophy of individualism, the potent liberalisms let loose on the world by Jean Jacques Rousseau, came to the fullest expression in New England. He was the completest embodiment of the *laissez-faire* reaction against a regimented social order, the severest critic of the lower economics that frustrate the dreams of human freedom. He was fortunate in dying before the age of exploitation had choked his river with its weeds; fortunate in not foreseeing how remote is that future of free men on which his hopes were fixed."

6 | CRUSADER FOR THE LOWLY

HARRIET BEECHER STOWE:
Uncle Tom's Cabin

On a single point only do the pro-and-con critics of *Uncle Tom's Cabin* agree. Without exception, all recognize the book's tremendous impact on its time, and its immense influence in instigating the American Civil War. At one extreme, a contemporary commentator described the work as "a monstrous distortion inspired by Abolitionist fanaticism and designed to excite sectional discord." And a well-known lecturer and writer, early in the present century, remarked that *"Uncle Tom's Cabin* has done more harm to the world than any other book ever written."

In contrast, the sentiment of a host of devoted admirers was expressed in a letter from Longfellow, characterizing *Uncle Tom's Cabin* as "one of the greatest triumphs recorded in literary history, to say nothing of its moral effect." Others hailed the book as "a triumph of reality," "immortal," and the author "unquestionably a woman of genius."

Never was a book more topical or better timed psychologically. The struggle over the slavery question had grown more tense—aggravated by the passage of the Fugitive Slave Law— the Abolitionists had for twenty years kept up a crescendo of antislavery agitation, Congress was split down the center by the increasing controversy, the clergy—North and South— boomed from their pulpits Biblical arguments for and against the "peculiar institution" of slavery. The surcharged moral climate awaited only a spark to set off a world-shaking explosion. *Uncle Tom's Cabin* furnished the spark.

Not only was the time ripe, but for generations heredity and environment had been shaping exactly the right person to inaugurate the great crusade against human slavery.

Daughter of one of the most noted divines of the nineteenth century, Lyman Beecher, sister of an even more sensational minister, Henry Ward Beecher, married to a minister, sister and mother of other ministers, Harriet Beecher Stowe spent virtually her entire life in an intensely religious atmosphere. Furthermore, her religious training was rigorously Calvinistic, in the spirit of Jonathan Edwards, Samuel Hopkins, and other New England Puritans. Constantly surrounded by fire-and-brimstone theology from her earliest childhood, Harriet could hardly avoid becoming a preacher—if not from a pulpit, at least with a pen. Throughout her prolific writings, including *Uncle Tom's Cabin,* the religious background was ever in evidence, inspiring her to evangelistic fervor and scriptural eloquence of expression.

Harriet Beecher Stowe was born in Litchfield, Connecticut, in 1811; and she received a better education in Hartford than was customary for women of the period. About two-thirds of it was religious in nature. She was an avid reader. Aside from theology, her favorite authors were Byron and Scott, both of whom influenced her later writing style.

The dynamic and restless Lyman Beecher transferred himself and his family from Litchfield to a pastorate in Boston when Harriet was fourteen, and a few years later moved again, to Cincinnati, where he had been called as President of the Lane Theological Seminary. There, Harriet remained until 1850, teaching school, getting married to a member of the Seminary faculty, Calvin Stowe, giving birth to six of her seven children, and occasionally contributing short sketches and stories for magazine publication.

The Cincinnati years were formative in many respects. Located across the Ohio River from large slave plantations in Kentucky, the city was the center of a raging slavery controversy. Anti-abolition mobs roamed the streets, destroying the presses of opposition newspapers, and mistreating free Negroes. Violent speeches, for and against slavery, were heard. Cincinnati was a refuge for escaping slaves, on their way north by underground railroad to freedom in Canada. The Seminary itself was a hotbed of antislavery sentiment, and only the fact that it was on a rough and muddy road, two miles from the city, saved it from mob attack. Lyman Beecher's home sheltered refugees on several occasions. Harriet heard direct from the runaway slaves stories of broken families, the cruelties of overseers, the horrors of the auction block, and the terrors of being hunted in flight.

On but one occasion did Mrs. Stowe see the slave-holding system in operation. On a brief visit with friends to Maysville, Kentucky, in 1833, she observed a number of plantations, with their great patriarchal manor houses and slave quarters. Here she found the model for the fictional Shelby plantation in *Uncle Tom's Cabin,* and obtained other impressions of the slave system's workings. From her brother Charles, a businessman who traveled to New Orleans and the Red River country, came more ammunition, for he brought back ugly tales of slavery in the Deep South. Harriet was indebted to Charles for the prototype of Simon Legree in *Uncle Tom's Cabin*, based on a ruffianly overseer whom Charles had met on a Mississippi River boat.

Harriet Stowe did not become an out-and-out Abolitionist during the Cincinnati years. Perhaps she shared her father's opinion that the Abolitionists were "made up of vinegar, aqua fortis and oil of vitriol with brimstone, saltpeter and charcoal to explode and scatter corrosive matter." In fact, Mrs. Stowe was an onlooker rather than an active protagonist in the slavery battle until she returned to New England. Calvin Stowe was appointed to a professorship at Bowdoin College in Maine, and there his family was transplanted in 1850.

All New England was then seething with indignation over passage of the Fugitive Slave Law, and especially over incidents connected with the law's enforcement in Boston. Southern slave-owners could pursue escaped slaves into free states, and officials in those states were required to aid them in recovering their property. Negroes who had long been legally free were rounded up and returned to their former masters, and their families were frequently broken up in the process.

A letter reached Harriet Stowe from her sister-in-law, Mrs. Edward Beecher, who implored her to "write something that would make a whole nation feel what an accursed thing slavery is." According to Stowe family tradition, Harriet at that moment resolved that "God helping me, I will write something. I will if I live." Meanwhile, one brother, Edward, was thundering against slavery from a Boston church, and another brother, Henry Ward, was holding spectacular auctions of slaves in his Brooklyn church, to redeem them from servitude.

The first portion of *Uncle Tom's Cabin* to be composed was the climax describing Tom's death. While attending church in Brunswick during a communion service, Mrs. Stowe related, the entire scene unrolled in her mind's eye. The same afternoon, she went to her room, locked the door and wrote out her vision. She ran out of writing paper, but used scraps of brown wrapping paper to complete her story. Subsequently, this account formed the chapter entitled "The Martyr" in *Uncle Tom's Cabin*. It was read to her children and husband, all of whom were deeply affected. Calvin Stowe is said to have exclaimed, "Hattie, this is the climax of that story of slavery which you promised sister Isabel you would write. Begin at the beginning and work up to this and you'll have your book."

After a few weeks, Harriet Stowe wrote Gamaliel Bailey, editor of the *National Era*, an abolition paper published in

Washington, D.C. Bailey had known the Beecher family in Cincinnati, where he edited another antislavery journal, the *Philanthropist,* until driven out by mob violence. In her letter Mrs. Stowe reported that she was planning to write a story called *Uncle Tom's Cabin,* or *The Man That Was a Thing* (a subtitle later changed to *Life Among The Lowly*), in serial form to run to three or four numbers. Bailey offered her three hundred dollars for publication rights and the *National Era* began serialization in June 1851.

A work which Mrs. Stowe had expected to finish in a month stretched on interminably. Scenes, incidents, characters, and conversations stored up in her memory from past experiences or reading came crowding in, while her powers of imagination and invention were at white heat. The weekly installments ran on for nearly a year before the weary author was able to bring the book to an end. Afterwards, she insisted that "the Lord Himself wrote it. I was but an instrument in his hand."

The essential plot of *Uncle Tom's Cabin* is not complex, though it involves many characters. In the opening scene, a benevolent Kentucky slave-owner, Mr. Shelby, in order to pay his debts, is compelled to sell some of his best slaves, including Uncle Tom, to a New Orleans slave-dealer named Haley. Overhearing a conversation between Shelby and Haley, a mulatto girl named Eliza learns that her child Harry is also to be sold. During the night she flees with the boy across the frozen Ohio river, and seeks freedom in Canada. Her husband, George Harris, a slave on a nearby plantation, also escapes and follows her. Eventually, after many adventures with pursuing slave-catchers, but aided by Quakers and other sympathetic whites along the way, they reach Canada and later Africa.

Uncle Tom is less fortunate. To avoid embarrassing his master, he refuses to run away, and is separated from his wife and children. On the trip down the Mississippi to New Orleans, Tom saves the life of little Eva, and in gratitude her father, St. Clare, buys him from the dealer. The next two years are pleasant ones for Tom as a servant in St. Clare's elegant New Orleans home, with the saintly child Eva, and her impish little Negro companion, Topsy. Then Eva dies, and, in her memory, St. Clare makes plans to free Tom and his other slaves. But St. Clare is accidentally killed trying to separate two quarreling men, and Mrs. St. Clare orders Tom sent to the slave market. Tom is bought at public auction by a brutal, drunken Red River planter named Simon Legree. Despite impeccable behavior and all efforts to please his cruel master, Tom soon incurs Legree's hatred, and is frequently beaten. Two female slaves, Cassy and Emmeline, decide to make their escape from the plantation and go into hiding. Legree accuses Tom of aiding them, and he suspects Tom of knowing where they are hidden. When Tom refuses to reveal any information, Legree has him flogged into insensibility. A couple of days later, young George Shelby, son of Tom's former owner, arrives to redeem Tom. It is too late. The effects of his vicious beating are mortal and Tom dies. After knocking Legree down, George Shelby returns to Kentucky and frees all of his slaves in the name of Uncle Tom, resolved to devote his future to the abolition cause.

Though the *National Era's* circulation was not large, *Uncle Tom's Cabin* won an enthusiastic and zealous following within a few months. Before the last chapter of the serial appeared, Mrs. Stowe's brain child came off the press in book form. The small publishing firm of John P. Jewett, in Boston, undertook the work with considerable trepidation, because of its length, its authorship by a woman, and the unpopular nature of the subject. To hedge against possible financial loss, Jewett offered the Stowes fifty per cent of the profits, in exchange for paying one-half the production costs. Instead, the Stowes elected to receive straight ten per cent royalties on copies sold —a decision that cost them a fortune.

Neither the author nor the publisher was optimistic about *Uncle Tom's* success. Mrs. Stowe expressed the hope that the book would bring in enough to buy her a new silk dress. The original edition was 5,000 copies in two volumes, with a woodcut of a Negro cabin as a frontispiece.

On the day of publication 3,000 copies were sold, the balance went the second day, while orders poured in. Within a week, 10,000 copies had been bought, and over 300,000 by the end of the first year in the United States alone. Eight power presses were running night and day to meet the demand, three paper mills were trying to supply the necessary paper, and still the publisher was "thousands of copies behind orders." Apparently the book was read by every reasonably literate person in the country.

Exceeding even the American sales was the popularity of *Uncle Tom's Cabin* abroad. A young employee of Putnam's sent a copy to an English publisher, receiving five pounds for his trouble. Pirated editions proliferated, since international copyright protection was lacking. Soon there were eighteen English publishing houses supplying the demand with forty different editions. Within a year it is estimated that a million and a half copies were sold in Great Britain and the Colonies, from none of which did Mrs. Stowe receive any royalty. Simultaneously, continental European publishers were busy reaping the golden harvest. Eventually, the book was translated into at least twenty-two languages, and was as phenomenally successful in France, Germany, Sweden, Holland, and other countries as it had been in English-speaking nations.

Furthermore, the novel was promptly dramatized and became one of the most popular plays ever produced on the American stage. Innumerable versions put on by countless theatrical troupes have toured the world during the past century. Again, Mrs. Stowe gained nothing financially, for the copyright law prevailing in 1852 gave her no control over dramatizations. As a matter of fact, she disapproved of the theater, and refused requested permission for her book to be made into a play.

Altogether, the smashing hit scored by *Uncle Tom's Cabin* surpasses anything in the annals of modern publishing. Only the Bible is believed to have beaten the novel's record. In fictional, dramatic, poetical, and musical form it became the property of millions, and circulated round the globe.

The impact of *Uncle Tom's Cabin* on contemporary opinion and passions was as striking as its huge sales. Mrs. Stowe's son and grandson later described its reception as "like the kindling of mighty conflagration, the sky was all aglow with the resistless tide of emotion that swept all before it and even crossed the broad ocean, till it seemed as if the whole world scarcely thought or talked of anything else."

From the South a storm of wrath, denials, and vituperation descended upon Uncle Tom's author. Soon her name was bracketed with the Prince of Evil. Newspapers carried columns of detailed criticism, designed to expose errors and fallacies in Mrs. Stowe's depiction of slavery. Typical of the comments was the *Southern Literary Messenger's* declaration that the book was a "criminal prostitution of the high functions of the imagination," and by her guilt as its author, Mrs. Stowe "placed herself without the pale of kindly treatment at the hands of Southern criticism." Thousands of angry and abusive letters came to Mrs. Stowe personally. At the beginning, *Uncle Tom's Cabin* circulated freely in the South, but after the bitter reaction, possession of a copy in that area became dangerous.

Ironically, Mrs. Stowe had hoped and believed that her novel might be a means of peacefully resolving the prolonged slavery dispute. After reading it, a Southern friend had written her, "Your book is going to be the great pacificator; it will unite North and South." In *Uncle Tom's Cabin* Mrs. Stowe attempted to present fairly both sides of the slavery controversy—the picturesque and patriarchal on the one hand, the cruel and sinister on the other. Two slave-holders depicted in the book, Mr. Shelby and Augustine St. Clare, are Southern gentlemen of peerless virtue. Little Eva, St. Clare's daughter, is probably the most angelic child in all literature. The arch-villain Simon Legree is a renegade Vermonter, and much of the book's comedy is provided by two other New Englanders, Miss Ophelia and Marks. Mrs. Stowe made it crystal clear that the Northerners had little understanding of the Negro in the concrete, however much they might sympathize with him in the abstract.

But these concessions were insufficient to appease Southern resentment. From every side violent attacks continued and Mrs. Stowe was accused of falsifying facts. It was pointed out, for example, that the Southern laws were as stringent against the murder of slaves as of whites, and statutes usually forbade the separation of children below the age of ten from their mothers. Also, slaves as property were too valuable to be seriously mistreated.

In the North, *Uncle Tom's Cabin* received a mixed reception. Even some who disliked slavery condemned the book because they feared it would stir up civil strife. Northern investors in the Southern cotton business censured it for fear it would endanger their investments. Their point of view was expressed by the New York *Journal of Commerce* in a scathing editorial questioning Mrs. Stowe's veracity. Generally, however, *Uncle Tom's Cabin* was accepted by Northern readers as a just indictment of the slavery system. As nothing else had done, the novel aroused the national conscience and humanitarian instincts. Its strong religious overtones drove home the argument that slavery dealt in human souls.

One of the immediate effects of *Uncle Tom's Cabin* was to make impossible the enforcement of the Fugitive Slave Law. Outside the South, nonco-operation with the law was virtually unanimous. More ominous, the book whipped up an enormous volume of antislavery sentiment and perhaps made inevitable the outbreak of the Civil War. Certainly it was a major cause of that catastrophic conflict, as Abraham Lincoln recognized when he greeted Mrs. Stowe, on a visit to the White House in 1862, as "the little lady who wrote the book that made this big war." Charles Sumner remarked, incidentally, that "if *Uncle Tom's Cabin* had not been written, Abraham Lincoln could not have been elected President of the United States."

The literary merits of *Uncle Tom's Cabin* received only cursory attention at first, though they have been much debated among later critics. The historian James Ford Rhodes noted that "the style is commonplace, the language is often trite and inelegant, sometimes degenerating into slang; and the humor is strained." A Southern critic, Stark Young, discussing Mrs. Stowe's use of Negro dialect, says, "She has seen plenty of blacks but cannot make them talk. Her ear is impossible; she has no sense of their rhythm or vividness." Van Wyck Brooks refers to the book's "obvious blemishes of structure and sentimentalism," despite which he characterizes it as "a great human document." Another modern commentator, Katharine Anthony, believes that *Uncle Tom's Cabin,* "As a romance and a picture of American manners . . . undoubtedly deserves high rank. Mrs. Stowe apparently had a fondness for the South. While she hated it for being on the side of slavery, she portrayed its atmosphere with fire and sympathy. She was the first American writer to take the Negro seriously and to conceive a novel with a black man as the hero. Although it was written with a moral purpose, the author forgot the purpose sometimes in the joy of telling her tale." But from a historical point of view, of course, the great significance of the novel is as a sociological document rather than as a literary classic or work of art. Certainly it is more than merely a story, as one caustic pen described it, "spattered with murder, lust, illicit love, suicide, sadistic torture, profanity, drunkenness, and barroom brawls."

Uncle Tom's Cabin at once made Mrs. Stowe an international celebrity. The year after the novel's publication, she made the first of three trips abroad, visiting England and Scotland. There she met and was entertained by hundreds of the nobility, royalty, and other eminent persons, among them Queen Victoria, Prince Albert, Dickens, George Eliot, Kingsley, Ruskin, Macaulay, and Gladstone. On her triumphal tour, she was received with like acclaim by the common people, who saw in her the champion of the underdog. In Edinburgh, she was presented with a national penny offering, amounting to 1,000 gold sovereigns, to help carry on her fight against slavery. Never before or since has an American author created so much excitement or been so applauded in the British Isles.

In an attempt to prove that the picture of slavery drawn in her book was not exaggerated or "a tissue of lies," as some charged, Mrs. Stowe compiled *A Key to Uncle Tom's Cabin,* which she said "will contain all the original facts, anecdotes, and documents upon which the story is founded, with some very interesting and affecting stories parallel to those of *Uncle Tom."* The work is divided into four parts. It begins with an explanation of the characters, to prove that they were true to life. The second part relates to slave laws, showing that existing statutes did not protect the slave. Then follows a narration of the experiences of individual slaves, the failure of public opinion to protect the slave, and a discussion of the demoralizing effect of slavery upon free labor in the South. Finally, there is a strong indictment of the churches for their divided and ineffectual stand on slavery.

The *Key* had the weakness and serious shortcoming that its materials had been collected after *Uncle Tom's Cabin* was written, and much of it was based on hearsay; it was not a popular success, and added little strength to the novel's condemnation of slavery. As an instance of poetic justice, the English publisher who had originally pirated *Uncle Tom's Cabin* printed 50,000 copies of the *Key,* anticipating another bonanza, and proceeded into bankruptcy.

Only one other work on slavery came from Mrs. Stowe's prolific pen. This was the novel, *Dred, a Tale of the Great Dismal Swamp,* published in 1856. In four weeks 100,000 copies were sold, though *Dred* never approached the popularity of *Uncle Tom's Cabin.* In *Dred,* the author's theme was the evil effects of the slave system upon the white man— both the owner and the poor white squatter. Miscegenation between the two races and its dire results for all the characters involved were dramatized. *Dred* is rich in sketches of poor whites, revivalist preachers, and plantation life, but there is no one central character, such as Uncle Tom, to win one's sympathy.

Henceforth, for the remainder of her long life of eighty-five years, Mrs. Stowe produced an endless flow of novels, stories, biographies, articles, and religious essays. For nearly thirty years she averaged a book annually, but the subject of slavery was largely abandoned. During the Civil War, her principal contribution was an open letter to the women of England, reminding them of their overwhelmingly favorable response to *Uncle Tom's Cabin* eight or nine years earlier, and reproaching them for pro-Southern sentiment and actions after the outbreak of the war. As a result, mass meetings were held throughout the British Isles, helping to change English ruling opinion toward the Union cause. Hence, Mrs. Stowe's letter may have played an important part in preventing English interference at a time when it could have endangered the Northern side.

In estimating Harriet Beecher Stowe's place in history, Kirk Monroe declared, "Not only does she stand in the foremost rank of famous women of the world, but, in shaping the destiny of the American people at a most critical period of their history, her influence was probably greater than that of any other individual. . . . Of course, the abolition of slavery was not, and could not be, accomplished by any one person," Monroe pointed out, as he reviewed the elements that had brought final victory, but "the greatest and most far-reaching of all these influences was that of *Uncle Tom's Cabin.*"

Perhaps as nearly a definitive evaluation of *Uncle Tom's Cabin* as is possible after the lapse of a century was made by another woman author, Constance Rourke:

> Battered though it has become through an overplus of excitement which has attended its career, defective though it is in certain essentials, it still has qualities which lift it above its contemporary position as a tract, qualities which should dismiss the easy, usual charge of exaggeration. Obviously the book lacks a genuine realism; but perhaps it should not be judged as realism at all. Obviously it lacks the hardiness and purity of view which belong to great writing; its emotion is never free, but intensive, indrawn, morbid, sentimental if one chooses, running an unchecked course which seemed created by hysteria. But the unbroken force of that emotion produced breadth; in its expansions and uncalculated balances, its flowing absorption in large sequences of action and its loose combinations of interwoven fates, the story at least brings to mind what is meant by the epical scale; it has above all that affecting movement toward unknown goals over long distances which becomes the irresistible theme of the greater narrative, rendered here with pathos because the adventure is never free, but always curtailed or fatefully driven.

"Removed from the atmosphere in which it was written," as Van Wyck Brooks asserted, "*Uncle Tom's Cabin* remained a great folk-picture of an age and a nation."

7 PROPHET OF THE PROLETARIAT

KARL MARX: *Das Kapital*

In his funeral eulogy for Karl Marx, Friedrich Engels concluded that "Marx was above all a revolutionary, and his great aim in life was to cooperate in this or that fashion in the overthrow of capitalist society and the State institutions which it has created." In these words, Marx's collaborator, disciple, and closest friend succinctly summed up the moving force in the famous social rebel's career.

It was a tumultuous age into which Marx was born. Revolt and unrest were in the air. The memory of one French Revolution was fresh, and another was imminent. The following decades were to be marked by widespread popular bitterness and discontent, and criticisms of existing institutions. By 1848, this mood had built up to explosive force, and revolutions erupted throughout Europe. Even in England, the Chartist Movement threatened established government. Pressure for the alleviation of abuses resulting from the new industrialism, and for abolition of the last vestiges of feudalism was everywhere felt. The times were perfectly adapted to Karl Marx's subversive, nonconformist temperament.

Marx was born in 1818 at Trier in the German Rhineland, the son of a prosperous lawyer. On both sides of the family, Karl was descended from rabbinic ancestors, but while he was still a child, the entire family was converted to Christianity. For the remainder of his life, perhaps in reaction against the handicaps imposed by his racial background, Marx was anti-Semitic in his outlook.

Young Marx studied law and philosophy at Bonn and Berlin, with the ultimate ambition of achieving a professorship. His increasingly unorthodox opinions, however, closed the door to him, and he turned to journalism. A new periodical, the *Rheinische Zeitung*, was being started in 1842, and Marx became first a contributor, and within a short time the editor. Attacks on the Prussian government and the paper's generally radical tone caused its suppression after only a little more than a year.

Marx moved on to Paris to study socialism and to write for another short-lived journal, the *Franco-German Year Books*. There he became acquainted with leading representatives of socialist and communist thought. The most important event of the period, from the standpoint of Marx's future career, was the beginning of his lifelong friendship with Friedrich Engels. A fellow-German, Engels was relatively wealthy, the son of a cotton manufacturer, and as devoted to socialist ideals as Marx himself. The foundation for Marx's later *Das Kapital* was laid by Engels in 1845 with the publication of his *Condition of the Working Classes in England*.

Marx's continued agitation against the Prussian government caused the French authorities to expel him as an undesirable alien. He took refuge in Brussels for three years, and then went back to Germany briefly. Exiled again, he returned to

Paris during the revolution of 1848. In that year, in collaboration with Engels, he wrote and published the celebrated *Communist Manifesto*. One of the most violent and influential pieces of radical literature ever printed, the pamphlet concludes with the stirring slogan:

> The communists consider it superfluous to conceal their opinions and their intentions. They openly declare that their aims can only be achieved by the violent overthrow of the whole contemporary social order. Let the governing classes tremble before the communistic revolution. The workers have nothing to lose but their chains. They have the whole world to gain. Workers of the world, unite!

Wherever Marx went, he was an active and aggressive agitator, organizing workers' movements, editing communist papers, and instigating rebellion.

The collapse of the European revolutions of 1848-49 made the continent too small to hold Marx. He emigrated to England in the summer of 1849, at the age of thirty-one, and spent the remainder of his life in London. Earlier, he had married Jenny von Westfalen, daughter of a Prussian official, and she remained for nearly forty years his faithful partner, sharing with him a period of incredible poverty, privation, and misfortune. Of their six children, only three survived to grow up, and of the three, two in later life committed suicide. Unquestionably, these years of extreme hardship colored Marx's views and account for much of the rancor and bitterness in his writings. Only frequent financial aid from Friedrich Engels saved the Marx family from actual starvation. Marx's only earned income was a guinea a week, received from the New York *Tribune* for a letter on European affairs, and intermittent pay for jobs of hack writing.

Despite the misery, importunate debtors, sickness, and want with which he was constantly surrounded in the drab Soho district of London, where he settled, Marx was as indefatigable as ever in his promotion of socialistic causes. Year after year, often for as much as sixteen hours a day, he went to the British Museum to accumulate the enormous mass of material for the work eventually to be titled *Das Kapital*. Discounting interruptions caused by other activities and illness, the book was over eighteen years in preparation. Engels, who was supporting the Marx family in the meanwhile, was hopeless that it would ever be completed. "The day the manuscript goes to press I shall get gloriously drunk," he said. Both he and Marx referred to it as "the damned book," and Marx admitted that it was "a perfect nightmare."

A major event in Marx's life during these years was the foundation, in 1864, of the International Working Men's Association, now known as the First International. This was an effort to bring the working classes of the world together into international association. Though retiring in public, Marx was the power behind the throne, and wrote most of the association's documents, addresses, rules, and program. Internal quarrels and rivalry for the leadership, together with the disrepute into which the organization fell after the collapse of the Paris Commune in 1871, led to its dissolution. Subsequently, it was succeeded by the Second International, representing western socialist groups, and the Third International, or Comintern, of the communist world.

The prolonged period of gestation for *Das Kapital* finally drew to a close. Late in 1866, the completed manuscript of volume one was sent to Hamburg, and in the fall of the following year, the printed work came off the press. It was written in German, and no English translation was available until about twenty years later. The first rendering into another language—appropriately, in the light of future events—was a Russian edition in 1872.

In Marx's day, England was the prime exhibit of the workings of the capitalist system. Examples to illustrate his economic theories were accordingly drawn almost entirely from that country. Horrible instances were plentiful, for the institution of capitalism in the mid-Victorian period was at its worst. Social conditions in factory communities were indescribably bad. Basing his findings upon official reports of government inspectors, Marx presented the facts accurately in *Capital*—to use the English title. Women pulled canal boats along the towpath with ropes over their shoulders. Women were harnessed, like beasts of burden, to cars pulling coal out of British mines. Children began to work in the textile mills when they were nine or ten years old, and labored twelve to fifteen hours a day. As the practice of night shifts came into vogue the beds in which the children slept were said never to get cold, for they were used in shifts. Tuberculosis and other occupational diseases killed them off at a high rate.

Protests over the terrible conditions were by no means limited to Marx. Such warm-hearted humanitarians as Charles Dickens, John Ruskin, and Thomas Carlyle wrote voluminously and at white heat, demanding reforms. Parliament was being aroused to corrective legislation.

Marx took much pride in his "scientific" approach to economic and social problems. As Engels said, "Just as Darwin discovered the law of evolution in organic nature, so Marx

discovered the law of evolution in human history." Economic
phenomena, stated Marx, "can be watched and recorded with
the precision proper to natural science." Frequently he refers
to the work of biologists, chemists, and physicists, and it was
clear that he aspired to become the Darwin of sociology or
perhaps the Newton of economics. By the scientific analysis
of society, Marx believed he had discovered how to transform
a capitalistic into a socialistic world.

Marx's "scientific" method contributed immensely to his
wide acceptance, for the concept of evolution in all fields had
caught the nineteenth-century imagination. By tying his class-
struggle theory of history to Darwin's theory of evolution,
Marx gave his ideas respectability and, at the same time, he
believed, made them irrefutable.

In the view of Marx and his followers, his profoundest contribution to the study of economics, history, and other social
sciences was the development of a principle called "dialectical
materialism," an abstruse, ambiguous term. Though more
fully explained in his earlier writings, *Capital* applies the
theory in detail.

The dialectic method was taken over by Marx from the
German philosopher Hegel. In essence, it maintains that everything in the world is in a constant state of change. Progress
is achieved by the reaction of opposing forces on each other.
Thus, for example, the English colonial system opposed by
the American Revolution produced the United States. As
Laski phrased it, "The law of life is the warring of contra-
dictions, with growth as its consequence."

This premise led Marx to the formulation of his theory of
historical materialism, or the economic interpretation of history. "The history of all existing society," argued Marx and
Engels, "is the history of class struggles. Freeman and slave,
patrician and plebeian, lord and serf, guildmaster and journey-
man, in a word, oppressor and oppressed, stood in sharp opposition each to the other. They carried on perpetual warfare."
In his eulogy of Marx, Engels elaborated further:

> He discovered the simple fact, heretofore hidden be-
> neath ideological overgrowths, that human beings must
> have food and drink, clothing and shelter, first of all, be-
> fore they can interest themselves in politics, science, art,
> religion and the like. This implies that the production of
> the immediately requisite material means of subsistence,
> and therewith the extant economic developmental phase
> of a nation or an epoch, constitutes the foundation upon

which the State institutions, the legal outlooks, the artistic and even the religious ideas, of those concerned, have been built up.

In brief, the struggle for food and shelter are omnipotent, determining everything else in human affairs.

The history of mankind, according to Marx, is primarily the story of the exploitation of one class by another. In prehistoric ages, there was a tribal or classless type of society. But in historic times, Marx argued, classes had grown up, and the masses of the human population had become, first, slaves, then serfs (the feudal state), and next propertyless wage slaves (the capitalistic era). Applying the theory of dialectical materialism, Marx was convinced that the inevitable further step was a revolt of the workers and "the dictatorship of the proletariat," followed by communal ownership and a return to a classless social organization.

In *Capital,* Marx developed his case against the capitalist system, to demonstrate why, in his estimation, its eventual destruction and disappearance were inescapable. Here he propounded what Communists generally regard as his second most important contribution to social science, the theory of labor value. Nor was this an original theory with Marx. Following such older economists as Adam Smith and David Ricardo, he asserted that labor is the source of all value. Marx quoted Benjamin Franklin, who, a century earlier, had remarked that "trade in general being nothing else but the exchange of labor for labor, the value of all things is most justly measured by labor." From Smith he took the definition of capital as "a certain amount of labour amassed and kept in reserve." Ricardo had likewise suggested that the value and price of any commodity should be determined by the amount of labor that goes into it.

Using this as a criterion, Marx developed his theory of "surplus value," first stated in his *Critique of Political Economy* (1859), and in revised form in *Capital.* The worker, lacking property, had only one commodity to sell—his own labor, and to avoid starvation, he must sell it. Given the existing economic system, the employer would purchase the commodity at the lowest possible price. Hence the actual value of the labor was invariably in excess of wages paid. A workingman paid a wage of four shillings a day actually earned that sum in some six hours, but was required to work ten hours. The extra four hours, therefore, were stolen from the worker by the capitalist. So interpreted, profit, interest, and rent were derived entirely from the surplus value of labor's toil, of which the workers have been robbed. It might logically be concluded then, that the capitalist system is nothing more than an evil scheme set up to exploit and to rob the working class.

Though Marx's theories of value and surplus value have been invaluable for purposes of propaganda and agitation, economists generally now consider them invalid and discredited. One of the factors that caused their rejection was the increased use of machinery, which brought about great variations in the amount of labor needed for various commodities. Freehof pointed out that "the chemist will make one discovery with regard to soil fertility and will multiply a hundred fold the productivity of ten million farm laborers. It was the chemist who created the productivity." Also in refutation of the theory, another critic suggested that "Men dive for pearls because they are valuable; pearls are not valuable because men dive for them." Marx does not acknowledge that science, technology, art, or organization add anything to values and prices.

As a matter of fact, economists have never agreed on a method of measuring value, despite two centuries of meditating and writing upon the subject. Demand and utility seem to be the most widely accepted criteria. As Barzun commented, modern economics "has destroyed Marx's theory, but has not replaced it by a tested, 'scientific' one."

His surplus value theory led Marx to the next steps in his thesis. In order to meet fierce competition, each capitalist tries to extract more and more surplus value from the workers by such devices as lengthening hours, or reducing wages, or using the "stretch-out." He introduces more and more machinery to eliminate labor and speed up production. By utilizing machinery which requires less physical strength to operate, men can be replaced by the cheaper labor of women and children. The consequences are thus described by Marx:

> They mutilate the laborer into a fragment of a man, degrade him to the level of an appendage of a machine, destroy every remnant of charm in his work and turn it into a hated toil; they estrange from him the intellectual potentialities of the labor process in the same proportion as science is incorporated in it as an independent power; they distort the conditions under which he works, subject him during the labor process to a despotism the more hateful for its meanness; they transform his lifetime into working time, and drag his wife and child beneath the wheels of the Juggernaut of capital.

So, Marx insists, the installation of machinery, to speed up and to increase production, not only fails to ease the worker's lot, but has such deleterious effects as causing unemployment (machines displacing men), the exploitation of women and children, overproduction of commodities, and killing the worker's interest in his job. Marx goes on to state:

> Machinery is the most powerful weapon for repressing strikes, those periodical revolts of the working class against the autocracy of capital. The steam engine was from the very first an antagonist that enabled the capitalist to tread under foot the growing claims of the workmen, who threatened the newly born factory system with a crisis. It would be possible to write quite a history of the inventions made since 1830, for the sole purpose of supplying capital with weapons against the revolts of the working class.

Giving the Malthusian theory a special twist, Marx says that overpopulation always follows in the path of capitalism. The system needs an "industrial reserve army" for periods of great production expansion, when new industries are being created or old ones revived. In the nature of things, the surplus labor force must endure prolonged periods of unemployment. Then appears capitalism's greatest curse: depressions and panics. Since the workers are paid bare subsistence wages, they are unable to buy all the goods the factories pour forth, markets become glutted, the labor force is reduced, and severe depressions ensue.

Seeking outlets for his overstocked warehouses, the capitalist next turns to foreign fields, and tries to find markets in backward countries abroad to unload the commodities his own workers cannot afford to purchase. This endeavor and the search for raw materials to keep the factories operating inexorably lead to international conflicts and imperialistic wars.

The ultimate outcome of capitalist strife and turmoil, Marx believed, is increased concentration and monopoly, for "one capitalist always kills many." The middle class would disappear, as small capitalists were swallowed up by the larger ones. Finally, there would remain only a handful of great capitalists confronting the proletarian multitude. When that time came, the proletariat would have its opportunity. One of the most vivid and memorable passages in *Capital* describes the steps leading up to the denouement:

While there is a progressive diminution in the number of capitalist magnates, there occurs a corresponding increase in the mass of poverty, oppression, enslavement, degeneration, and exploitation. But at the same time there is a steady intensification of the wrath of the working class—a class which grows ever more numerous, and is disciplined, unified, and organized by the very mechanism of the capitalist method of production. Capitalist monopoly becomes a fetter on the method of production which has flourished with it and under it. The centralization of the means of production and the socialization of labor reach a point where they prove incompatible with their capitalist husk. This bursts asunder. The knell of capitalist private property sounds. The expropriators are expropriated.

The class struggle would end with the triumph of the proletariat.

Having captured the state, the proletariat would establish its dictatorship. This stage, however, Marx prophesied, "is but the transition to the abolition of all classes and to the creation of a society of the free and equal." How long it would be necessary for the period of dictatorship to continue is not specified—a point of considerable interest in view of Soviet Russia's thirty-eight years under an iron-handed authoritarian regime which shows no sign of relaxing its grip. In fact, Marx is extremely vague in describing the nature of his classless society. After the state had carried out its role of education and organization, government would "wither away." There would be no force or struggle, peace and plenty would prevail for everyone. The chief aim of society would be "the full and free development of every individual," and the guiding principle would be "From each according to his abilities, to each according to his needs!"

The inconsistency and glaring contrast of this beautiful dream of utopia with the preceding period of bloody, ruthless class warfare has been commented upon by numerous critics. In any case, as Hallett wrote:

The "class-less society" of Marx is as dull as the heaven of the orthodox Victorian; and it inspires as little credence and as little enthusiasm. Once the world revolution has been relegated to the background, it is difficult to find in the dry bones of Marxism anything to stir men's passions or steel them to fresh endurance or fresh endeavour.

Nevertheless, Marxism has all the force of a religion to millions of devout Communists. Dialectical materialism serves as a creed to supersede all other faiths. The older religions, such as Christianity, declared Marx, teach a passive acceptance of one's lot in life, glorifying resignation, meekness, and humility. They act, therefore, as "the opium of the people," blinding the proletariat to its destiny and placing major obstacles on the road to revolution.

How much truth is there in Marx? This is a question that has occupied innumerable social scientists, theologians, and other writers and thinkers for the past century. In many essentials, time has shown fundamental errors in his theories and predictions. No non-Marxian economist any longer takes seriously his labor theories of value and surplus value, a foundation piece in Marx's thought. In no country has there developed the conflict of classes, leading to proletarian revolution, prophesied by Marx. A well-known Marxist, Sidney Hook, emphasized that this doctrine, too, is basic to the Communist creed, for he wrote, "If the facts of the class struggle can be successfully called into question, the whole theoretical structure of Marx crashes to the ground."

The capitalistic system has followed an entirely different course, at least in the most enlightened nations, from that forecast by Marx. Instead of increased misery, poverty, and suffering among the working class, the reverse has occurred. Strong labor unions and government regulation have arisen to hold the excesses of capitalist competition and enterprise in check. Despite Marx's contempt for the "economists, philanthropists, humanitarians, improvers of the condition of the working class, organizers of charity, members of societies for the prevention of cruelty to animals, temperance fanatics, hole-and-corner reformers of every imaginable kind," such people have succeeded in eliminating the worst evils of capitalism, and made the system work with as much smoothness as could reasonably be expected in any exceedingly complex man-made institution. As a recent report of the Twentieth Century Fund commented: "Of all the great industrial nations, the one that has clung the most tenaciously to private capitalism has come closest to the socialist goal of providing an abundance to all in a classless society, a level of material well-being which is beyond even the comprehension of the vast majority of the world's people."

Marx pinned strong hopes on weakening national ties among the "proletariat," aiming to substitute for them a sense of international solidarity among the workers everywhere. Failure to achieve this perhaps desirable goal has been demonstrated

in two world wars and by the nationalistic fervor characteristic of the current world scene—nowhere more evident than
in Russia, China, and other Communist areas. In Marx's judgment, the proletarian revolution would occur first in the most
highly industralized nations, e.g., England, Germany, and the
United States, while Russia was least ripe for revolt—another
prediction not borne out by subsequent events.

The dialetic method used by Marx has had considerable
weight with later historians, though, as William Henry Cham-
berlin commented:

> Marx's method of historical materialism fails to ac-
> count for the obvious differences between peoples which
> are in the same stage of economic development. It leaves
> out of account such vital factors as race, religion, and
> nationality. It does not reckon with the immense im-
> portance of human personality. It is doubtful whether a
> single historical event could be correctly interpreted in
> terms of this theory.

Nevertheless, while recognizing the fallacies in Marx's
thought, it would still be difficult to overestimate his impact
on our times. In certain important respects, his influence on
the capitalistic world has been beneficial. By emphasizing
the abuses of the industrial system and playing up the danger
of a workers' revolution, fundamental reforms have been
effected. In short, the constant reiteration by Communists and
Socialists of capitalist shortcomings has forced the correction
of many of those evils, and thereby vastly diminished, if not
eliminated, the likelihood of the proletarian revolt prophesied
by Marx.

But it is the consequences of Marxism's conquest of Russia,
China, and other vast areas, bringing an estimated nine
hundred million people under its sway, that have posed the
most urgent problems for the modern world. Ironically, Marx
had great scorn for Russians in general and for Russian revo-
lutionaries in particular. His conclusions regarding the Tsarist
rule of his day are singularly apt for Communist Russia: "The
policy of Russia is changeless. Its methods, its tactics, its ma-
neuvers may change, but the pole star of its policy—world
domination—is a fixed star."

Actually, present-day Russia fulfills few of Marx's ideas and
ideals for communism. As President Truman remarked, in
1950, Russia is not a Communist state nor was Stalin a real
Communist. There is, for example, a dictatorship by the Communist party, or rather a hierarchy thereof, rather than a true

dictatorship of the proletariat. The political state which, according to Marx, would soon "wither away" becomes more all-powerful with the passage of time. Beginning with Lenin, the Communist leaders have found it easier to preach Marx than to practice him. While continuing to pay lip service to Marxian philosophy, they have modified the dogma inherited from Marx, as political circumstances and expediency seemed to require. Viewing the activities of his disciples, Marx once said, "I am not a Marxist," and it appears probable that he would have had strong doubts about the application of his theories in the mid-twentieth century. A favorite Socialist saying is that "if Marx had lived under Stalin, he would not have lived long."

Only the first volume of "the Bible of the working classes" was published in Marx's lifetime. After his death in 1883, his copious, but incomplete and badly organized notes for volumes two and three were taken over by Engels. The second volume appeared in 1885 and the third in 1894, the year before Engels died. These contain elaborations and applications of the main thesis, dealing with the "circulation of capital" and the "process of capitalist production as a whole." It is upon the first volume, however, that Marx's reputation rests, and the last two volumes are relatively little read. Still another work, *The Theory of Surplus Value*, which was to have formed the fourth volume of *Capital*, was edited from Marx's manuscripts by Karl Kautsky, and published in Germany, 1905-10.

Capital is admittedly hard reading. One critic (Barzun) describes it as "badly written, ill put together, lacking in order, logic, or homogeneity of material." Another (Croce) mentions "the strange composition of the book, the mixture of general theory, of bitter controversy and satire, and of historical illustrations or digressions," and considers the work "unsymmetrical, badly arranged and out of proportion." A third (Standen), while declaring that "the scheme of the three volumes is magnificent on a grand scale," concedes that "the manner of presentation of *Capital* can be irritating, with its long digressions and ponderous slowness."

It is doubtful that any figure in history has inspired more violently contradictory opinions than Karl Marx. There is practically no middle ground between the view which holds him to have been "a diabolically inspired Jew who plotted the downfall of civilization," and the diametrically opposite picture of him as "the lovable saint who selflessly devoted himself to the world's disinherited class of the nineteenth century." One bitter critic has stated that "In the name of human prog-

ress, Marx has probably caused more death, misery, degradation and despair than any man who ever lived."

What is the secret, then, of Marx's appeal for and influence
and power over millions of the earth's inhabitants? Neill has
suggested that Marx is "the symbolical leader of the have-nots
in their struggle against the haves." Barzun believes that "The
strength of Marx is precisely that he shared the feelings of
the downtrodden, that the prejudice of equality was in his
very liver, and joined to it the ambition and jealousy of power,
both ready to destroy the present moral order in the name of
a higher which he saw." Another interpretation comes from
Harold Laski: "At bottom, the main passion by which he
was moved was the passion for justice. He may have hated
too strongly, he was jealous and he was proud. But the mainspring of his life was the desire to take from the shoulders of
the people the burden by which it was oppressed." Yet another
perceptive evaluation comes from Freehof, who wrote, "The
great constructive gift of Karl Marx to modern society, socialistic and capitalistic alike, is his picture of the inevitability
of a society in which poverty and suffering will cease. This
ideal has become a challenge to every social system. Even a
social system like ours, which rejects his economics, nevertheless accepts that ideal in its own way. Thus, the man who
himself lived in misery gave the world the hope for the complete abolition of poverty. This is the accomplishment of Karl
Marx. That is the way in which he has changed the mind
of the modern world."

8 LEVIATHAN AGAINST ELEPHANT

ALFRED T. MAHAN:

The Influence of Sea Power Upon History

When a contemporary critic described Admiral Alfred T.
Mahan's *The Influence of Sea Power Upon History* as "an
admirable book, but the most incendiary of modern times,"
he displayed remarkable perception. More than any other individual, Mahan shaped the modern navies of the world. His
pen has been termed "mightier than a flotilla," while "the
super-dreadnoughts are his children, the roar of the 16-inch

guns are but the echoes of his voice." Certainly, the writings of
no other historian have exerted such direct and widespread
influence as did those of Mahan.

Throughout recorded time, Mahan demonstrated, sea power
has been the deciding factor in world dominion. Command
of the sea is essential for any nation aspiring to play a major
role in world affairs, and to achieve maximum prosperity and
security at home. Land powers, without access to the sea, no
matter how great, are doomed to eventual collapse and decay,
for the land, Mahan pointed out, "is almost all obstacle, the
sea almost all open plain." A nation capable of controlling
this plain by its naval power and of maintaining a strong
merchant marine can exploit the world's wealth.

What manner of man was "the incendiary Mahan"? Perhaps the last person one would select as a revolutionist, un-
settler of the status quo, or disturber of the peace. Born in
1840, the son of a professor of military and civil engineering
at West Point, and a graduate of Annapolis, Mahan had spent
long, monotonous years as a career naval officer, alternating
between shore and sea duty. Except for limited action during
the American Civil War, he never experienced armed conflict. His perspective was broadened, however, by service in
Brazil and the Orient, and by travels in Europe.

Following these travels, another fifteen years went by without distinction, save for a small volume, *The Gulf and Inland
Waters,* relating to Civil War naval history, which Mahan was
assigned to write in 1883. Then came the break that would
establish his fame and bring about a radical change in his
future career. Mahan was invited by Admiral Stephen B. Luce
to lecture on tactics and naval history at the newly formed
War College in Newport.

Here was exactly the kind of opportunity for which Mahan
had been waiting. Never notably successful as a naval officer,
bored with naval routine, still only a captain in rank (he was
promoted to Rear Admiral after retirement), the new assign-
ment seemed heaven-sent. He was given a year's freedom for
reading and thinking before reporting at Newport; and then
in September 1886, before a small group of officers, he began
the series of lectures which was destined to be published in
matured form, four years later, as *The Influence of Sea Power
Upon History, 1660-1783.*

In a letter to his English publisher, Mahan noted that the
term "sea power" was chosen by design for his title "to compel
attention and to receive currency. . . . I deliberately discarded the adjective 'maritime' as being too smooth to arrest men's
attention or stick in their minds." It is also apparent that the

word "power" hit a responsive chord in an age of steam and electricity and power politics. Thus the title, *The Influence of Sea Power,* was selected with care to make a specific impression upon its readers.

This celebrated book, upon which Mahan's reputation primarily rests, is, in essence, a narration and explanation of the rise and progress of British sea power from the middle of the seventeenth century to the close of the Napoleonic wars.

Mahan begins by tracing in broad outline the rise and decline of the great maritime powers, reviewing in some detail the elements necessary for a nation aiming to achieve power at sea. These conditions he reduces in number to six: geographical position, physical conformation (including natural production and climate), extent of territory, number of population, character of the people, and character of the government.

Elaborating upon these "elements of sea power," Mahan showed in each instance how Britain had gained strength over her opponents. According to his interpretation, sea power is far more than naval power, comprising not only a military fleet but commercial shipping and a strong home base. "The history of sea power," wrote Mahan, "while embracing in its broad sweep all that tends to make a people great upon the sea or by the sea, is largely a military history." Nevertheless, he continually emphasized that navies, campaigns, and battles are only a means to an end. Neither a flourishing merchant marine nor a successful navy is possible without the other. National prosperity depends upon the combination.

In considering geographical position, a matter of prime importance, Mahan stressed the vast advantages accruing to a nation so located "that it is neither forced to defend itself by land nor induced to seek extension of its territory by way of the land . . . as compared with a people one of whose boundaries is continental." Examples are England on one side, and France and Holland on the other. Early in her modern history, Holland's strength was exhausted by having to maintain a large army and to carry on wars to preserve her independence. France was weakened by dividing her wealth and man power between building up naval power and projects of continental expansion. Her position was made more vulnerable, also, by fronting on both the ocean and the Mediterranean, preventing her from making use of a united fleet. Its location on two oceans, Mahan pointed out, placed the United States in a similar position of weakness. A central position, with ports near major trade routes and strong bases for operations against potential enemies, is a great strategic asset. Again, England, with her control of the Channel and North Sea trade routes, was enabled to gain supremacy.

In analyzing his second element, physical conformation, Mahan stated, "The seaboard of a country is one of its frontiers; and the easier the access offered by the frontier to the region beyond, in this case the sea, the greater will be the tendency of a people toward intercourse with the rest of the world by it." Numerous and deep harbors, however, are vital. Because England and Holland had not been generously treated by nature in soil or climate, they perforce took to the sea, while France, endowed with "delightfulness and richness of the land," and the United States, likewise blessed, had fewer inducements to look seaward.

The third and last "natural condition" affecting the development of a nation as a sea power was extent of territory. By this phrase Mahan meant "not the total number of square miles which a country contains, but the length of its coastline and the characters of its harbors." The proportion of the country's population to the extent of its seacoast was also of paramount significance. An illustration is taken from the American Civil War:

> Had the South had a people as numerous as it was warlike, and a navy commensurate to its other resources as a sea power, the great extent of its sea coast and its numerous inlets would have been elements of great strength . . . the South not only had no navy, not only was not a seafaring people, but . . . its population was not proportioned to the extent of the sea-coast which it had to defend.

After reviewing the three natural conditions affecting sea power, i.e., geographical position, physical conformation, and extent of territory, Mahan turned next to a consideration of the people and their government. Here stress was still placed on the number of population, but a further distinction was made, for "it is not only the grand total, but the number following the sea, or at least readily available for employment on ship-board and for the creation of naval material that must be counted." Historical instances were provided by England and France. The population of France was considerably greater than that of England, but the latter's maritime and commercial orientation and proclivities gave her a decided edge over the predominantly agricultural population of France. Mahan concluded that "a great population following callings related to the sea is, now as formerly, a great element of sea power," and he found the United States deplorably "deficient in that element."

The effect of national character and aptitudes upon the development of sea power was Mahan's fifth point. "Almost without exception," he wrote, history shows that "aptitude for commercial pursuits must be a distinguishing feature of the nations that have at one time or another been great upon the sea." Though the English and Dutch were often contemptuously referred to as "nations of shopkeepers," they gained far more permanent and substantial rewards from their maritime trade than did the gold-seeking Spanish and Portuguese, or the thrifty, hoarding French, unwilling to risk investments in foreign commerce. "The tendency to trade," remarked Mahan, "involving of necessity the production of something to trade with, is the national characteristic most important in the development of sea power."

National genius was marked too, Mahan believed, by the ability to establish healthy colonies. In this respect the British were superior to the French, because "The English colonist naturally and readily settles down in his new country, identifies his interest with it, and though keeping an affectionate remembrance of the home from which he came, has no restless eagerness to return." Neither were the Spanish effective colonizers, because they were primarily concerned with the rapid exploitation of the new country's wealth, rather than with full development of its resources.

Finally, Mahan considers the character of the government and its institutions in relation to the growth of sea power. The form of government and the character of rulers, he believed, "have exercised a very marked influence upon the development of sea power." While preferring the processes of democratic governments, Mahan noted that "despotic power, wielded with judgment and consistency, has created at times a great sea commerce and a brilliant navy with greater directness than can be reached by the slower processes of a free people. The difficulty . . . is to insure perseverance after the death of a particular despot." Because England had reached the greatest height of sea power of any modern nation, a study of government policies there was considered by Mahan to be especially pertinent. For the most part, English government action over several centuries had consistently been directed toward control of the sea. Regardless of the reigning monarch or of political parties, the English recognized the basic importance to the nation of the maintenance of naval supremacy.

After an extended historical review of the actions of various governments as they pertained to the sea careers of their peoples, Mahan decided that government influence works in two ways: first, in times of peace:

> The government by its policy can favor the natural growth of a people's industries and its tendencies to seek adventure and gain by way of the sea; or it can try to develop such industries and such sea-going bent, when they do not naturally exist; or, on the other hand, the government may by mistaken action check and fetter the progress which the people left to themselves would make.

Second, in times of war, sea power is determined by the attitude of the government toward creating, equipping, and adequately maintaining "an armed navy, of a size commensurate with the growth of its shipping and the importance of the interest connected with it." Likewise essential was "the maintenance of suitable naval stations, in those distant parts of the world to which armed shipping must follow the peaceful vessels of commerce." The United States, Mahan found, was weak in that it lacked foreign bases of either a colonial or military nature.

Thus having examined and reflected upon the six basic features affecting sea power, Mahan was ready to proceed to a detailed analysis of European naval wars of the period 1660-1783—approximately a century and a quarter. The remainder of his book is devoted to this historical review. For background, Mahan described the general conditions prevailing in Europe in the late seventeenth century, with particular reference to Spain, France, Holland, and England—the nations that were to be principally involved in future struggles for sea power. In Mahan's eyes, the history of Europe during the tumultuous years that followed was largely a contest among the western powers for the control of the sea. Beginning his survey with the Dutch War of Charles II, he emphasized the extent to which England's commercial interests were involved in the War of the Spanish Succession, from which England emerged as a Mediterranean power, holding Gibraltar and Port Mahon. In the Seven Years' War, Wolfe's success was made possible by the fleet, which opened the St. Lawrence and prevented the arrival of reinforcements from France. The fundamental meaning of sea power was demonstrated again during the American Revolution, when England, with divided naval forces, was unable to cope with the combined might of France and Spain, and the American colonies were thus able to win their freedom.

Mahan's main thesis, recurring throughout his work, is that as between sea power and land power, a relentless sea blockade has always proved more decisive than an invincible land army.

"In developing the tactical details of the various battles," his leading biographer, Captain W. D. Puleston, commented, "Mahan made every endeavor to be exact. As his examples were taken from the sailing-ship era, he was at pains to familiarize himself with the technique of sailing and the precise meaning of the old sea terms, which even in his midshipman days had been falling into disuse." In his autobiography Mahan describes the mechanical means he employed, such as paper ship models, to reproduce and re-enact sea battles under sail.

In *The Influence of Sea Power Upon History* Mahan's principal aim was, as he stated to his former commanding officer, Admiral Luce, "to write a critical *military* history of the naval past, not a chronicle of naval events." He might have added also that one of his objects was to indicate the interrelation of naval and political history, for he was fully convinced that the economic power which went with control of the sea gave its possessor a dominant position in world affairs. "Thus England," as Pratt remarked, "because she cultivated sea power while her opponents neglected it, was enabled to thwart the overweening schemes of Louis XIV and Napoleon and, as Mahan firmly believed, to rescue civilization from those who would have destroyed it."

The Influence of Sea Power Upon History won world recognition immediately after publication—though far greater abroad than in the United States. Within a short time, translations were available in German, Japanese, French, Italian, Russian, and Spanish. Everywhere the book provided effective ammunition for the period of great naval expansion just getting under way, especially in Great Britain, Germany, and America.

As various critics have suggested, a question will always remain as to whether Mahan's work would have had such a tremendous impact if it had appeared in another period or in a different setting. Without doubt, the times were most propitious, and Mahan's dictums on the significance of maritime might fell upon fertile soil, fitting perfectly the belligerent tendencies of the age. The great powers were flexing their biceps for a disastrous naval race and for the acquisition of new colonial possessions. How natural it was then that Mahan should have been so readily accepted as a prophet. His heavily documented proof that command of the sea was a prerequisite for any nation's welfare furnished justification for policies already adopted or under consideration. As one British writer phrased it, his teaching "was as oil to the flame of colonial expansion everywhere leaping into life."

In Britain, critics hailed Mahan's book as "the gospel of England's greatness." Puleston pointed out that "It might have been written to order for the British Cabinet, so clearly did it support all their contentions." One admiral asserted that for the improved position of the British Navy after 1900, "We have not to thank either Conservatives or Liberals, but Mahan and no one else." In a tribute to Mahan at the time of his death in 1914, the London *Post* declared that Britain "owes to the great American a debt which can never be repaid, for he was the first elaborately and comprehensively to formulate the philosophy of British sea-power."

These comments will be more readily appreciated when it is realized that at the time Mahan was writing his *Influence of Sea Power Upon History* the English Navy had gone through a long period of financial neglect, its personnel had been reduced to a skeleton force, and its might was being rapidly outstripped by more modern French and Italian ships. Britain's navy was described by one seaman as "a menagerie of unruly and curiously assorted ships," over two-thirds of them unarmored. Mahan's support for a modernized, powerful English fleet was therefore extremely timely, and greatly accelerated the movement for naval reorganization and strengthening.

English admiration and esteem for Mahan were demonstrated during two visits which he paid to Britain, in ·1893 and 1904. He was a guest of honor at state dinners given by Queen Victoria and the Prime Minister, was the first foreign guest of honor ever entertained by the Army and Navy Club, and both Oxford and Cambridge awarded him honorary degrees within a week's time.

But since *The Influence of Sea Power Upon History* was not, as one critic suggested it should have been, published in a language intelligible only to Americans and Englishmen, its impact on Germans and Japanese was as forceful as on the British. Kaiser Wilhelm II reported, "I am just now not reading but devouring Captain Mahan's book. It is on board all my ships. . . . Our future lies upon the water; the trident must be in our fist." Mahan's work became the inspiration for the new German Navy. One of his biographers, Taylor, stated, "There is ample evidence that in the last few months of his life Mahan suffered mental distress about the war [World War I] and the part he had played—although entirely unpremeditated—in stimulating the growth of the German Navy."

Likewise in Japan, every captain of a Japanese ship of war was served out a copy of Mahan's book as part of his equipment. The Japanese were eager to learn Western ways, and began an extensive correspondence with Mahan on the building of navies, the size of guns, and other naval matters. An invitation from the Japanese to become their official naval adviser was declined by Mahan. Nevertheless, taking their cue from him, the Japanese set out to become the supreme naval power of the Far East.

Among the leading countries, only the United States, which Mahan was most anxious to influence, was slow to accept his teachings. Mahan was convinced that the United States must enter into vigorous competition with other powers over foreign markets, build a huge navy, acquire naval bases overseas, and expand by acquiring colonies outside the western hemisphere. Hawaii, he contended, should be annexed and used as an American base. The Caribbean, he pointed out further, bore the same relation to America as did the Mediterranean to Europe, and its importance to the United States would be accentuated by completion of the Panama Canal. Throughout *The Influence of Sea Power Upon History* the author gave special attention to the United States and noted its potentialities as a sea power. "Mahan had written his book," said Captain Puleston, "to rekindle among his own countrymen their former interest in sea power. He believed Americans had been so engrossed in developing the interior of the continent that they had unnecessarily thrown away a great heritage. He did not want his country to follow the example of France under Louis XIV and become primarily a land power."

Mahan's arguments made two converts in key positions: Theodore Roosevelt and Henry Cabot Lodge. Roosevelt in the White House and Lodge in the Senate became enthusiasts for a great American navy. Roosevelt found a perfect expression of his philosophy of the "big stick," in Mahan's writings, and he used the sea power theories to help him win American public opinion to a policy of expansion across the seas. The influence of Mahan on the huge program of naval construction in the United States, beginning in the eighteen-nineties, is clear and marked.

Following his first great popular success, Mahan's prolific pen poured forth a cascade of books and magazine articles. Volumes of books and collected essays number some twenty, supplemented by scores of periodical contributions. Most significant were additions to his "sea-power series," notably *The Influence of Sea Power Upon the French Revolution and Empire, 1793–1812,* regarded by critics as a more thorough and carefully documented work than *The Influence of Sea Power Upon History;* biographies of Farragut and Nelson; and *Sea Power in Its Relations to the War of 1812.*

Mahan readily conceded that his ideas of sea power were not original, and he referred, for example, to what Bacon and Raleigh had written three centuries before on the same theme. Much earlier, such ancients as Thucydides, Xerxes, and Themistocles had recognized the importance of the concept. To a greater extent than any previous writer, however, Mahan succeeded in his special approach, which was, in his own words, "an analysis of history, attempting to show from current events, through a long series of years, precisely what influence the command of the sea had had upon definite issues. . . . This field had been left vacant, yielding me my opportunity." Though, as various commentators have suggested, Mahan's view of history was too narrow, ignoring many vital factors, he provided a new outlook on politics and economics.

Granting that Mahan's doctrines were reasonably valid for his own time and for the preceding centuries, have they been made obsolete by the technological advances of the twentieth century? In particular, has the coming of air power, A-bombs, and H-bombs superseded sea power in today's world? Experts are divided in their opinions. In World War II, sea power played an outstanding part, but it had to be closely co-ordinated with air power, for ships unprotected from the air were highly vulnerable. The postwar development of the "hell-bomb" has cast some shadow on the future of navies. One such bomb could conceivably wholly incapacitate a concentrated fleet. However, Soviet Russia's development of a great fleet of submarines and America's emphasis on aircraft carriers furnish evidence that sea power may still have a place, even in an atomic age.

In the judgment of scholars, Mahan's permanent rank as a historian will not be on a par with his contemporary fame. His pre-eminent success was as a propagandist. By the time of his death, the United States had reached the goals he had set for it, i.e., the building of a great navy, the construction of the Panama Canal, and the acquisition of bases in the Caribbean and Pacific. He had witnessed the triumph of his philosophy that "Whoever rules the waves rules the world," with the major nations engaged in a mad competition for sea power. As one acute critic observed, "No other single person has so directly and profoundly influenced the naval doctrines and the national policies of so many nations"; while a French naval expert declared that Mahan "profoundly modified in his own lifetime the history of the age in which he lived."

9 HEARTLAND AND WORLD ISLAND

SIR HALFORD J. MACKINDER:

"The Geographical Pivot of History"

Within little more than a decade after Admiral Mahan had demonstrated, so convincingly and conclusively, the historical invincibility of sea power, the applicability of his doctrine to the future was seriously undermined, if not invalidated, by two new factors. One, in the material realm, was the Wright brothers' first successful experiments, in 1903, with a powered airplane. The second, in the realm of ideas, was a scientific paper, written in 1904, by an English geographer, Halford Mackinder, later celebrated as "the father of geopolitics."

In neither case did the world recognize immediately the monumental significance of these two events; nevertheless, the face of the globe was to be irretrievably changed by them.

No more improbable setting could be conceived for the dissemination of revolutionary theories than the meeting of the Royal Geographical Society in London, January 25, 1904, at which Mackinder read his famous paper, "The Geographical Pivot of History." Filling only twenty-four printed pages, the work was no more than an ordinary pamphlet in length, but its remarkable analysis of the interrelations of geography and politics, past and present, throughout the world introduced concepts that subsequently swayed the thinking of political and military leaders, economists, geographers, and historians everywhere.

At the end of the World War I, Mackinder developed his argument in considerably expanded detail in *Democratic Ideals and Reality*, though without essential modification of his original thesis. This book and his earlier essay are the foundation stones for the modern "science" of geopolitics— the combination of geography and political science.

Mackinder was forty-three years old when his renowned lecture was delivered. The son of a country doctor, he had been sent to Epsom College in 1874, and from there to Oxford. After a brilliant scholastic record, he became a traveling lecturer on geography for two years for the Oxford University Extension movement. There followed an appointment as Reader in Geography at Oxford, where he attracted hundreds of students by his dynamic teaching methods. Mainly because of his urgings, the Royal Geographical Society financed the establishment of the first British School of Geography at Oxford, in 1899, with Mackinder as its Director. In those years he also found time to win fame as a mountain climber, making the first daring ascent of Mt. Kenya in East Africa. Concurrently with his post at Oxford, Mackinder served as a Reader in Economic Geography at the University of London, a position which led to his becoming Director of the London School of Economics from 1903 to 1908. Always keenly interested in politics, he was elected to several terms in Parliament, from 1910 to 1922. His entire career, however, was primarily in academic circles, and devoted to promoting the scientific study of geography, especially geography as seen "from the human standpoint."

In "The Geographical Pivot of History," destined to have such wide repercussions, Mackinder first presented his theory of closed space, an idea popularized forty years later by Wendell Willkie in his "One World" slogan. Mackinder believed that "the Columbian epoch," a period of four centuries of geographic exploration and expansion, had ended at the beginning of the twentieth century. "In 400 years," he wrote, "the outline of the map of the world has been completed with approximate accuracy."

Pursuing the same thought in *Democratic Ideals and Democracy,* Mackinder stated:

We have lately attained to the North Pole and found that it is in the midst of a deep sea, and to the South Pole, and have found it upon a high plateau. With these final discoveries the book of the pioneers has been closed. No considerable fertile new land, no important mountain-range, and no first-class river can any more be the reward of adventure. Moreover, the map of the world had hardly been sketched before claims to the political ownership of all the dry land had been pegged out. . . . The missionary, the conqueror, the farmer, the miner, and, of late, the engineer, have followed so closely in the traveller's footsteps that the world. in its remoter borders.

has hardly been revealed before we must chronicle its virtually complete political appropriation. In Europe, North America, South America, Africa, and Australasia there is scarcely a region left for the pegging out of a claim of ownership, unless as the result of a war between civilized or half-civilized powers.

In the eighteen-nineties, the brilliant American historian, Frederick Jackson Turner, had expressed a similar, though more limited, closed-space concept with his writings on the passing of the frontier and its significance in American history. Now, Mackinder maintained, the frontier had vanished throughout the world.

The probable effects of his premise were thus described by Mackinder:

From the present time forth, in the post-Columbian age, we shall again have to deal with a closed political system, and none the less that it will be one of world-wide scope. Every explosion of social forces, instead of being dissipated in a surrounding circuit of unknown space and barbaric chaos, will be sharply reechoed from the far side of the globe, and weak elements in the political and economic organism of the world will be shattered in consequence. . . . Every shock, every disaster or superfluity, is now felt even to the antipodes, and may indeed return from the antipodes. . . . Every deed of humanity will henceforth be echoed and reechoed . . . round the world.

In the closed system characteristic of our era, and the almost limitless mobility which has accompanied it, both on land and in the air, the age of dominant sea power, in Mackinder's view, had gone. If this were true, then an age of land power had arrived. Where was the natural center for the new epoch? In the world's greatest land mass, of course; that is, the immense area of Eurasia, termed by Mackinder the "pivot region of the world's politics." Among five maps used to illustrate his essay, the last is entitled "The Natural Seats of Power," and delineates the "pivot area." Mackinder envisaged the geographical pivot as the north and interior of Euro-Asia, extending from the Arctic to the central deserts and westward to the broad isthmus between the Baltic and Black Seas.

According to the historical analysis, with which much of his paper is concerned, Europe and the rest of the world have, for centuries, been under constant pressure from the pivot area.

It was under the pressure of external barbarism that Europe achieved her civilization. I ask you, therefore, for a moment to look upon Europe and European history as subordinate to Asia and Asiatic history, for European civilization is, in a very real sense, the outcome of the secular struggle against Asiatic invasion. The most remarkable contrast in the political map of modern Europe is that presented by the vast area of Russia occupying half of the Continent and a group of smaller territories tenanted by the Western Powers.

Tracing the ebb and flow of early European history, Mackinder continued:

For a thousand years a series of horse-riding peoples emerged from Asia through the broad interval between the Ural mountains and the Caspian sea, rode through the open spaces of southern Russia, and struck home into Hungary in the very heart of the European peninsula, shaping by the necessity of opposing them the history of each of the great peoples around—the Russians, the Germans, the French, the Italians, and the Byzantine Greeks.

From the point of view of permanent influence, the Mongol invasions of the fourteenth and fifteenth centuries left the deepest impress, overrunning much of central Europe, Russia, Persia, India, and China. These invasions came from what Mackinder called the "pivot area," and "all the settled margins of the Old World sooner or later felt the expansive force of mobile power originating in the steppe."

Projecting his story to our own times, Mackinder saw the pivot area as increasing its weight in world affairs, coincidentally with its growth in economic and military power. Viewed historically, he saw as evidence "a certain persistence of geographical relationship," for—

Is not the pivot region of the world's politics that vast area of Euro-Asia which is inaccessible to ships, but in antiquity lay open to the horse-riding nomads, and is today about to be covered with a network of railways? There have been and are here the conditions of a mobility of military and economic power of a far-reaching and yet limiting character. Russia replaces the Mongol Empire. Her pressure on Finland, on Scandinavia, on Poland, on Turkey, on Persia, on India, and on China replaces the centrifugal raids of the Steppe-men. In the world at large she occupies the central strategical position held by Germany in Europe. She can strike on all sides and be struck on all sides, save the North.

Outside the pivot area, Mackinder defines two "crescents." In a great inner crescent, are placed Germany, Austria, India, and China, while in an "outer crescent" are found Britain, South Africa, Australia, the United States, Canada, and Japan. In reality, the power of the pivot area was not equivalent to the peripheral states, but, and here Mackinder voiced his greatest fear, "This might happen if Germany were to ally herself with Russia." In that event, the pivot state could expand over the marginal lands of Euro-Asia, use "vast continental resources for fleet-building, and the empire of the world would then be in sight."

Mackinder concluded his notable address by emphasizing that he spoke as a geographer. "The actual balance of political power at any given time is," he pointed out, "of course, the product, on the one hand, of geographical conditions, both economic and strategic, and, on the other hand, of the relative number, virility, equipment, and organization of the competing peoples." In his estimation, "the geographical quantities in the calculation are more measurable and more nearly constant than the human." The geographical significance of the pivot position would not be altered if it were occupied by some other people than the Russian.

Were the Chinese, for instance, organized by the Japanese, to overthrow the Russian Empire and conquer its territory, they might constitute the yellow peril to the world's freedom just because they would add an oceanic frontage to the resources of the great continent, an advantage as yet denied to the Russian tenant of the pivot region.

Writing at the close of the first World War, Mackinder felt "that the War has established, and not shaken, my former points of view." In *Democratic Ideals and Reality* he pursued further the concept of the "pivot area," now referred to it as the "Heartland," set in the center of the "World-Island."

As Mackinder viewed them, Europe, Asia, and Africa are not three continents but one: The "World-Island." Since man's thinking in the past has been dominated by the sea, this massive area has not been regarded as an island because it was impossible to circumnavigate it. "An ice-cap, two thousand miles across, floats on the Polar Sea," Mackinder pointed out, "with one edge aground on the shoals off the north of Asia. For the common purposes of navigation, therefore, the continent is not an island." Except for this fact and its vast size, however, it does not differ from other islands. Both in area and population, the World-Island overshadows the remainder of the earth. Of the land, the World-Island has two-thirds, while North and South America, Australia, and lesser regions have the rest. Furthermore, seven-eighths of the earth's population are contained on the World-Island, while the other land areas have only one-eighth. The Old World then, Mackinder observed, is "incomparably the largest geographical unit on our globe."

Citing "the proportions and relations" of the World-Island, Mackinder continued:

It is set as it were on the shoulder of the earth with reference to the North Pole. Measuring from Pole to Pole along the central meridian of Asia, we have first a thousand miles of ice-clad sea as far as the northern shore of Siberia, then five thousand miles of land to the southern part of India, and then seven thousand miles of sea to the Antarctic cap of ice-clad land. But measured along the meridian of the Bay of Bengal or the Arabian Sea, Asia is only some three thousand five hundred miles across. From Paris to Vladivostok is six thousand miles, and from Paris to the Cape of Good Hope is a similar distance.

Not only are the two Americas and Australia relatively small from the standpoint of area, Mackinder argued, but the man power and natural resources available to them are far inferior to the "Great Continent" or World-Island. "What if the Great Continent, the whole World-Island or a large part of it," asks Mackinder, "were at some future time to become a single and united base of sea power? Would not the other insular bases be outbuilt as regards ships and outmanned as regards seamen?" Though Germany had been defeated, the possibility still existed "that a large part of the Great Continent might some day be united under a single sway, and that an invincible sea power might be based upon it." Had Germany won, Mackinder warned, "she would have established her sea power on a wider basis than any in history, and in fact on the widest possible base."

Mackinder's Heartland had substantially the same boundaries as his earlier "pivot area." The Heartland is the central region of Europe and Asia, remote from and beyond the control of sea power. It "includes the Baltic Sea, the navigable Middle and Lower Danube, the Black Sea, Asia Minor, Armenia, Persia, Tibet and Mongolia. Within it, therefore, were Brandenburg-Prussia and Austria-Hungary, as well as Russia—a vast triple base of manpower, which was lacking to the horse-riders of history." The Baltic and Black seas were included by Mackinder because it had been shown during World War I that they could not be reached or controlled by outside sea power.

The Heartland, Mackinder goes on to say, by the way of further definition, has "one striking physical circumstance which knits it graphically together; the whole of it, even to the brink of the Persian Mountains overlooking torrid Mesopotamia, lies under snow in the winter time. . . . At mid-winter, as seen from the moon, a vast white shield would reveal the Heartland in its largest meaning." This area, Mackinder was convinced, was the key to the World-Island. Extending roughly from the Himalayas to the Arctic Ocean, and from the Volga to the Yangtze, it stretched 2,500 miles north and south and another 2,500 miles east and west. Invulnerable to sea power because of its inland position, the Heartland could, if properly developed and organized militarily, become the seat and pivot of effective world power.

His arguments were reduced by Mackinder to an oft-quoted formula:

"Who rules East Europe commands the Heartland:
Who rules the Heartland commands the World-Island:
Who rules the World-Island commands the World."

To prevent any one nation, especially Russia or Germany, from becoming supreme in the Heartland following World War I, Mackinder advocated setting up a barrier of buffer states from the Baltic to the Black Sea. The independent states, as visualized by Mackinder, were to be Esthonia, Lithuania, Poland, Great Bohemia, Hungary, Great Serbia, Great Roumania, Bulgaria and Greece—a list only slightly at variance with the decisions of the Paris Peace Conference. In the light of recent history, of course, Mackinder made a bad guess. The buffer zone did not accomplish its purpose. First Germany and then Russia broke through the barrier.

During World War II, in 1943, four years before his death, Mackinder for the third time examined the Heartland theory. In an article, "The Round World and the Winning of the Peace," he found his concept "more valid and useful today than it was either twenty or forty years ago." He went on to prophesy that "if the Soviet Union emerges from the war as conqueror of Germany, she must rank as the greatest land power on the globe. Moreover, she will be the Power in the strategically strongest defensive position. The Heartland is the greatest natural fortress on earth. For the first time in history it is manned by a garrison sufficient both in number and quality."

Nowhere were Mackinder's theories more avidly seized upon than in Nazi Germany. As interpreted by Karl Haushofer, prolific writer on geopolitical subjects, Mackinder's root idea of the Heartland set in a World-Island dominated German political thought for two decades, 1925-1945.

Haushofer came into prominence as early as 1908, when he was sent to Japan as a military observer for the German General Staff. Concentrating upon mastery of Far Eastern affairs, he became recognized as an expert. Through exceptional linguistic ability he learned to speak six foreign languages, including Chinese, Japanese, Korean, and Russian. Also, he traveled widely to gain first-hand acquaintance with the Middle and Far East. During World War I Haushofer rose rapidly in military rank, retiring as a major general. After the German surrender, and for the remainder of his career, he engaged in writing and in teaching political geography and military history at the University of Munich. From his pen came innumerable books, pamphlets, and articles expounding upon two key words in Nazi ideology: *Geopolitik,* dealing with the dynamics of world political change, and *Lebensraum,* the German people's need for living space, for room to expand and grow.

It is not certain when Haushofer first encountered Mackinder's work—probably in the early nineteen-twenties. Immediately Haushofer recognized that he had found his master, and freely acknowledged his debt. Writing in 1937, for example, he described Mackinder's 1904 paper as "as the greatest of all geographical world views" and added that he had never "seen anything greater than these few pages of a geopolitical masterpiece." Two years later he argued for a German-Russian alliance, pointing out that Mackinder, taking the British view, had expressed fear of the power these two countries united might exert. Haushofer frequently repeated Ovid's maxim, "It is a duty to learn from the enemy." At least four times, he reproduced Mackinder's map of the Heartland in the periodical *Zeitschrift für Geopolitik,* and admitted without hesitation that his own ideas were based upon the foundation supplied by Mackinder.

Their mutual friend, Rudolf Hess, was the link between Haushofer and Hitler. While Hitler was in jail, following the abortive Beer Hall Putsch of 1923, he was visited on several occasions by Haushofer. That Hitler absorbed some of Haushofer's geopolitical indoctrination is revealed by various passages in *Mein Kampf*. With the Nazi triumph a decade later, Haushofer was in a key position to influence German policy. Appointed head of the Nazi Geopolitical Institute, he recruited a huge staff to comb the earth for data on the nature, living conditions, and cultural influences of peoples, and other geographic information of potential military importance.

Fascinated by Mackinder's ideas, Haushofer was obsessed with the conviction that Germany must win control of the Heartland. His blueprints called for a "transcontinental bloc," reaching from the Rhine to the Yangtze. Central to his scheme was to be a monster alliance of Germany, Japan, China, Russia, and India against the British Empire. His teachings were strongly endorsed and supported by the German General Staff. The signing of the Nazi-Soviet Pact in 1939 seemed to make Haushofer's dream come true, but his whole policy was tossed overboard when Hitler committed the most decisive blunder of World War II by ordering his generals to attack the Soviet Union. Shortly after the war ended, Haushofer and his wife committed suicide at their Bavarian home.

As was natural, the implication by critics that he had helped to lay the foundation of Nazi militarism was resented by Mackinder. In a 1944 speech, he remarked:

> It has, I am told, been rumored that I inspired Haushofer, who inspired Hess, who in turn suggested to Hitler while he was dictating *Mein Kampf* certain geo-political ideas which are said to have originated with me. Those are three links in a chain, but of the second and third I know nothing. This however I do know from the evidence of his own pen that whatever Haushofer adopted from me he took from an address ["The Geographical Pivot of History"] I gave before the Royal Geographical Society just forty years ago, long before there was any question of a Nazi Party.

The spread of geopolitical doctrines was not confined, of course, to Germany. Hardly less active have been the Russians. A flourishing geopolitical bureau, Moscow's Institute for

World Economy and Politics, has long concerned itself with the conflict between the United States and the World-Island, which the Soviet Union hopes to dominate. It is of interest in this connection to recall Mackinder's view of Russia in 1919 when the Communist government was young. The leopard, he was convinced, never changes his spots. The British and American brand of government and the ideals of the League of Nations "are all of them opposed to the policies cast in the tyrannical molds of East Europe and the Heartland, whether Dynastic or Bolshevik. It may be the case that Bolshevik tyranny is an extreme reaction from Dynastic tyranny, but it is none the less true that the Russian, Prussian, and Hungarian plains, with their widespread uniformity of social conditions, are favorable alike to the march of militarism and to the propaganda of syndicalism."

The validity of Mackinder's geographical theories has been frequently debated, and the flaws in his argument pointed out. An obvious defect is Mackinder's failure to take into account the immense potentialities of air power. In his later writing he recognized that the conquest of the air had forced a new kind of unity on the world, but insisted this development supported rather than weakened the Heartland—World Island thesis. Critics maintain, however, that air power has become such a formidable weapon that the conception of the Heartland has lost its strategic significance. Air lines now crisscross the oceans and the continent. As Herrick commented:

> The air is universal. Within range of the necessary bases, it is one vast highway to be traversed at will over land and sea alike. Air power can be blocked only by air power; it knows no Heartland from which it is inevitably excluded. . . . Today's strategical formula might well read: *Who rules the planes commands the bases: who rules the bases commands the air: who rules the air commands the world.*

This view is reinforced by examination of a globe, where one sees the proximity of the Heartland and North America. "Seen from North America and in terms of new communications," Weigert points out, "inaccessibility and vastness no longer conceal the Heartland from us. It lies no longer behind an impenetrable wall of isolation." Modern long-range aircraft have conquered the arctic regions in the fifty years since Mackinder first delivered his ominous warnings. Further, the very size of the Heartland is a serious handicap to a defending power. The great length of Soviet Russia's land and sea frontiers, for example, increases vulnerability to hostile aircraft and presents a defense problem of enormous complexity. While being able, in Mackinder's words, to "strike on all sides," she can also "be struck on all sides."

Another blind side shown by Mackinder was his failure to realize the powerful place occupied by the Americas. At the time he was writing *Democratic Ideals and Reality*, he had just recently witnessed, in World War I, a demonstration of American vigor and strength. Apparently preoccupied with the Heartland–World-Island way of looking at the earth, however, he could see the New World only as peripheral, as "merely satellites of the old continent."

Nevertheless, despite Mackinder's shortcomings as a seer, there are weighty arguments sustaining his judgments. The Soviet Union has established an iron rule of the Heartland, and through agricultural and industrial development, mineral exploitation, railway and airfield construction has made the area one of the strongest in the world, economically and militarily. On the other hand, though proceeding under the forced draft of several five-year plans for the past two decades, the region has not yet attained the productive efficiency of the United States. Also, though ruling the Heartland, the Soviet Union is still remote from its goal of commanding the World-Island, much less the world.

Criticism has exposed the weakness of some details of Mackinder's views, but it has not invalidated his basic premises. As "the first to provide us with a global concept of the world and its affairs," in John C. Winant's phrase, he will be long remembered. "There is," declared Mackinder, "no complete geographical region either less than or greater than the whole of the earth's surface." He was instrumental in obtaining wide acceptance of the belief he expressed as early as 1889, that the "political geographer's is the crowning chapter of geography." His primary concern was to persuade his own countrymen and peoples of other democracies that geographical facts are of basic importance in the growth of peoples and states. He believed and taught that the world cannot be made safe for democracy unless the geographical realities are fully understood. Upon Mackinder's ideas of the world and its regions, the foundations of modern geography are laid.

10 | STUDY IN MEGALOMANIA

ADOLF HITLER: *Mein Kampf*

The funeral pyre which consumed the mortal remains of Adolf Hitler and Eva Braun, on April 30, 1945, deep underground in the Berlin chancellery was a climax that might have been imagined by the operatic composer Hitler most ardently admired, Richard Wagner, for a new Götterdämmerung, or *Twilight of the Gods*. The scene rang down the curtain on a vast melodrama that had opened a generation earlier, when the future Führer began his march to power.

At the time the Nazi Party under Hitler's leadership took over the reins of government in Germany in 1933, after more than a decade of agitation and violence, the world was appalled by its actions. The regime was coldly ruthless in establishing its control; all vestiges of democratic government were abolished; dissenting views mercilessly suppressed; churches, fraternal orders, and labor unions persecuted or "co-ordinated"; Jews murdered in large numbers; and territorial threats against ostensibly friendly neighboring nations thundered in waves of propaganda.

Yet, if non-Germans had taken the trouble to peruse a fat tome entitled *Mein Kampf* ("My Struggle"), they would have found the entire program spelled out in all its shocking detail. Thanks to the protection of international copyright, its author had succeeded in restricting the full story to the original German. It is improbable, though, that even if the unexpurgated text had been freely available in English, French, and other languages, many persons would have taken seriously "the fantastic dream of a frenzied visionary"—so vast in scope and incredibly ambitious did it appear. *Mein Kampf* has rightly been called the "propagandistic masterpiece of the age" and, viewed from the standpoint of a trial judge, the "most incriminating book of the twentieth century." A great nation and its allies committed themselves to carrying out the fanatical ideas in the book. By the outbreak of World War II, 5,000,000 copies had been distributed in Germany alone.

Growing up in Vienna (as another Viennese, Sigmund Freud, might have predicted), Hitler formed at a tender age the impressions, prejudices, and hatreds that were to govern him for the remainder of his life. All are poured out in *Mein Kampf*. The opening chapters provide a brief but significant sketch of those early years. Born in 1889, at Braunau, Austria, just across the river from the German border, Hitler always felt himself a German rather than an Austrian, and especially despised the easygoing Viennese. According to his own account, the first years were full of privation, suffering, failure, frustration, and maladjustment. His formal schooling ceased at thirteen, and both parents were lost about the same time. In Vienna, his struggles to become an artist and, failing that, an architect were handicapped by lack of education and lack of talent.

During the Vienna period, Hitler claims to have read widely, with emphasis on history. His ideas were influenced particularly by a book on the Franco-Prussian War, which inspired in him a fervent pride in the German race and convinced him of the God-given destiny of that people. At the same time he began to form an intense dislike for the Jews, and complete contempt for the Slavs and all other "non-Aryans." The Jew is primarily an international-minded money-maker and exploiter, usually a Socialist or Communist, Hitler declared, while the Slavs are an inferior race, with no culture of their own.

Association with the Social Democrats in Vienna caused Hitler to loathe Socialist and Communist propaganda, and, though he was an apt student of the party's tactics, his hatred of Marxism was lifelong. Despite his omnivorous reading habits, there is no evidence that he ever opened *Das Kapital*. Scarcely less profound was his detestation of democracy and democratic institutions, an aversion which began when he attended sessions of the Austrian Reichsrath in Vienna and observed what he regarded as its inefficient methods.

Finally, no longer willing to breathe the abominable cosmopolitan air of Vienna, Hitler settled in 1912 in Munich, which he called "a thoroughly German city." Two years later, to his delight, the World War came. He enlisted in a Bavarian regiment, and before the war ended had been wounded, gassed, twice decorated, and promoted to the rank of corporal. Germany's defeat both grieved and enraged him—a defeat, he believed, that had been caused by Jews, Marxists, and pacifists. The creation of a democratic German government following the war likewise angered and embittered him. It was then that Hitler resolved to become a politician.

Hitler's entry into politics came after his return to Munich. For a time he served as a paid political informer for the army or *Wehrmacht*. He was invited to, and accepted, membership in a small group called the German Workers' party, soon renamed the National Socialist German Workers' party, the nucleus of the Nazi party. Within a short time, by internal maneuvering, Hitler gained tight control of the organization, and abolished the "senseless" practice of making party decisions by vote of the members. The Party's program, as it developed under Hitler's command, was designed to win the sympathies of the working classes, to exterminate "the international poisoners," to abolish legislative bodies, and to establish the principle of blind, unquestioning obedience to a leader or *Führer*.

By 1923, with 27,000 party members, and supported by a military clique under General Ludendorff, while the Stresemann government appeared to be tottering, Hitler concluded that the time had come to seize power. He had his followers stage the famous Beer Hall Putsch in Munich. The attempt ended in complete fiasco, and sixteen of Hitler's adherents were shot down in the streets. Hitler himself was arrested and sentenced to five years in prison, a term later reduced to one year.

As a prisoner in the Bavarian fortress at Landsberg, Hitler had leisure for the the first time to write his autobiography. Actually, *Mein Kampf* is a spoken rather than a written book. Sharing the prison with Hitler was his loyal disciple, Rudolph Hess, and to Hess was dictated directly on to a typewriter the first volume of the work. Dedicated to the sixteen Nazis who had fallen in the Munich uprising, the book was originally titled "Four and a Half Years of Struggle Against Lies, Stupidity, and Cowardice." The second volume was completed in 1926 at Berchtesgaden.

Otto Tolischus has described the contents of *Mein Kampf* as "10 per cent autobiography, 90 per cent dogma, and 100 per cent propaganda"—a fair analysis. It seems incredible today that such a crude, long-winded, badly written, contradictory, and repetitious book could have captured the emotions of a highly cultured nation. But the situation was made to order. Ludwig Lore's comments are enlightening:

The German people in 1933 were in a mood that made them dangerously susceptible to the fascist bacillus. They had tried to find a way back to normal living and national self-respect and had found the way blocked by prejudice and blind misunderstanding. The great nations were interested only in reparations. The German labor parties which might have helped were split into half a dozen warring camps. All this was played against a background colored by a century of high-pressure nationalism. The German people had reached a point where order and security seemed to matter more than a political freedom that had become synonymous with brawls and bloodshed. Hitler understood these things and used them for his purposes, aided by a phenomenal capacity for organization and propaganda and by the readiness of Germany's great industrialists to finance his campaigns. Once established, the German's innate respect for authority made it simple to establish Fascist leadership.

Mein Kampf's theme song, recurring again and again, is race, race purity, race supremacy—though nowhere did Hitler attempt to define race. Mankind, he said, is divided into three groups: the culture-creators, of whom there is only one example, the Aryan or Nordic (more specifically the German); the culture-bearers, such as the Japanese; and the culture-destroyers, e.g., Jews and Negroes. It was never intended by nature, Hitler claimed, that all races should be equal, any more than individuals are equal. Some are created superior to others. The Germans, as the world's strongest race, should rule over the inferior races of the earth. A few characteristic passages from *Mein Kampf* will illustrate Hitler's views on "inferior" races.
Writing of the Austrian Empire:

I was repelled by the conglomeration of races which the capital showed me, repelled by this whole mixture of Czechs, Poles, Hungarians, Ruthenians, Serbs, Croats, and everywhere, the eternal mushroom of humanity— Jews and more Jews.

About Africans:

. . . it is criminal lunacy to keep on drilling a born half-ape until people think they have made a lawyer out of him, while millions of members of the highest culture-race must remain in entirely unworthy positions; . . . it is a sin against the will of the Eternal Creator if His most gifted beings by the hundreds and hundreds of thousands are allowed to degenerate in the present proletarian morass, while Hottentots and Zulu Kaffirs are trained for intellectual professions.

Hindu nationalists "individually always impressed me as gabbling pomposities without any realistic background."

Poles, Czechs, Jews, Negroes, and Asiatics are lumped together as unworthy of German citizenship, even though they may be born in Germany and speak the German language. France was regarded with special contempt:

> . . . racially; . . . she is making such great progress in negrification that we can actually speak of an African state arising on European soil. The colonial policy of present-day France cannot be compared with that of Germany in the past. If the development of France in the present style were to be continued for three hundred years, the last remnants of Frankish blood would be submerged in the developing European-African mulatto state.

It is in the attacks on the Jews, however, that Hitler's race prejudice reaches its frenzied height, as, for example, in this passage:

> The Jewish train of thought in all this is clear. The Bolshevization of Germany—that is, the extermination of the national folkish Jewish intelligentsia to make possible the sweating of the German working class under the yoke of Jewish world finance—is conceived only as a preliminary to the further extension of this Jewish tendency of world conquest. As often in history, Germany is the great pivot in the mighty struggle. If our people and our state become the victim of these bloodthirsty and avaricious Jewish tyrants of nations, the whole earth will sink into the snares of this octopus; if Germany frees herself from this embrace, this greatest of dangers to nations may be regarded as broken for the whole world. . . .
> In general, the Jews will always fight within the various national bodies with those weapons which on the basis of the recognized mentality of these nations seem most effective and promise the greatest success. In our national body, so torn with regard to blood, it is therefore the more or less "cosmopolitan," pacifistic-ideological ideas, arising from this fact; in short, the international tendencies which they utilize in their struggle for power . . . until they have turned one state after another into a heap of rubble on which they can then establish the sovereignty of the eternal Jewish empire.

To maintain the pristine purity of the Aryan, i.e., the German master race, there must be no "bastardization" by admixture with inferior stocks. The decline of great nations in the past, asserted Hitler, had invariably resulted from the mixture of blood and the loss of race purity. To prevent such a calamity, it is the state's duty to intervene. Even though "cowards and weaklings" may protest the invasion of their rights, the state must "see that the nation's blood be kept pure so that humanity may reach its highest development. The state must lift marriage from the abyss of racial shame and sanctify it as an institution for the procreation of likenesses of God instead of monstrosities which are a cross between men and apes."

Fanatically believing in the innate superiority of the Aryan "race" over all others, Hitler preached that it is the duty, and privilege, of the master race to conquer, exploit, dispossess, or exterminate other races for its own advantage. Since Germany was crowded and needed *Lebensraum,* more living space, it was her right, as the great Nordic power, to grab Slavic land, remove the Slavs, and settle Germans on it. All humanity in the long run would benefit through having the habitat of the highest race extended and the scattered Germanic peoples united under one rule. "Only an adequately large space on this earth assures a nation of freedom of existence. . . . Germany will either be a world power or there will be no Germany."

The vast expansion visualized by Hitler would take place principally at the expense of Russia. Looking hungrily to the east, he speculated on what could be accomplished "if the Ural, with its immeasurable raw material and the Ukraine with its immeasurable grain fields lay within Germany." It was Germany's duty to rescue the Russian people from the Bolshevist leaders. "If we speak of soil in Europe today," continued Hitler, "we can primarily have in mind only Russia and her vassal border states. Here Fate itself seems desirous of giving us a sign. By handing Russia to Bolshevism, it robbed the Russian nation of that intelligentsia which previously brought about and guaranteed its existence as a state. . . The giant empire in the east is ripe for collapse."

Power, Hitler said, is the justification for invasion.

> . . . no people on this earth possesses so much as a square yard of territory on the strength of a higher will or superior right. . . . State boundaries are made by man and changed by man. The fact that a nation has succeeded in acquiring an undue amount of soil constitutes no higher obligation that it should be recognized eternally. At most it proves the strength of the conquerors and the weakness of the nations. And in this case, right lies in this strength alone.

Hitler recognized that there were other possible solutions than territorial expansion to Germany's rapid population growth. One alternative would be contraceptive limitation of births—rejected because it was not in accord with the master race theory. Another, followed by Germany's prewar rulers, was to expand factory production for foreign markets, that is increased industrialization, a solution not acceptable to Hitler, for he wanted Germany to feed herself and be self-sufficient. Furthermore, he was violently opposed to the creation of a large urban proletariat, the result of a great factory system. A third way out was to increase the productivity of the already available land, but this, argued Hitler, was but a partial and temporary answer. The only real remedy, he concluded, was for Germany to acquire new territory beyond existing frontiers, enabling more Germans to live on the land.

Hitler's long-range goals in population and territory were summarized in this paragraph:

> . . . Today we count eighty million Germans in Europe! This foreign policy will be acknowledged as correct only if, after scarcely a hundred years, there are two hundred and fifty million Germans on this continent, and not living penned in as factory coolies for the rest of the world, but: as peasants and workers, who guarantee each other's livelihood by their labor.

In short, Hitler foresaw the German population as more than tripled in the next hundred years, and, per capita, possessing twice as much room as was then available. The idea of a widely spaced population also appealed to Hitler for "military-geographical" reasons, because it would be less vulnerable to an enemy. (Shades of Mackinder-Haushofer!)

To attain the objectives set by his soaring ambition, Hitler proposed to use three methods: propaganda, diplomacy, and force. Nowhere in *Mein Kampf* is the author more revealing of himself and his tactics than in his discussion of propaganda techniques, correctly believed by him to be one of the Nazis' most effective and formidable weapons. Max Lerner called Hitler "probably the greatest master of propaganda and organization in modern history," adding that, "to find his equal one must go back to Loyola and the Jesuits." To perfect his own understanding of the propaganda art, Hitler studied the propaganda techniques of the Marxists, the organization and methods of the Catholic Church, British propaganda of World War I, American advertising, and Freudian psychology. He wrote:

The function of propaganda . . . is not to weigh and ponder the rights of different people, but exclusively to emphasize the one right which it has set out to argue for. Its task is not to make an objective study of the truth, in so far as it favors the enemy, and then set it before the masses with academic fairness; its task is to serve our own right, always and unflinchingly. It was absolutely wrong to discuss war-guilt from the standpoint that Germany alone could not be held responsible for the outbreak of the catastrophe; it would have been correct to load every bit of the blame on the shoulders of the enemy, even if this had not really corresponded to the true facts, as it actually did. . . . The purpose of propaganda is not to provide interesting distraction for blasé young gentlemen, but to convince, and what I mean is to convince the masses.

The importance of concentration and repetition was stressed.

The receptivity of the great masses is very limited, their intelligence is small, but their power of forgetting is enormous. In consequence of these facts, all effective propaganda must be limited to a very few points and must harp on these in slogans until the last member of the public understands what you want him to understand by your slogan. As soon as you sacrifice this slogan and try to be manysided, the effect will piddle away, for the crowd can neither digest nor retain the material offered. In this way the result is weakened and in the end entirely cancelled out.

Hitler's faith in propaganda is illustrated by his statement that "It is possible by means of shrewd and unremitting propaganda, to make people believe that heaven is hell—and hell heaven." For its greatest potential propaganda must be adapted to the most limited intelligence, "aimed always and primarily at the emotions, and very little at men's alleged reason." Propaganda has "no more to do with scientific accuracy than a poster has to do with art. . . . The greater the mass of men to be reached, the lower its intellectual level must be."
Also useful to the propagandist are certain psychological tricks. One should not, for example, attempt to convert a crowd to a different point of view in the morning. Dim lights are useful, and in the evening when people are tired and their powers of resistance low, their "complete emotional capitulation" is relatively easy to achieve. Another mighty tool is

mass suggestion, when the mob has a chance to join in parades and spectacular demonstrations, so typical of the Nazi regime. As Hitler put it:

> . . . the gigantic mass demonstrations, these parades of hundreds of thousands of men, which burned into the small, wretched individual the proud conviction that, paltry worm as he was, he was nevertheless a part of a great dragon, beneath whose burning breath the hated bourgeois world would some day go up in fire and flame and the proletarian dictatorship would celebrate its ultimate final victory.

Hitler's supreme contempt for the masses appears again and again, in such phrases as "an empty-headed herd of sheep," "the incarnation of stupidity," and his frequently expressed belief that mankind in the mass is lazy, cowardly, feminine, emotional, and incapable of rational thought.

The ultimate in Hitlerian propaganda technique is the principle of the big lie. The doctrine is "wholly correct," Hitler declared, "that the very greatness of the lie is a factor in getting it believed. . . . With the primitive simplicity of the masses a great lie is more effective than a small one, because they often lie in small matters, but would be too ashamed to tell a great big lie. Hence it will never occur to the broad mass to suspect so large a lie, and the mass will be quite unable to believe that anyone could possibly have the infernal impudence to pervert the truth to such an extent." In brief, the bigger the lie, the more likely it will be believed by the masses.

Another major propaganda principle is that of the single devil. Do not confuse the populace by offering too many enemies for it to hate at the same time. Concentrate upon one adversary, and focus the people's hatred upon this enemy. For Hitler, of course, the Jew served as the universal scapegoat. Regardless of whether he was ranting against democracy, Marxism, the Versailles Treaty, France, or some other favorite target, the Jew was always present, scheming and plotting, trying with devilish ingenuity to undermine Germany and Aryan culture. A sample is this hysterical outburst:

> . . . France is and remains by far the most terrible enemy. This people, which is basically becoming more and more negrified, constitutes in its tie with the aims of Jewish world domination an enduring danger for the existence of

the white race in Europe. For the contamination by Negro blood on the Rhine in the heart of Europe is just as much in keeping with the perverted sadistic thirst for vengeance of this hereditary enemy of our people as is the ice-cold calculation of the Jew thus to begin bastardizing the European continent at its core and to deprive the white race of the foundations for a sovereign existence through infection with lower humanity.

The task of the propagandist is facilitated, Hitler said, by state control of education. Too much book-learning is an error. Physical education and physical health should take first place. Second is the development of character, especially such military virtues as obedience, loyalty, strength of will, self-control, capacity for sacrifice, and pride in responsibility. Relegated to third place is intellectual activity. For girls, training must be for motherhood. The concept of education for all was repugnant to Hitler who described it as a disintegrating poison invented by liberalism for its own destruction. Each class and each subdivision of a class had only one possible education. He thought that the great mass of people should enjoy the blessings of illiteracy.

For the last group, education is to be limited to an indoctrination with "general ideas, carved by eternal repetition into the heart and memory of the people." Always the guiding principle is that the child belongs to the state, and the sole object of education is to train tools for the state.

Hitler's views on popular education are of a piece with his opinion of democracy in general. At every opportunity he ridiculed the ineffectiveness of the democratic state:

> The Western democracy of today is the forerunner of Marxism which without it would not be thinkable. It provides this world plague with the culture in which its germs can spread. In its most extreme form, parliamentarianism created a "monstrosity of excrement and fire," in which, however, sad to say, the "fire" seems to me at the moment to be burned out. . . . For there is one thing which we must never forget: in this, too, the majority can never replace the man. It is not only a representative of stupidity, but of cowardice as well. And no more that a hundred empty heads makes one wise man will an heroic decision arise from a hundred cowards.

Hitler saw democracy as "the deceitful theory that the Jew would insinuate—namely, the theory that all men are created

equal"; while any doctrine of universal suffrage and equal
rights is "pernicious and destructive."
Hitler substituted the leader principle for democracy. He
put heads over the mass who were supposed to obey orders
without question. Over all was the Führer, taking full responsibility for all he did or failed to do.
Having drawn his blueprint for Germany and the world in
Mein Kampf, Hitler faithfully adhered to it, except for one
important, though, as it turned out, temporary deviation—
the Nazi-Soviet Pact of 1939. How difficult it must have
been for him to swallow the Russian agreement is indicated
by this diatribe in *Mein Kampf.*

> Never forget that the rulers of present-day Russia are
> common blood-stained criminals; that they are the scum
> of humanity which, favored by circumstances, overran a
> great state in a tragic hour, slaughtered and wiped out
> thousands of her leading intelligentsia in a wild blood
> lust . . .

Since Hitler, in *Mein Kampf,* had so plainly revealed his
intentions years before he came to power in Germany, and
more than a decade prior to the beginning of World War II,
why did the statesmen of the world pay so little heed to his
warnings? In part, he was ignored because of the general
atmosphere of appeasement, wishful thinking, and peace-at-
any-price that prevailed. Another factor was an amazing
story of international censorship. Because Hitler refused to
authorize a complete translation of *Mein Kampf,* only a much
expurgated, bowdlerized version was available in English until
1939. In that year, on the eve of war, two American publishers, one with Hitler's approval and one without, brought
out uncensored editions. In France, in 1936, Hitler, through
his publisher, sued and restrained the issue of a full translation, pleading infringement of copyright. A condensed edition
published in London omitted most of the passages attacking
France, eliminated a section justifying war, and so softened
the tone of the book as to be false and misleading.
Meanwhile, millions of copies of the complete *Mein Kampf*
were being sold and circulated in Germany. Every newly
married couple was presented with a copy, while every member
of the Nazi party and every civil servant was expected to
possess the book. Later editions in Germany did, however,
leave out the attacks on Russia and France, to conceal Hitler's purposes and to lull potential enemies to sleep.
Viewing *Mein Kampf* retrospectively, historians would

maintain that Hitler had no understanding of history, anthropologists that his racial views were nonsense, educators that his theories of education were altogether medieval and reactionary, political scientists would protest his authoritarian doctrines of government and his misrepresentation of democracy, while literary experts would hold that he did not know how to write a paragraph or organize a chapter. Weigert summed it up in this way:

> The half-educated Hitler was a mosaic of influences: the amoral statecraft of Machiavelli, the mystic nationalism and romanticism of Wagner, the organic evolution of Darwin, the grossly exaggerated racialism of Gobineau and Houston Stewart Chamberlain, the messianic complex of Fichte and Hegel, the military braggadocio of Treitschke and Bernhardi, and the financial conspiracy of the Prussian Junker caste. . . . Haushofer served as a channel of unification between theory and action.

And yet, despite such glaring defects, *Mein Kampf* is, as one of its bitterest critics, Hendrik Willem Van Loon, described it, "one of the most extraordinary historical documents of all time," combining "the naiveté of Jean-Jacques Rousseau with the frenzied wrath of an Old Testament prophet." Norman Cousins called it "by far the most effective book of the twentieth century. . . . For every word in 'Mein Kampf.' 125 lives were to be lost; for every page, 4,700 lives; for every chapter, more than 1,200,000 lives." Its power was derived, of course, from the fact that it was the political bible of the German people, and guided the policies of the Third Reich from 1933 until the end of World War II.

It is the world's misfortune that Hitler's ideas did not expire with him. Their adherents are still numerous in Germany, while Communist governments have borrowed and are making extensive use of many of them. Dictators everywhere will continue to find primary source material for their evil purposes in *Mein Kampf,* in the same manner that, for the past four centuries, they have been drawing upon Machiavelli.

The World of Science

11 | CELESTIAL REVOLUTION

NICOLAUS COPERNICUS:
De Revolutionibus Orbium Coelestium

Since primitive ages, man has been fascinated by the pageant of the skies—the sun, the moon, the planets, the stars, and their ceaseless movements. The rising and setting of the sun, the waxing and waning of the moon, the succession of the seasons, the advance and retreat of the planets were not only observable facts, but in numerous respects affected mankind's daily existence. It is not strange, therefore, that a vast body of legends, and even religions, grew up around celestial phenomena.

As civilizations advanced, philosophers attempted to explain the moving heavens in rational terms. Most advanced of the ancient scientists and thinkers on matters of astronomy were the Greeks, starting with Pythagoras in the fifth and Aristotle in the fourth centuries, B.C. An Egyptian, Claudius Ptolemy, living in Alexandria about A.D. 150, organized and systematized the classical learning of his own and preceding eras into a comprehensive set of theories. For nearly 1,500 years, the Ptolemaic system, as set forth in "The Almagest," dominated the minds of men and was universally accepted as the true conception of the universe.

Ptolemy's theory was built around the notion that the earth was a fixed, inert, immovable mass, located at the center of the universe, and all celestial bodies, including the sun and the fixed stars, revolved around it. The earth, it was believed, was the hub of a system of spheres. To these the planets were rigidly attached. The stars were attached to another sphere outside this system, and all rotated each twenty-four hours.

The complicated motions of the planets were explained by epicycles, with the planetary spheres rotating in the opposite direction from the sphere of stars, but pulled along by a stronger force. Saturn was considered the most distant planet, nearest to stellar space, and consequently took longest to complete a revolution. The moon, being nearest the center, completed a revolution in the briefest time. Rosen describes the Ptolemaic conception in these terms:

The traditional doctrine held that the planets, moving eastward most of the time, periodically slowed down until they actually came to a halt, then reversed themselves a second time, resuming their eastward journey, and repeating this cycle of changes endlessly.

The universe was thus a closed space bounded by a spherical envelope. Beyond this universe there was nothing.

General assent to the Ptolemaic theories was made easier by two factors, both a reflection of human nature: first, the system rested upon natural appearances, upon things as they were seen by any casual observer; and, second, they fed man's ego. How pleasing it was to believe that the earth was the center of the heavens, with the planets and stars revolving about it. The whole universe seemed to be made for man.

This beautiful structure remained substantially intact until the coming of the great era of intellectual awakening in Europe —the Renaissance. Its destruction was the work of Nicolaus Copernicus, "a churchman, a painter and a poet, a physician, an economist, a statesman, a soldier, and a scientist"—one of the "universal men" for whom the Renaissance was celebrated.

Copernicus' seventy-year life span, 1473-1543, was one of the most exciting and adventurous periods in Europe's history. Columbus discovered new continents. Magellan circumnavigated the globe, Vasco da Gama made the first sea voyage to India, Martin Luther waged the Protestant Reformation, Michelangelo created a new world of art, Paracelsus and Vesalius laid the groundwork for modern medicine, and Leonardo da Vinci, "that tremendous universal genius" flourished as painter, sculptor, engineer, architect, physicist, biologist, and philosopher. What a fitting age for another brilliant mind, Copernicus, to give the world a new system for the universe.

Nicolaus Copernicus was born on the banks of the Vistula in Torun, Poland, an old Hanseatic League city. His early

career was largely directed by an influential uncle, Lucas
Watzelrode, later the prince-bishop of Ermeland. A long
and varied education for Nicolaus began with the preparatory
school at Torun, and continued, in 1491, at the University
of Krakow. He had been attracted to this institution by its
reputation as one of the leading European centers for mathematics and astronomy. Five years later he traveled to Italy
to continue his education at Bologna, one of the oldest and
most famous of European universities. The study of canon
law and astronomy occupied his time. Subsequently, he spent
a year in Rome, lecturing on mathematics and astronomy.
About five years in Padua and Ferrara, studying medicine
and church law, completed Copernicus' academic career.
His degree of Doctor of Canon Law was received from Ferrara in 1503.

Meanwhile, through his uncle's influence, Copernicus had
been nominated canon in the cathedral of Frauenburg, and
it was there that he spent the remaining thirty-seven years of
his life, after returning from Italy in 1506.

Copernicus' canonical duties were multifarious: he carried on an active medical practice among churchmen and
laity; aided in the military defense of his district in the recurring wars between Poles, Prussians and Teutonic knights;
participated in the peace conferences which followed; ad-
vised on the reform of the coinage and currency; administered
the remoter parts of the diocese; and for relaxation, painted
and translated Greek poetry into Latin.

Astronomy, then, was only one of the varied activities
carried on by the versatile Copernicus. But increasingly it
became his primary interest, as he developed his ideas on
astronomical phenomena—ideas which apparently had come
to him early in life and had been intensified by his studies at
Krakow and in Italy. His investigations were carried on quietly
and alone, without help or consultation. For an observatory,
he used a turret on a protective wall built around the cathedral.

Astronomical instruments available to Copernicus were
crude and primitive. His work was done nearly a century before the telescope was invented. For measuring purposes, he
possessed a sundial; a triquetrum (an awkward three-sided
wooden affair) which he made himself, to obtain the altitudes
of the stars and planets; and an astrolabe, a sphere within
vertical and horizontal rings. Further, the climate was un-
favorable to astronomical observations; proximity to the Baltic
Sea and rivers brought fogs and clouds. Completely clear
days and nights were rare. Nevertheless, on every possible

occasion, year after year, Copernicus labored over his calculations.

The revolutionary theory which Copernicus was attempting to prove or disprove through his prolonged studies went directly contrary to the time-honored and revered Ptolemaic system. The theory was, in short, that the earth was not stationary but rotated on an axis once daily and traveled around the sun once yearly. So fantastic was such a concept in the sixteenth century that Copernicus did not dare to advance it until he was convinced his data were irrefutable. Hence the delay of more than thirty years before the Copernican system was revealed to the world.

Actually, certain of the ancient Greek astronomers had suggested that ours might be a sun-centered rather than an earth-centered universe. Aristarchus, "the ancient Copernicus," in the third century, b.c., for example, accounted for the daily rising and setting of the sun by supposing that the earth turned around once a day on its axis. But his hypothesis, along with those of other astronomers with similar ideas, was rejected by Aristotle and Ptolemy in favor of a geocentric or earth-centered scheme. These early theories were known to Copernicus from his reading of classical literature, and may well have inspired him to a re-examination of the problem. To Copernicus, it seemed that Aristarchus, 1,800 years before, had given a much simpler explanation of the motions of the sky than were contained in the complicated Ptolemaic system.

Perhaps as early as 1510, Copernicus wrote a short general account of his new theory. Entitled the *Commentariolus* or "Little Commentary," the tract was not published during the author's lifetime, but a number of handwritten copies were circulated among students of astronomy. At least two of the manuscripts are still extant. In the *Commentariolus* Copernicus indicated that he had begun his researches because it appeared to him that the Ptolemaic theories of the cosmos were too complex, too irrational, and did not provide satisfactory explanations for celestial phenomena. The main conclusions to which Copernicus had come were reported: the earth was not the center of the solar system, but only of the moon orbit, and all the planets revolved around the sun. The "Little Commentary" represented a distinct stage in the development of the great astronomer's ideas.

It is conceivable that Copernicus' master work, on which he had toiled for thirty years, might never have reached the printing press, and consequently would have been lost to the world, except for the efforts of a young German scholar. In the summer of 1539 there came to Frauenburg to visit

Copernicus a twenty-five-year-old professor of mathematics from the University of Wittenberg. This was George Joachim Rheticus. Attracted by Copernicus' growing fame, Rheticus had come to verify at first hand the true merits of his reputation. He expected to remain only a few weeks, but he was warmly welcomed by Copernicus and actually stayed for over two years. He speedily became convinced that his host was a genius of the first rank. For three months he studied Copernicus' writings and discussed them with the author. Rheticus then wrote an account of the Copernican ideas and sent it, in the form of a letter, to his former teacher Johann Schöner, at Nuremberg. The letter was printed at Danzig in 1540. The *Narratio Prima*, or "First Account," by Rheticus, was the first published statement of the Polish astronomer's world-shaking theories. Actually, the little book dealt in detail only with a portion of the Copernican system, that is, with a consideration of the earth's movements. Rheticus had anticipated following his "First Account" with other "accounts," but these were never required. His admiration, amounting almost to adulation, was shown by the warm praise he gave his "Dominus Doctor" throughout his treatise.

Up to this point, Copernicus had been extremely reluctant to permit publication of his complete work. He was a perfectionist, and felt every observation had to be checked and rechecked; the original manuscript, rediscovered in Prague in the middle of the nineteeth century, after being lost for 300 years, shows evidence of a half-dozen extensive revisions. In addition to these hesitations, Copernicus may also have been deterred by the potential disapproval of the Church. The Protestant Reformation and the intellectual ferment of the Renaissance were making religious circles suspicious of revolutionary theories as well as of any ideas that might cause other departures from orthodox teachings. Copernicus, a faithful churchman, had no desire to play the heretic or the martyr.

So favorably received, however, was the *Narratio Prima,* and so urgent were the pleadings of Rheticus and others to permit full publication, that Copernicus finally yielded. The manuscript was entrusted to Rheticus, who was to take it to Nuremberg and see it through the press. Before this task could be accomplished, however, he was appointed to a professorship at the University of Leipzig, and a local Lutheran clergyman, Andreas Osiander, was assigned the responsibility.

Apparently Osiander was worried about the radical ideas expressed by Copernicus. Without authorization and anonymously, he proceeded to remove Copernicus' introduction to Book I. For it he substituted his own preface, stating that the book merely contained hypotheses for the convenience of astronomers; it was not necessarily true or even probable that the earth moves; in other words, the book was not to be taken seriously. Osiander was doubtless well intentioned in his attempt to avoid hostile criticism; and, as Mizwa pointed out. "Perhaps, unwittingly, Osiander rendered a much greater service than he realized for the preservation of this great work. Because of this spurious and disarming foreword, cleverly addressed as though in the name of the author, 'to the reader of the hypotheses of this work,' the church overlooked the revolutionary importance of *De Revolutionibus* and did not put it on the Index until 1616."

Before the printing was finished, Copernicus suffered a severe stroke. A well-authenticated story relates that, in one of the most dramatic moments in history, a messenger arrived in Frauenberg bringing from Nuremberg the first copy of Copernicus' masterpiece and placed it in his hands only a few hours before the author's death. The date was May 24, 1543. The book was entitled *De Revolutionibus Orbium Coelestium*, "Concerning the Revolutions of the Heavenly Spheres." Like other scholarly productions of the time, it was written in Latin.

Wisely and diplomatically, Copernicus dedicated his work to Pope Paul III. It is obvious from the dedicatory statement that Copernicus anticipated some difficulties.

I can well believe, most holy father, that certain people, when they hear of my attributing motion to the earth in these books of mine, will at once declare that such an opinion ought to be rejected. Now, my own theories do not please me so much as not to consider what others may judge of them. Accordingly, when I began to reflect upon what those persons who accept the stability of the earth, as confirmed by the opinion of many centuries, would say when I claimed that the earth moves, I hesitated for a long time as to whether I should publish that which I have written to demonstrate its motion, or whether it would not be better to follow the example of the Pythagoreans, who used to hand down the secrets of philosophy to their relatives and friends in oral form. As I well considered this, I was almost impelled to put the finished work wholly aside, through the scorn I had reason to anticipate on account of the newness and apparent contrariness to reason of my theory.

My friends, however, dissuaded me from such a course and admonished me that I ought to publish my book

which has lain concealed in my possession not only nine
years, but already into four times the ninth year. Not a
few other distinguished and very learned men asked me to
do the same thing, and told me that I ought not on account of my anxiety, to delay any longer in consecrating
my work to the general service of mathematicians. . . .

I do not doubt that clever and learned men will agree
with me if they are willing fully to comprehend and to
consider the proofs which I advance in the book before
us. In order, however, that both the learned and the un-
learned may see that I fear no man's judgment, I wanted
to dedicate these, my night labors, to your Holiness, rather
than to anyone else, because you, even in this remote cor-
ner of the Earth where I live, are held to be the greatest
in dignity of station and in love for all sciences and for
mathematics, so that you, through your position and
judgment, can easily suppress the bites of slanderers,
although the proverb says that there is no remedy against
the bite of calumny. It may fall out, too, that idle bab-
blers, ignorant of mathematics, may claim a right to pronounce a judgment on my work, by reason of a certain
passage of Scripture basely twisted to suit their purpose.
Should any such venture to criticize and carp at my
project I heed them not and look upon their judgments
as rash and contemptible.

His conception of the universe is summarized by Copernicus
in these words:

Most distant of all is the Sphere of the Fixed Stars, containing all things and for that very reason immovable;
in truth the frame of the Universe, to which the motion
and position of all other stars are referred. Though some
men think it to move in some way, we assign another reason why it appears to do so in our theory of the movement of the Earth. Of the moving bodies first comes
Saturn, who completes his circuit in 30 years. After him,
Jupiter, moving in a twelve year revolution. Then, Mars,
who revolves biennially. Fourth in order an annual cycle
takes place in which we have said is contained the Earth
with the lunar orbit as an epicycle. In the fifth place
Venus is carried around in nine months. Then Mercury
holds the sixth place, circulating in the space of eighty
days. In the middle of all dwells the Sun. Who, indeed,
in this most beautiful temple would place the torch in
any other or better place than one whence it can illumi-

nate the whole at the same time? . . . We find, therefore, under this orderly arrangement a wonderful symmetry in the Universe, and a definite relation of harmony in the motion and magnitude of the orbs, of a kind it is not possible to obtain in any other way.

An outline of the contents of *De Revolutionibus* will show the plan of its development. Following the dedicatory preface to Pope Paul III, and the fake introduction by Osiander, the work is divided into six "Books," or main divisions, each subdivided by chapters. In Book I are Copernicus' views of the universe, arguments in favor of his heliocentric or suncentered theory, including the idea that the earth, like other planets, revolves around the sun, and a discussion of the seasons. Several chapters at the end of this book constitute a textbook on trigonometry, and the principles of this branch of mathematics were utilized by Copernicus in later sections.

Book II deals with the motions of the celestial bodies, measured mathematically, and closes with a catalog of stars, showing the position of each in the sky—a list taken over from Ptolemy for the most part, though with some corrections.

The other four books contain detailed descriptions of the motions of the earth, the moon, and the planets. In each case, explanation of the motions is accompanied by a geometrical diagram showing the course followed by the sphere on the basis of Copernicus' calculations.

One of the principal reasons advanced against the theory of a moving earth had been stated by Ptolemy. The earth must remain stationary, he contended, for otherwise anything floating in the air, such as a cloud or a bird, would be left behind, and an object tossed in the air would descend a considerable distance westward. Most cataclysmic of all, if the earth turned at such a tremendous speed, it would soon break into pieces, disintegrate, and fly off into space. Before Galileo's discovery of the mechanics involved and Newton's law of gravitation, these ancient Ptolemaic arguments were difficult to refute. Copernicus answered them by suggesting that the air around the earth is carried along by the earth's motion and that it is more logical to assume that the earth turns instead of the entire universe, for if the earth did not rotate, the sky would have to revolve to produce day and night. The defense was further reinforced by a philosophical speculation: nature is not self-destructive, and God would not have created a universe merely to have it destroy itself.

For Copernicus, the sun was inert and passive, stationary

amid revolving planets, much like Ptolemy's conception of the earth. The sun's only functions were to supply light and heat. The universe was strictly limited. Outside the sphere of the stars, as Ptolemy had taught, space ceased to exist. The concept of infinite space was probably as unknown to Copernicus as it had been 1,400 years earlier to Ptolemy. Neither did he depart from Ptolemy's system of epicycles. There was a different center for each of the orbits, and the sun was not placed in the true center of any of the planetary orbits. These were features of the Copernican system to be corrected by later astronomers.

Acceptance of the Copernican system was slow, both among scientists and the general populace. With a few exceptions, expressions of contemporary opinion were in violent opposition. According to one tale, the printer's shop where *De Revolutionibus* was being printed was attacked by university students who tried to destroy the press and the manuscript; the printers barricaded themselves to finish the job. A burlesque play ridiculing Copernicus was produced by a group of strolling players at Elbing; it depicted the astronomer as having given his soul to Satan.

More serious, however, was the reaction of the powerful church organizations. The new theories upset the standard philosophical and religious beliefs of the medieval era. If the Copernican doctrines were true, man no longer occupied a central place in the universe; he had been removed from his pedestal, and his home was reduced to but one of many planets.

But because it was occupied with other matters and in part perhaps because of Osiander's misleading preface, the Catholic Church took no immediate action against the Copernican treatise. Less restrained were the Reformation leaders. Martin Luther severely criticized Copernicus on a number of occasions. He referred to him as "the new astronomer who wants to prove that the Earth goes round, and not the Heavens, the Sun, and the Moon; just as if someone sitting in a moving wagon or ship were to suppose that he was at rest, and that the Earth and the trees were moving past him. But that is the way nowadays; whoever wants to be clever must needs produce something of his own, which is bound to be the best since *he* has produced it! The fool will turn the whole science of Astronomy upside down. But, as Holy Writ declares, it was the Sun and not the Earth which Joshua commanded to stand still." Luther's loyal disciple Melanchthon remarked disparagingly of Copernicus, "He stopped the sun and set the earth in motion."

John Calvin was equally emphatic in his condemnation, quoting Psalm 93: "The world also is established, that it cannot be moved," and demanded indignantly, "Who will venture to place the authority of a Copernicus above that of the Holy Spirit?"

Not until 1615 did the Catholic Church take stern measures against the *De Revolutionibus,* and its action then was in the nature of reprisal against such advocates of the Copernican theories as Galileo and Bruno. The Copernican principles were disposed of in this fashion:

The first proposition, that the sun is the center and does not revolve about the earth, is foolish, absurd, false in theology, and heretical, because expressly contrary to Holy Scripture. The second proposition, that the earth revolves about the sun and is not the center, is absurd, false in philosophy and from a theological point of view at least, opposed to the true faith.

The following year, 1616, the writings of Copernicus were placed on the Index of prohibited books "until they should be corrected," and, at the same time, "all writings which affirm the motion of the Earth" were condemned. For more than two centuries, Copernicus remained on the Index. The ban was finally removed in 1835.

The fates suffered by Galileo and Bruno may well have deterred others from embracing the Copernican system. Giordano Bruno, an ardent follower of Copernicus, went beyond the latter in advocating the theory that space is boundless and that the sun and its planets are only one of many similar systems. He suggested further that there might be other inhabited worlds, with rational beings equal or superior to ourselves. For such blasphemy, Bruno was tried before the Inquisition, condemned, and burned at the stake in February 1600. Only slightly less drastic was the treatment of the great Italian astronomer Galileo, who, in 1633, under threat of torture and death by the Inquisition, was forced on his knees to renounce all belief in Copernican theories, and was sentenced to imprisonment for the remainder of his days.

The hesitation of Catholic and Protestant theologians to accept the Copernican theory was matched by the attitude of philosophers and scientists. One of the founders of modern scientific methods, Francis Bacon, for example, argued against the conception of the earth rotating on an axis and circling in an orbit around the sun. The hold of Aristotle and Ptolemy on the European universities was unbroken long after *De Revo-*

lutionibus saw the light. Actually, as Stebbins points out, "The slow adoption of the Copernican system was characteristic of all countries. In America the Ptolemaic and Copernican systems were taught concurrently at Harvard and also at Yale."

Nevertheless, slowly and gradually the Copernican theories won inevitable acceptance. Continued investigations by such dedicated scientists as Giordano Bruno, Tycho Brahe, Johann Kepler, Galileo Galilei, and Isaac Newton during the succeeding decades constructed a pyramid of irrefutable evidence. Defects in the Copernican system were removed by these and other investigators as better instruments for observation were perfected, and as each individual could build upon the researches of his predecessors.

The greatest astronomer immediately following Copernicus was a Dane, Tycho Brahe. Tycho did not subscribe to the theory that the earth revolves around the sun, but, with excellent instruments given to him by the King of Denmark, he was able to make astronomical observations and measurements far superior to those of Copernicus. On the basis of these data, his German assistant, Johann Kepler, after Tycho's death, was able to formulate his three famous laws: (a) that planets travel in ellipses, rather than in circles, with the sun in one focus; (b) that as the earth or other planet revolves around the sun in its elliptical orbit it does not move uniformly, but in such a way that as it is nearest the sun it moves fastest; (c) the distance of a planet from the sun is proportional to the period of its revolutions around the sun.

Galileo was the first observer to apply the telescope to astronomy, and many of his telescopic discoveries substantiated the findings of Copernicus. A scientific foundation was provided by Galileo when he established fundamental principles in dynamics, the science of motion. Conclusive proof of the validity of the Copernican theory was furnished by Sir Isaac Newton, with his discovery of the law of gravitation and his formulation of the laws under which the planets moved. And some of the remaining mysteries of the universe were unveiled by Einstein's theory of relativity in the twentieth century.

In the light of numerous modifications made by scientists in later centuries, the question is frequently and reasonably asked: Is the Copernican theory true? Undeniably, Copernicus left his system incomplete and inaccurate at various points. His conception of the perfectly circular motion of the celestial bodies was demonstrated to be erroneous; instead, they move in ellipses. Copernicus thought of the universe with very finite limitations, contrary to the modern theory of an infinite number of solar systems. In other details, likewise, the principles stated by Copernicus over four centuries ago do not conform to present-day knowledge. But in its essential feature—the choice of the sun as the center of our planetary system— Copernicus discovered fundamental truth and furnished a foundation for the modern science of astronomy.

Copernicus' place in the history of science is lastingly established. His influence on his contemporaries and on all subsequent thought entitle him to a pre-eminent position. As Goethe wrote:

Of all discoveries and opinions, none may have exerted a greater effect on the human spirit than the doctrine of Copernicus. The world had scarcely become known as round and complete in itself when it was asked to waive the tremendous privilege of being the center of the universe. Never, perhaps, was a greater demand made on mankind—for by this admission so many things vanished in mist and smoke! What became of our Eden, our world of innocence, piety and poetry; the testimony of the senses; the conviction of a poetic—religious faith? No wonder his contemporaries did not wish to let all this go and offered every possible resistance to a doctrine which in its converts authorized and demanded a freedom of view and greatness of thought so far unknown, indeed not even dreamed of.

Finally, consider the judgments of three notable living American scientists. Commented Vannevar Bush, "Publication of the master work of Copernicus . . . marked a turning point of such great importance as to influence every phase of human thought. It affords an outstanding example of the effect of scientific truth in the freeing of man's mind and in clearing his vision for future conquests of ignorance and intolerance." Nobel prize winner Harold C. Urey affirmed, "All superlatives fail when describing the work of Nicolaus Copernicus. He broke with a conception of the solar system that had stood for one thousand years, and introduced an entirely new concept of the relation of the planets to the sun. In so doing he initiated the whole modern method of scientific thought, and modified our thinking on all phases of human life."

Lastly, there is the opinion of the distinguished astronomer Harlan True Stetson:

It is always embarrassing to survey the long list of true notables that have contributed to the progress of science in the world's history and to give any small number as preeminently outstanding. Yet, if I were called upon to select three names, I should say without much hesitation, Copernicus, Newton, and Darwin. These three have certain characteristics in common that make them inseparable in the triumph of progress. These characteristics are imagination, the boldness of genius, and an originality exhibiting extraordinary comprehensiveness of the concept. Of the greatest of these, all things considered, I believe the laurels would go to Copernicus, for it was he who laid the foundations of modern astronomy without which Newton could not have built his law of gravity and he opened the gates to a revolutionary type of thinking challenging the orthodox which had to take place before the doctrine of evolution could gain a foothold in our thinking.

12 DAWN OF SCIENTIFIC MEDICINE

WILLIAM HARVEY: De Motu Cordis

Biological science and research at the beginning of the seventeenth century were little more advanced than had been the study of astronomy prior to Copernicus. Physicians and medical schools still practiced and taught the anatomical and physiological theories concerning the heart, arteries, veins, and blood handed down from the great Asiatic-Greek physician Galen in the second century.

For more than a thousand years, no substantial additions had been made to man's knowledge of blood circulation and the functions of the heart. Aristotle had taught that blood originated in the liver, went from there to the heart, and then through the body to the veins. The heart, he believed, was also the source of body heat and the seat of intelligence. Erasistratus of the Alexandrian school maintained that the arteries carried a subtle kind of air or spirits. This conception had been corrected by Galen, who discovered that the arteries carried blood, not air, but for centuries after his time physicians were convinced that a spirit of some sort had a part in the blood system, perhaps animating the heart.

Only the boldest of scientists dared to question the precedents and sayings received from the ancients. Galen's writings were regarded as of almost divine origin—not to be disputed or doubted. According to Galen, too, the liver was the center of the blood system. Digested food was carried to the liver and there transformed into blood, with "natural spirits" added. Blood moved backward and forward in the body, by way of both the veins and the arteries, like the slow ebb and flow of the tides. Arterial blood from one side of the heart mixed with venous blood from the other side through minute pores.

To natural facts there had become attached, over the centuries, much superstitious lore about the blood. More than any other part of the body, blood possessed a sacred quality, as is shown by its use in religious sacrifices and the pouring of blood upon the altars of the gods.

By 1600, however, change was everywhere in the air. The Renaissance in Europe brought not only a revival of literature, but an intellectual awakening immediately affecting the natural sciences. It was the age of Galileo, Kepler, Harvey, Bacon, and Descartes. In Italy, fifty years earlier, "the founder of modern anatomy," Andreas Vesalius, proved that the "pores" described by Galen were nonexistent, and that there was no direct connection between the two chambers of the heart. About the same time, Servetus, later burned at the stake by John Calvin, stated his belief that the blood circulates through the lungs, but he did not recognize the heart as a pumping organ. The pulmonary circulation idea was likewise suggested by Realdo Colombo, anatomy professor at Rome. Another important link was supplied by Fabricius of Padua in 1603, when he discovered that the veins have valves, though he misunderstood their purpose, surmising they were merely meant to slow the flow of blood into the extremities.

Thus, these and a few other brave souls had the temerity to cast doubt on ancient dogma that had held medical progress enchained throughout the medieval era. None, on the other hand, was able to arrive at the whole truth. Each made a significant contribution toward unveiling the mystery of blood circulation and heart functions, but in every instance stopped short, with a partial and incomplete answer. The task of discovering and formulating an orderly, systematic, and scientific set of principles fell to the brilliant and incisive mind of an English physician, William Harvey.

The renascence of learning came to England later than to the Continent, particularly Italy, but at the time of Harvey's birth in 1578, the nation was entering one of its greatest periods. During the coming century, Queen Elizabeth would reign, Britain's naval might would be established by the defeat of the Spanish Armada, English explorers would open up new lands, and Shakespeare, Donne, Spenser, Dryden, Milton. Jonson, and Bacon would flourish in the literary world. The repression of thought, characteristic of preceding centuries, was beginning to lift, and men's minds were free, within certain limits, to create new ideas and to open new fields.

For the study of medicine, it was natural for Harvey to go to Italy. The renowned university at Padua has been called the alma mater of the Renaissance, and for generations it was the medical center of Europe. There, after graduating from Cambridge, young Harvey spent four years, principally under the guidance of a famous and inspiring teacher, Fabricius, discoverer of valves in the veins. He learned to dissect and experiment on various kinds of animals, and it is probable that his lifetime interest in blood circulation was first aroused by Fabricius' theories.

Returning to England in 1602, Harvey began a career destined to last for the next fifty years, as physician, lecturer, and writer. He married the daughter of Queen Elizabeth's personal physician, and subsequently served as a fellow of the Royal College of Physicians, physician to St. Bartholomew's Hospital, and physician to James I and Charles I.

Throughout his life, however, Harvey was more fascinated by medical research and experimentation than the practice of medicine. In 1616 he began lecturing before the College of Physicians on the circulation of the blood. His manuscript lecture notes still survive, written in an almost illegible mixture of Latin and English. The notes describe some of his experiments and reveal that by this date he had already become convinced of the validity of his now celebrated theories on blood circulation. "The movement of the blood," he wrote, "is constantly in a circle, and is brought about by the beat of the heart."

Twelve years passed before Harvey was ready to publish his conclusions. Why the long delay in reporting such a notable discovery to the world? There are various conjectures. Sir William Osler suggested that "Perhaps it was the motive of Copernicus, who so dreaded the prejudices of mankind that for thirty years he is said to have detained in his closet the *Treatise of Revolutions*." In Harvey's own words, his theory of general circulation of the blood "is of so novel and unheard-of character, that I not only fear injury to myself from the envy of a few, but I tremble lest I have mankind at large for my enemies, so much does wont and custom, that has become as another nature, and doctrine once sown and that has struck deep root and rested from antiquity, influence all men."

Neither was Harvey a man to rush into print lightly, for, in his opinion, "The crowd of foolish scribblers is scarcely less than the swarms of flies in the height of summer, and threatens with their crude and flimsy productions to stifle us as with smoke."

But eventually, after years of further experimentation and observation, Harvey decided the time was ripe. In 1628, in Frankfurt, Germany, there appeared a small volume of seventy-two pages, considered by many authorities not given to overstatement to be the most important medical book ever written. Naturally, it was in Latin, the universal scholarly language. The full title was *Exercitatio Anatomica de Motu Cordis et Sanguinis in Animalibus,* "Anatomical Exercise on the Motion of the Heart and Blood in Animals." Exactly why it was issued in Germany is not known—perhaps because the annual book fair held in Frankfurt would insure its more rapid circulation amongst scientists on the continent. Harvey's atrocious handwriting was doubtless to blame for numerous typographical errors.

Two dedications graced *De Motu Cordis.* The first is to Charles I, in which the king in his kingdom is compared to the heart in the body, and this is followed by an address to Doctor Argent, President of the Royal College, "and the rest of the doctors and physicians, his most esteemed colleagues." In the latter statement, Harvey expresses the view that truth should be accepted regardless of its source and that truth is of more value than antiquity. "I profess," he said, "both to learn and to teach anatomy, not from books but from dissections; not from the positions of philosophers but from the fabric of nature." In this sentence, Harvey caught the design and spirit of modern scientific methodology.

An introduction and seventeen brief chapters, which make up the main body of the book, give a clear, connected account of the action of the heart and of the circular movement of the blood around the body. The introduction reviews the theories of Galen, Fabricius, Realdo Colombo, and other earlier writers, effectively demonstrating their errors.

In his first chapter, Harvey related some of the problems that had confronted him in his research:

When I first gave my mind to vivisections, as a means of discovering the motions and uses of the heart, and sought to discover these from actual inspection, and not from the writings of others, I found the task so truly arduous, so full of difficulties, that I was almost tempted to think, with Fracastorius, that the motion of the heart was only to be comprehended by God. For I could neither rightly perceive at first when the systole [contraction] and when the diastole [dilation] took place, nor when and where dilation and contraction occurred, by reason of the rapidity of the movement, which in many animals is accomplished in the twinkling of an eye, coming and going like a flash of lightning.

Harvey at length became convinced that the heart's movements could be studied with less difficulty in the colder animals, such as toads, frogs, serpents, small fishes, crabs, shrimps, snails, and shellfish, than in the warm-blooded animals. In the former, he saw that the movements were "slower and rarer." The same phenomena were easily observable in dying warm-blooded animals, as the heart's action slowed down.

On the basis of his experiments Harvey noted that the heart's contraction forces the blood out; as the heart contracts, the arteries dilate to receive the blood. The heart, a muscle serving as a kind of pump, forces continuous circulation of the blood. The blood impelled into the arteries gives rise to the pulse, "as when one blows into a glove." Contrary to the ancient ebb and flow belief, the movement is all in one direction. Harvey demonstrated that the blood passes from the left side of the heart through the arteries to the extremities, and then back by way of the veins to the right side of the heart. The direction of the circulation he determined by tying ligatures around arteries and veins at various points. The momentous discovery, in short, was that the same blood carried out by the arteries is returned by the veins, performing a complete circulation.

Harvey's description of this process is picturesque:

These two motions, one of the ventricles, another of the auricles, take place consecutively, but in such a manner that there is a kind of harmony and rhythm preserved between them, the two concurring in such wise that but one motion is apparent, especially in the warmer blooded animals, in which the movements in question are rapid. Nor is this for any other reason than it is in a piece of machinery, in which, though one wheel gives motion to another, yet all the wheels seem to move simultaneously; or like the mechanism in firearms, where the trigger being touched, down comes the flint, strikes the steel, elicits a spark, which falling among the powder, it is ignited, upon which the flame extends, enters the barrel, causes the explosion, propels the ball, and the mark is attained—all of which incidents, by reason of the celerity with which they happen, seem to take place in the twinkling of an eye.

In thinking of the blood's movements as circular, Harvey may conceivably have been influenced by the ancient philosophers, such as Aristotle, who taught that the circular motion is perfect and the noblest of all movements. Harvey's contemporary, the astronomer Giordano Bruno, concluded that the circle is "the fundamental symbol and pattern of all life and action in the cosmos." It is significant that Harvey in his treatise uses such phrases as "motion as it were in a circle" and "motion of the blood we may be allowed to call circular."

Harvey's line of reasoning on the circulation was remarkably accurate on the whole, but there was one missing link. How did the blood get from the arteries to the veins? Harvey knew that the blood went to the arteries from the left heart and from the veins back to the right heart. However, he said, "I have never succeeded in tracing any connection between the arteries and veins by a direct anastomosis of their orifices." Lacking a microscope, he could not see the capillaries, the minute vessels through which the blood cells pass from the arteries to the veins, though he was convinced there must be such channels. The riddle was solved a few years after Harvey's death by an anatomy professor at Bologna, Marcello Malpighi. Examining a frog's lung under the newly-invented microscope, Malpighi saw the network of capillaries connecting the arteries and veins, exactly as Harvey had predicted. Thus the final step in demonstrating the circulation of the blood was completed.

To win over the skeptics, further proofs of circulation were produced by Harvey. One was the application of what is known to scientists as the quantitative method. He demonstrated that in an hour's time the heart, in its some 4,000 beats, pumps out far more than the total amount of blood in the body. If the blood sent out by the heart in a single day is measured, the quantity is much in excess of all the food taken in and digested —thereby disproving the ancient Galen's theory. "In short," wrote Harvey, "the blood could be furnished in no other way than by making a circuit and returning."

Additional evidence of circulation comes from the effect of poisons on the body.

We see in contagious diseases, in poisoned wounds, the bites of serpents or mad dogs, in the French pox, and the like the whole body may become diseased while the place of contact is often unharmed or healed. . . . Without doubt the contagion first being deposited in a certain spot is carried by the returning blood to the heart, from which later it is spread to the whole body. . . . This may also explain why some medical agents applied to the skin have almost as much effect as if taken by mouth.

Harvey's use of animals for experimental purposes was an innovation. He believed that "Had anatomists only been as conversant with the dissection of the lower animals as they are with that of the human body, the matters that have hitherto kept them in a perplexity of doubt would, in my opinion, have met them freed from every kind of difficulty." Harvey may be rightly regarded as one of the founders of the science of comparative anatomy. He mentions, for example, experiments on sheep, dogs, deer, pigs, birds, chicks in eggs, snakes, fish, eels, toads, frogs, snails, shrimps, crabfish, oysters, mussels, sponges, worms, bees, wasps, hornets, gnats, flies, and lice.

I have observed that there is a heart in almost all animals, not only in the larger ones with blood, as Aristotle claims, but in the smaller bloodless ones also, as snails, slugs, crabs, shrimps, and many others. Even in wasps, hornets, and flies, have I seen with a lens a beating heart at the upper part of what is called the tail, and I have shown it living to others. In these bloodless animals the heart beats slowly, contracting sluggishly as in moribund higher animals. This is easily seen in the snail, where the heart lies at the bottom of that opening on the right side which seems to open and close as saliva is expelled. . . . There is a small squid . . . caught at sea and in the Thames, whose entire body is transparent. Placing this creature in water, I have often shown some of my friends the movements of its heart with great clearness.

Aside from his remarkable discoveries, Harvey's greatest contribution to science and medical research was his introduction of experimental or laboratory methods. He laid the foundation upon which for more than three centuries physiology and medicine have been built. The essence was as Harvey himself stated, "to search and study out the secrets of Nature by way of experiment." Medicine had a history going back several millenniums before the birth of Harvey. Physicians had learned to recognize and to describe accurately the principal diseases afflicting mankind. Observation, while important, is not in itself enough, and frequently leads to erroneous conclusions. This was the major difference between Harvey and his predecessors. Going beyond superficial observation, little handicapped by superstitions or by reverence for antiquated theories, Harvey drew up hypotheses and tested them by experiments. He was the first to adopt the scientific method of experiment for the solution of a biological problem. All his successors of significance since 1628 have followed the same path.

The contemporary reception of Harvey's discoveries is of interest. His book was not a literary sensation; its profound import was probably not recognized even by Harvey himself. Some opposition rising from conservatism and prejudice was expressed. A contemporary Walter Winchell, John Aubrey, wrote that "he had heard him [Harvey] say that after his book on the Circulation of the Blood came out, he fell mightily in his practice; 'twas believed by the vulgar that he was crack-brained, and all the physicians were against him."

The attitude of one of the intellectuals of the time was expressed by Sir William Temple, writing of the work of Copernicus and Harvey:

> Whether either of these be modern discoveries or derived from old foundations is disputed; nay, it is so too, whether they are true or no; for though reason may seem to favour them more than the contrary opinions, yet sense can hardly allow them, and to satisfy mankind both these must concur. But if they are true, yet these two great discoveries have made no change in the conclusions of Astronomy nor in the practice of Physic, and so have been but little use to the world, though, perhaps, of much honour to the authors.

For the most part, Harvey ignored his critics. The prolonged hostility of the University of Paris medical school, however, finally induced him to break his silence. John Riolan, professor of anatomy in the Paris school, had persuaded the faculty there to prohibit the teaching of Harvey's doctrine. In an attempt to overcome his objections, Harvey addressed to Riolan two *Anatomical Disquisitions* on the subject of the circulation of the blood. These were published in a small book in 1649, twenty-one years after *De Motu Cordis*. Therein, Harvey replied in detail to those who had condemned his work.

In the second of the *Disquisitions*, Harvey laments:

> But scarce a day, scarce an hour has passed since the birthday of the circulation of the blood that I have not heard something for good or for evil, said of this my dis-

covery. Some abuse it as a feeble infant and yet unworthy
to have seen the light; others again think the baby deserves
to be cherished and cared for. These oppose it with much
ado, those patronize it with abundant commendation.
One party holds that I have completely demonstrated
the circulation of the blood by experiments, observations, and ocular inspection against all force and strength
of argument; another thinks it scarcely sufficiently illustrated, not yet cleared of all objections. There are some,
too, who say that I have shown a vainglorious love of
dissection of living creatures, and who scoff at and deride
the introduction of frogs and serpents, flies and other of
the lower animals upon the scene. . . . To return evil
speaking with evil speaking, however, I hold to be unworthy in a philosopher and searcher after truth. I believe
that I shall do better and more advisedly if I meet so
many indications of ill breeding with the light of faithful
and conclusive observation.

Fortunately, Harvey lived to see general acceptance of his
theories among those competent to judge them. His election
to the presidency of the College of Physicians in 1654, three
years before his death, is evidence of his high standing among
his professional colleagues.

Also indicative of contemporary opinion is the Latin in-
scription on Harvey's tomb:

William Harvey, to whose honorable name all academies rise up out of respect, who was the first after many
thousand years to discover the daily movement of the
blood, and so brought health to the world and immortality
to himself, who was the only one to free from false philosophy the origin and generation of animals, to whom
the human race owes its acquirements of knowledge, to
whom Medicine owes its very existence, chief Physician
and friend of their Serene Highnesses James and Charles,
Monarchs of the British Isles, a diligent and highly successful Professor of Anatomy and Surgery at the College
of Medicine at London; for them he built a famous
Library and endowed it and enriched it with his own
patrimony. Finally after triumphal exertions in observation, healing and discovery, after various statues had been
erected to him at home and abroad, when he had trav-
ersed the full circle of his life, a teacher of Medicine
and of medical men, he died childless on June 3 in the

year of grace 1657, in the eightieth year of his age, full of years and fame.

There has been little of a *basic* nature added to Harvey's discovery of the circulation, though, of course a vast body of knowledge has accumulated dealing with the physiology of the heart, blood vessels, and lungs. Much is known now concerning the heart's structure, its behavior in health and disease, its complex movements, and the functions of the blood that were not even imagined in Harvey's day.

Nevertheless, as Kilgour commented:

The direct contributions of Harvey's discovery to medicine and surgery are obviously beyond measuring. It is the basis for all work in the repair of damaged or diseased blood vessels, the surgical treatment of high blood pressure and coronary disease, the well-known "blue baby" operation, and so on. It is general physiology, however, that is most in his debt. For the notion of the circulating blood is what underlies our present understanding of the self-stabilizing internal environment of the body. In the dynamics of the human system the most important role is played by the fluid whose circulation Harvey discovered by a feat of great insight.

Perhaps no one has better summed up the meaning of Harvey's career to the progress of medicine than a great medical leader of our own time. In the annual Harveian Oration delivered at the Royal College of Physicians in London, in 1906, Sir William Osler said of *De Motu Cordis*:

. . . . it marks the break of the modern spirit with the old traditions. No longer were men to rest content with careful observation and with accurate description; no longer were men to be content with finely spun theories and dreams, which "serve as a common subterfuge of ignorance"; but here for the first time a great physiological problem was approached from the experimental side by a man with modern scientific mind, who could weigh evidence and not go beyond it, and who had the sense to let the conclusions emerge naturally but firmly from the observations. To the age of the hearer, in which men had heard, and heard only, had succeeded the age of the eye, in which men had seen and had been content only to see. But at last came the age of the hand—the thinking, devising, planning hand; the hand as an instrument of the mind, now reintroduced into the world in a modest little monograph of seventy-two pages, from which we may date the beginning of experimental medicine.

13 SYSTEM OF THE WORLD

SIR ISAAC NEWTON:

Principia Mathematica

Of all the books which have profoundly influenced human affairs, few have been more celebrated and none read by fewer people than Sir Isaac Newton's *Philosophiae Naturalis Principia Mathematica, Mathematical Principles of Natural Philosophy.* Deliberately written in the most abstruse and technical Latin, profusely illustrated by complex geometrical diagrams, the work's direct audience has been limited to highly erudite astronomers, mathematicians, and physicists.

One of Newton's chief biographers has stated that when the *Principia* was published in the last quarter of the seventeenth century there were not more than three or four men living who could comprehend it; another generously stretched the number to ten or a dozen. The author himself admitted that it was "a hard book," but he had no apologies, for he planned it that way, making no concessions to the mathematically illiterate.

Yet, notable men of science hold Newton to be one of the great intellectual figures of all time. Laplace, a brilliant French astronomer, termed the *Principia* "pre-eminent above any other production of human genius." Lagrange, famous mathematician, asserted that Newton was the greatest genius who ever lived. Boltzmann, a pioneer of modern mathematical physics, called the *Principia* the first and greatest work ever written on theoretical physics. An eminent American astronomer, W. W. Campbell, remarked, "To me it is clear that Sir Isaac Newton, easily the greatest man of physical science in historic time, was uniquely the great pioneer of astro-physics." Comments from other leading scientists over the past two-and-a-half centuries have been phrased in like superlatives. The layman must necessarily accept these judgments on faith, and on the basis of results.

Newton was born almost exactly a century after the death of Copernicus, and in the same year as Galileo's death. These giants in the world of astronomy, together with Johannes Kepler, furnished the foundations upon which Newton continued to build.

Newton was a mathematical wizard in an age of gifted mathematicians. As Marvin pointed out, "the seventeenth century was the flowering age of mathematics, as the eighteenth was of chemistry and the nineteenth of biology, and the last four decades of the seventeenth saw more forward steps taken than any other period in history." Newton combined in himself the major physical sciences—mathematics, chemistry, physics, and astronomy—for in the seventeenth century, before the era of extreme specialization, a scientist could encompass all fields.

Newton, born on Christmas Day, 1642, in his early years saw the rise and fall of Oliver Cromwell's Commonwealth Government, the Great Fire which practically destroyed London, and the Great Plague which wiped out a third of the city's population. After eighteen years spent in the little hamlet of Woolsthorpe, Newton was sent to Cambridge University. There he was fortunate to come under the guidance of an able and inspiring teacher, Isaac Barrow, Professor of Mathematics, who has been called Newton's "intellectual father." Barrow recognized, encouraged, and stimulated the growing genius of young Newton. While still in college, Newton discovered the binomial theorem.

Because of the plague, Cambridge was closed in 1665, and Newton returned to the country. For the next two years, largely cut off from the world, he devoted himself to scientific experimentation and meditation. The consequences were astounding. Before he had reached the age of twenty-five, Newton had made three discoveries that entitle him to be ranked among the supreme scientific minds of all time. First was the invention of the differential calculus, termed "fluxions" by Newton, because it deals with variable or "flowing" quantities. The calculus is involved in all problems of flow, movement of bodies, and waves, and is essential to the solution of physical problems concerned with any kind of movement. "It seemed to unlock the gates guarding the storehouse of mathematical treasures; to lay the mathematical world at the feet of Newton and his followers."

Newton's second major discovery was the law of composition of light, from which he proceeded to analyze the nature of color and of white light. It was shown that the white light of the sun is compounded of rays of light of all the colors of the rainbow. Color is therefore a characteristic of light, and the appearance of white light—as Newton's experiments with a prism demonstrated—comes from mixing the colors of the spectrum. Through knowledge gained from this discovery, Newton was able to construct the first satisfactory reflecting telescope.

Even more noteworthy was Newton's third revelation: the law of universal gravitation, which is said to have stirred the imaginations of scientists more than any theoretical discovery of modern times. According to a well-known anecdote, the flash of intuition which came to Newton when he observed the fall of an apple led to formulation of the law. There was nothing particularly new in the idea of the earth's attraction for bodies near its surface. Newton's great contribution was in conceiving the gravitation law to be universal in application —a force no less powerful in relation to celestial bodies than to the earth—and then producing mathematical proof of his theory.

Curiously enough, Newton published nothing at the time on these three highly significant discoveries on the calculus, color, and gravitation. Possessed of an extremely reticent, even secretive nature, he had an almost morbid dislike of public attention and controversy. Consequently, he was inclined to suppress the results of his experiments. Whatever he published later was done under pressure from friends, and afterward he nearly always regretted surrendering to their entreaties. Publication led to criticism and discussion of his work by fellow-scientists, something which Newton, with his sensitive nature, completely detested and resented.

Following the enforced isolation and leisure of the plague years, Newton returned to Cambridge, received a master's degree, and was appointed a fellow of Trinity College. Shortly thereafter his old teacher, Barrow, withdrew, and Newton, at the age of twenty-seven, became professor of mathematics, a position which he held for the next twenty-seven years. For the next decade or two little was heard of Newton. It is known that he continued his investigations of light, and published a paper on his discovery of the composite nature of white light. Immediately he became involved in controversy, first because his conclusions on the subject of light were in opposition to those then prevailing; and, second, because he had included in the paper a statement on his philosophy of science. In the latter, he had expressed the point of view that the chief function of science is to carry out carefully planned experiments, to record observations of the experiments, and lastly to prepare mathematical laws based on the results. As Newton

stated it, the "proper method for enquiring after the proper-
ties of things is to deduce them from experiments." While these
principles are in complete accord with modern scientific research, they were by no means fully accepted in Newton's
day. Beliefs founded on imagination, reason, and the appearance of things, usually inherited from ancient philosophers,
were preferred to experimental evidence.

Attacks on his paper by such established scientists as Huy-
gens and Hooke so angered Newton that he resolved to escape
future irritations by doing no more publishing. "I was so
persecuted," he said, "with discussions arising from the publication of my theory of light, that I blamed my own imprudence
for parting with so substantial a blessing as my quiet to run
after a shadow." He even expressed an acute distaste for
science itself, insisting that he had lost his former "affection"
for it. Later, he had to be "spurred, cajoled and importuned"
into writing his greatest work, the *Principia*. In fact, creation
of the *Principia* appears to have come about more or less by
chance.

In 1684, through computations by Picard, the earth's exact
circumference was determined for the first time. Using the
French astronomer's data, Newton applied the principle of
gravitation to prove that the power which guides the moon
around the earth and the planets around the sun is the force
of gravity. The force varies directly with the mass of the attracted bodies and inversely as the square of their distances.
Newton went on to show that this accounts for the elliptical
orbits of the planets. The pull of gravity kept the moon and
the planets in their paths, balancing the centrifugal forces of
their motions.

Again, Newton failed to reveal his phenomenal discovery
of nature's greatest secret. As it happened, however, other
scientists were engaged in a search for a solution of the same
problem. Several astronomers had suggested that the planets
were bound to the sun by the force of gravity. Among these
was Robert Hooke, Newton's severest and most persistent
critic. But none of the theorists had been able to offer mathematical proof. By now Newton had won considerable reputation as a mathematician, and he was visited at Cambridge
by the astronomer Edmund Halley who requested his help.
When Halley stated the problem, he learned that it had been
solved two years before by Newton. Further, Newton had
worked out the principal laws of motion of bodies moving
under the force of gravity. Characteristically, though, Newton
had no intention of publishing his findings.

Halley at once recognized the significance of Newton's accomplishment, and used all his powers of persuasion to convince the stubborn Newton that his discovery should be developed and exploited. Moved by Halley's enthusiasm and with his own interest rekindled, Newton began the writing of his masterpiece, the *Principia,* termed by Langer "a veritable reservoir of mechanistic philosophy, one of the most original works ever produced."

Not the least remarkable feature of the *Principia* was that its composition was completed in eighteen months, during which, it is said, Newton was so engrossed that he often went without food and took little time to sleep. Only the most intense and prolonged concentration could have brought forth such a monumental intellectual achievement in so brief a period. It left Newton mentally and physically exhausted.

Furthermore, during the time of writing, Newton's peace of mind was intensely disturbed by the usual controversies, particularly with Hooke, who maintained he should receive credit for originating the theory that the motion of the planets could be explained by an inverse square law of attraction. Newton, who had finished two-thirds of the *Principia,* was so incensed by what he considered an unjustified claim, that he threatened to omit the third and most important section of his treatise. Again Halley used his influence and prevailed on Newton to complete the work as first planned.

The role played by Edmund Halley in the whole history of the *Principia* deserves the highest commendation. Not only was he responsible for inducing Newton to undertake the work in the first place, but he obtained an agreement with the Royal Society to publish it, and unselfishly dropped everything he was doing to supervise the final printing. Finally, when the Royal Society reneged on its promise to finance the publication, Halley stepped in and paid the entire expense out of his own pocket, though he was a man of moderate means, with a family to support.

Surmounting all obstacles, the *Principia* came from the press in 1687, in a small edition, selling for ten or twelve shillings a copy. The title page bore the imprimatur of Samuel Pepys, then President of the Royal Society, "although it is to be doubted," remarked one commentator, "whether the learned diarist could have understood so much as a single sentence of it."

Any brief summary of the *Principia* in nontechnical language is a difficult, if not impossible, undertaking, but some highlights may be indicated. The work as a whole deals with the motions of bodies treated mathematically, in particular, the application of dynamics and universal gravitation to the solar system. It begins with an explanation of the differential calculus or "fluxions," invented by Newton and used as a tool for calculations throughout the *Principia*. There follow definitions of the meaning of space and time, and a statement of the laws of motion, as formulated by Newton, with illustrations of their application. The fundamental principle is stated that every particle of matter is attracted by every other particle of matter with a force inversely proportional to the square of their distances apart. Also given are the laws governing the problem of bodies colliding with each other. Everything is expressed in classical geometrical forms.

The first book of the *Principia* is concerned with the motion of bodies in free space, while the second treats of "motion in a resisting medium," such as water. In the latter section, the complex problems of the motion of fluids are considered and solved, methods discussed for determining the velocity of sound, and wave motions described mathematically. Herein is laid the groundwork for the modern science of mathematical physics, hydrostatics, and hydrodynamics.

In the second book Newton effectively demolished the world system of Descartes, then in popular vogue. According to Descartes' theory, the motions of the heavenly bodies were due to vortexes. All space is filled with a thin fluid, and at certain points the fluid matter forms vortexes. For example, the solar system has fourteen vortexes, the largest of them containing the sun. The planets are carried around like chips in an eddy. These whirlpools were Descartes' explanation for the phenomena of gravitation. Newton proceeded to demonstrate experimentally and mathematically that "the Vortex Theory is in complete conflict with astronomical facts, and so far from explaining celestial motions would tend to upset them."

In his third book, entitled "The System of the World," Newton was at his greatest as he dealt with the astronomical consequences of the law of gravitation.

In the preceding books I have laid down the principles of philosophy [science]; principles not philosophical but mathematical. . . . These principles are the laws and conditions of certain motions, and powers or forces. . . . I have illustrated them here and there . . . with . . . an account of such things as are of more general nature . . . such as the density and the resistance of bodies, spaces void of all bodies, and the motion of light and sound. It remains that, from the same principles, I now demonstrate the frame of the System of the World.

Explaining why he had not popularized his work, Newton revealed that—

> Upon this subject I had, indeed, composed the third Book in a popular method, that it might be read by many, but afterwards, considering that such as had not sufficiently entered into the principles could not easily discern the strength of the consequences, nor lay aside the prejudices to which they had been many years accustomed, therefore, to prevent the disputes which might be raised upon such accounts, I chose to reduce the substance of this Book in the form of Propositions (in the mathematical way), which should be read by those only who had first made themselves masters of the principles established in the preceding Books; not that I would advise anyone to the previous study of every Proposition of those Books; for they abound with such as might cost too much time, even to readers of good mathematical learning.

For this reason, the style of the *Principia* has been described as "glacial remoteness, written in the aloof manner of a high priest."

At the outset, Newton makes a fundamental break with the past by insisting that there is no difference between earthly and celestial phenomena. "Like effects in nature are produced by like causes," he asserted, "as breathing in man and in beast, the fall of stones in Europe and in America, the light of the kitchen fire and of the sun, the reflection of light on the earth and on the planets." Thus was discarded the ancient belief that other worlds are perfect and only the earth is imperfect. Now all were governed by the same rational laws, "bringing order and system," as MacMurray said, "where chaos and mystery had reigned before."

A mere listing of the principal topics covered in the third book is impressive. The motions of the planets and of the satellites around the planets are established; methods for measuring the masses of the sun and planets are shown; and the density of the earth, the precession of the equinoxes, theory of tides, orbits of the comets, the moon's motion, and related matters discussed and resolved.

By his theory of "perturbations" Newton proved that the moon is attracted by both the earth and the sun, and therefore the moon's orbit is disturbed by the sun's pull, though the earth provides the stronger attraction. Likewise, the planets are subject to perturbations. The sun is not the stationary center of the universe, contrary to previous beliefs, but is attracted by the planets, just as they are attracted to it, and moves in the same way. In later centuries, application of the perturbations theory led to the discovery of the planets Neptune and Pluto.

The masses of different planets and the masses of the sun Newton determined by relating them to the earth's mass. He estimated that the earth's density is between five and six times that of water (the figure used by scientists today is 5.5), and on this basis Newton calculated the masses of the sun and of the planets with satellites, an achievement which Adam Smith called "above the reach of human reason and experience."

Next, the fact that the earth is not an exact sphere, but is flattened at the poles because of rotation, was explained, and the amount of flattening was calculated. Because of the flattening at the poles and the slight bulge at the equator, Newton deducted that the force of gravity must be less at the poles than at the equator—a phenomenon that accounts for the precession of the equinoxes, the conical motion of the earth's axis, resembling a gyroscope. By studying the shape of the planet, furthermore, the possibility of estimating the length of day and night on the planet was shown.

Another application of the law of universal gravitation was Newton's exploration of the tides. When the moon is fullest, the earth's waters experience their maximum attraction, and high tide results. The sun also affects the tides, and when the sun and moon are in line, the tide is highest.

Still another subject of popular interest on which Newton shed light was comets. His theory was that comets, moving under the sun's attraction, travel elliptical paths of incredible magnitude, requiring many years to complete. Henceforth, comets, which were once regarded by the superstitious as evil omens, took their proper place as beautiful and harmless celestial phenomena. By using Newton's theories of comets, Edmund Halley was able to identify and to predict accurately the reappearance about every seventy-five years of the famous "Halley's Comet." Once a comet has been observed, its future path can be accurately determined.

One of the most amazing discoveries made by Newton was his method for estimating the distance of a fixed star, based on the amount of light received by reflection of the sun's light from a planet.

The *Principia* made no attempt to explain the *why* but only the *how* of the universe. Later, in response to charges that his was a completely mechanistic scheme, making no provision for ultimate causes or for a Supreme Creator, Newton added a confession of faith to the second edition of his work:

This most beautiful system of the sun, planets, and comets could only proceed from the counsel and dominion of an intelligent and powerful Being. . . . As a blind man has no idea of colours, so have we no idea of the manner by which the all-wise God perceives and understands all things.

The function of science, he believed, was to go on building knowledge, and the more complete our knowledge is, the nearer are we brought to an understanding of the Cause, though man might never discover the true and exact scientific laws of nature.

Brilliant achievement as the *Principia* was, Newton's most ardent admirers concede that it was not written in a vacuum. As Cohen stated:

The great Newtonian synthesis was based on the work of predecessors. The immediate past had produced the analytical geometry of Descartes and Fermat, the algebra of Oughtred, Harriot and Wallis, Kepler's law of motion, Galileo's law of falling bodies. It had also produced Galileo's law of the composition of velocities—a law stating that a motion may be divided into component parts, each independent of the other (for example the motion of a projectile is composed of a uniform forward velocity and a downward accelerated velocity like that of a freely falling body). The afore-mentioned are but a few of the ingredients present and waiting for the grand Newtonian synthesis. But it remained for the genius of Newton to add the master touch; to show finally, and once and for all, in just what manner the ordered universe is regulated by mathematical law.

It was evident that the world needed, as Jeans described him, "a man who could systematize, synthesize and extend the whole, and it found him in superlative excellence in Newton." Newton himself recognized that his "System of the World," his mechanics of the universe, was built upon the work begun by Copernicus and so notably carried forward by Tycho Brahe, Kepler, and Galileo. "If I have seen farther than other men," Newton said, "it is by standing on the shoulders of giants."

In fact, the probable cause of the controversies that dogged Newton's life was the intellectual ferment prevailing in his time. The air was full of new theories, and many able scientists were exploring them. It is not surprising that two men would make the same discovery almost simultaneously and quite independently. Precisely this appears to have happened in Newton's two principal controversies, those with Leibniz and Hooke. Leibniz invented the differential calculus, and Hooke advanced a theory of universal gravitation, both somewhat later than Newton's, but announced to the world first, because Newton had neglected to publish his work.

The contemporary reception of the *Principia* was more cordial in England and Scotland than on the Continent, but everywhere slow. As Newton had foreseen, an understanding of it required great mathematical ability. The extraordinary nature of the performance was acknowledged, however, even by those who had only a dim conception of Newton's contribution. Gradually, scientists everywhere accepted the Newtonian system, and by the eighteenth century it was firmly established in the world of science.

After the *Principia,* Newton appears to have lost any active interest in scientific research, though he lived for forty years after its publication. During this period he was the recipient of many honors: appointed Master of the Mint, knighted by Queen Anne, elected President of the Royal Society from 1703 until his death in 1727, saw publication of the second and third editions of the *Principia,* and, in general, was held in the highest respect and esteem.

Scientific discoveries in the twentieth century have modified or shown inadequacies in Newton's work, especially in relation to astronomy. Einstein's theory of relativity, for example, maintains that space and time are not absolute, as Newton had taught. Nevertheless, as various authorities in science and technology have pointed out, the structure of a skyscraper, the safety of a railroad bridge, the motion of a motor car, the flight of an airplane, the navigation of a ship across the ocean, the measure of time, and other evidences of our contemporary civilization still depend fundamentally on Newton's laws. As Sir James Jeans wrote, the Newtonian principles are "inadequate only with reference to the ultra-refinements of modern science. When the astronomer wishes to prepare his 'Nautical Almanac,' or to discuss the motions of the planets, he uses the Newtonian scheme almost exclusively. The engineer who is building a bridge or a ship or a locomotive does precisely what he would have done had Newton's scheme never been proved inadequate. The same is true of the electrical engineer, whether he is mending a telephone or designing a power-station. The science of everyday life is still wholly Newtonian; and it is impossible to estimate how much this science owes to Newton's clear and penetrating mind having set it on the right road, and this so firmly and convincingly that none who understood his methods could doubt their rightness."

The tribute paid Newton by Einstein should remove any question of rival philosophies: "Nature to him was an open book, whose letters he could read without effort. In one person he combined the experimenter, the theorist, the mechanic and, not least, the artist in expression."

Newton's own estimate of his career, made near the end of a long life, was characteristic of his modesty: "I do not know what I may appear to the world, but to myself I seem to have been only like a boy on the seashore, and diverting myself in now and then finding a smoother pebble or a prettier shell than ordinary, while the great ocean of truth lay all undiscovered before me."

14 SURVIVAL OF THE FITTEST

CHARLES DARWIN: *Origin of Species*

By curious coincidence, the year 1809 witnessed the births of more extraordinary leaders than perhaps any other single year in history. Each was destined to gain pre-eminence in his career. Two of them, Charles Darwin, "The Newton of Biology," and Abraham Lincoln, "The Great Emancipator," were born on the same day and nearly in the same hour. Other remarkable individuals who first saw the light in this year included Gladstone, Tennyson, Edgar Allan Poe, Oliver Wendell Holmes, Elizabeth Barrett Browning, and Felix Mendelssohn.

Of these celebrated names, and in fact among all the millions born in the nineteenth century, none, with the possible exception of Karl Marx, did as much as Darwin to change the main trends of thought, and to produce a new outlook in human affairs. "Darwinism" is a concept as firmly fixed in the popular mind as Marxism, Malthusianism, and Machiavellianism.

Though the basic principles of Darwin's theories are today almost universally accepted in the scientific world, controversies have raged around them for nearly a century. The fundamentalist-modernist battles of the nineteen-twenties, culminating in the Scopes "monkey trial" in Tennessee, are among the most publicized instances of a war which began in 1859.

Only recently have there been signs of an armistice in the hostilities.

As a youth, Darwin showed little promise of becoming a world-famed scientist. He was descended from a family of distinguished scholars and professional men, but even his father expressed strong doubt that he would ever amount to anything. In grammar school, young Charles was bored by the study of dead languages and by the rigid classical curriculum. He was rebuked by the headmaster for wasting his time on chemical experiments and in collecting insects and minerals. Following in his father's footsteps, he was sent to Edinburgh University at sixteen to study medicine. After two years there, he decided that the medical profession was not for him. Whereupon he was transferred to Cambridge to train for the ministry in the Church of England.

From the point of view of formal study, Darwin considered the three Cambridge years wasted. But he did have the good fortune to form firm friendships with two influential teachers. With Henslow, professor of botany, and Sedgwick, professor of geology, he spent much time in field excursions, collecting beetles, and in natural history observations.

It was through Sedgwick that Darwin received an offer to sail as naturalist on board the naval ship *Beagle,* starting out on an extensive surveying expedition in the southern hemisphere. Looking back on this voyage in later years, Darwin rated it "by far the most important event in my life." It determined his whole career. The idea of becoming a clergyman "died a natural death" on the *Beagle.*

During the next five years, from 1831 to 1836, the *Beagle* touched on nearly every continent and major island, as she circled the world. Darwin was called upon to serve as geologist, botanist, zoologist, and general man of science—superb preparation for his subsequent life of research and writing. Everywhere he went, he made extensive collections of plants and animals, fossil and living, earth-dwelling and marine forms. He investigated, with the eye of a naturalist, the flora and fauna of land and sea—the pampas of Argentina, the dry slopes of the Andes, the salt lakes and deserts of Chile and Australia, the dense forest of Brazil, Tierra del Fuego, and Tahiti, the deforested Cape Verde Islands, geological formations of the South American coast and mountains, active and dead volcanoes on islands and mainland, coral reefs, fossil mammals of Patagonia, extinct races of man in Peru, and the aborigines of Tierra del Fuego and Patagonia.

Of all the regions visited, none impressed Darwin as forcibly as the Galápagos Islands, 500 miles off the west coast of South

America. On these isolated, uninhabited, and rather barren volcanic islands, he saw giant tortoises, elsewhere found only as fossils, huge lizards long since extinct in other parts of the world, enormous crabs, and sea lions. He was particularly struck by the fact that the birds were similar to those on the neighboring continent, but not identical. Furthermore, there were variations among the different species of birds from island to island.

The strange phenomena of the Galápagos Islands, added to certain facts previously noted in South America, reinforced the ideas on evolution beginning to take shape in Darwin's mind. According to his own account:

> I had been deeply impressed by discovering in the Pampean formation great fossil animals covered with armour like that on the existing armadillos; secondly, by the manner in which closely allied animals replace one another in proceeding southwards over the Continent; and thirdly, by the South American character of most of the productions of the Galápagos archipelago, and more especially by the manner in which they differ slightly on each island of the group; none of the islands appearing to be very ancient in a geological sense.

Never again could Darwin accept as credible the teachings of Genesis, that every species had been created whole and had come down through the ages unchanged.

Immediately upon his return to England, Darwin began keeping a notebook on evolution, collecting facts on variation of species, the beginning of the *Origin of Species*. The first rough draft of his theory was written out in thirty-five pages in 1842, and enlarged in 1844 to a fuller sketch of 230 pages. In the beginning, the great riddle was how to explain the appearance and disappearance of species. Why did species originate, become modified with the passage of time, diverge into numerous branches, and often vanish from the scene completely?

The key to the mystery for Darwin came through a chance reading of Malthus' *Essay on Population*. Malthus had shown that mankind's rate of increase was retarded by such "positive checks" as disease, accidents, war, and famine. It occurred to Darwin that similar factors might keep down the populations of animals and plants.

> Being well prepared to appreciate the struggle for existence which everywhere goes on from long-continued observation of the habits of animals and plants, it at once

struck me that under these circumstances favourable species would tend to be preserved, and unfavourable ones to be destroyed. The result of this would be the formation of new species. Here then I had at last got a theory by which to work.

Thus was born the famous Darwinian doctrine of "natural selection," "struggle for existence," or "survival of the fittest," the foundation stone for the *Origin of Species*.

For twenty years Darwin compiled his notebooks, substantiating his theories. He read a vast range of literature—whole series of periodicals, travel books, books on sport, horticulture, breeding of animals, and general natural history. "When I see the list of books of all kinds which I read and abstracted, including whole series of Journals and Transactions, I am surprised at my industry," wrote Darwin. He talked with expert breeders of animals and plants, and sent lists of questions to everyone who might have useful information. Skeletons of many kinds of domesticated birds were prepared, and the age and weight of their bones compared with those of wild species. Tame pigeons were kept and extensive crossing experiments made. He experimented with floating fruits and seeds in sea water, and investigated other questions relating to seed transport. All the botanical, geological, zoological, and paleontological knowledge he had acquired on the *Beagle* expedition was brought to bear on the problem. To this mass of data were added Darwin's own ideas as he gave constant thought to his revolutionary theories.

Strong support for the principle of natural selection, Darwin thought, came from a study of "artificial selection." In the case of domestic animals and plants—horses, dogs, cats, wheat, barley, garden flowers, etc.—man has selected and bred the varieties that were most advantageous to his own needs. So radically modified have domestic animals, crops, and flowers become in the process, they can scarcely be recognized as related to their wild ancestors. New species are developed by selection. The breeder picks out animals and plants possessing the characters he wants, breeds only these generation after generation, and eventually produces species different from any that had previously existed. Dogs as unlike as the dachshund, the collie, the spaniel, and the greyhound, for example, were descended from the wolf.

If evolution could be brought about by artificial selection, reasoned Darwin, is it not possible that nature functions in the same manner, by natural selection? In nature, however, the breeder's place is taken by the struggle for existence. Among all forms of life, Darwin observed, an enormous number of individuals must perish. Only a fraction of those that were born can survive. Some species furnish food for other species. The battle goes on ceaselessly, and the fierce competition eliminates animals and plants unfitted to survive. Variations in species take place to meet the conditions necessary for survival.

So intent was Darwin in building a tower of irrefutable proof for his theories that he neglected publication until the eighteen-fifties. Then, at the urging of close friends, he began preparation of a monumental work to be issued in several volumes. But when the task was approximately half finished a thunderbolt struck. Darwin received a letter from Alfred Russel Wallace, a fellow-scientist, who was carrying on natural history explorations in the Malay Archipelago. Wallace revealed that he, too, was meditating on the origin of species, and like Darwin had been inspired by reading Malthus. With the letter was enclosed an "Essay on the Tendency of Varieties to Depart Indefinitely from the Original Type." It was precisely a statement of Darwin's own theory, for, said Darwin, "if Wallace had had my MS. sketch written out in 1842, he could not have made a better short abstract! Even his terms now stand as heads of my chapters."

Darwin was in a dilemma. It was obvious that both men had arrived at identical conclusions quite independently, though Darwin had given years of study and thought to the subject, while Wallace's ideas had come to him in a sudden flash of intuition. At length it was decided that papers by both Darwin and Wallace would be presented at the next meeting of the Linnaean Society. Accordingly, the first public announcement of the theory of evolution by natural selection was made on the evening of July 1, 1858. Shortly thereafter, both papers were issued in the Society's *Journal*.

Spurred on by the Wallace incident, Darwin abandoned the huge work on which he had been engaged, and settled down to writing what he called an "Abstract." Near the end of 1859, the book that was to become a milestone in the history of science was published by John Murray in London. The first edition was 1,200 copies, all of which were sold the first day. Other editions followed, until, by the end of Darwin's lifetime (in 1882), 24,000 copies had been sold in England alone, and it had been translated into almost every civilized language. The original was entitled *On the Origin of Species by Means of Natural Selection, or the Preservation of Favoured Races in the Struggle for Life*. Time has shortened this unwieldy title to *Origin of Species*.

The fundamentals of Darwin's theory are discussed in the first four chapters of the *Origin*. The following four consider possible objections to the theory, after which several chapters deal with geology, the geographic distribution of plants and animals, and pertinent facts concerning classification, morphology, and embryology. The final chapter summarizes the entire argument.

At the outset, the *Origin of Species* describes the changes that have taken place in domesticated animals and plants as a result of human control. The variations that have come about by "artificial selection" are compared with changes in nature, or "natural selection." Wherever there is life, it is concluded, change is constant. No two individuals are ever exactly identical.

To variation there is added the struggle for existence. Some striking illustrations are used to demonstrate how far the ability of all living organisms to reproduce outstrips their capacity to survive. Even the slowest breeding animals, like elephants, would soon fill the world. If every elephant grew to maturity and reproduced naturally, "After a period of from 740 to 750 years," said Darwin, "there would be nearly nineteen million elephants alive, descended from the first pair." From this and other examples, it is deduced that "As more individuals are produced than can possibly survive, there must in every case be a struggle for existence, either one individual with another of the same species, or with the individuals of distinct species, or with the physical conditions of life." There is no exception to the rule that every plant, fish, bird, and animal, including the human race, produces infinitely more seed than will ever be born or could be accommodated in a crowded world. The rate of increase is geometrical.

The interdependence of species is also graphically illustrated. Darwin found that pollination by "humble-bees" is necessary for the fertilization of heartsease flowers and some kinds of clover.

> The number of humble-bees in any district depends in a great measure upon the number of field-mice, which destroy their combs and nests. . . . Now the number of mice is largely dependent, as every one knows, on the number of cats. . . . Hence it is quite credible that the presence of a feline animal in large numbers in a district might determine, through the intervention first of mice and then of bees, the frequency of certain flowers in that district.

The *Origin of Species* proceeds to show how the principle of "natural selection" operates to check population increases. Some individuals in a species will be stronger, can run faster, are more intelligent, more immune to disease, or better able to endure the rigors of climate than their fellows. These will survive and reproduce as the weaker members perish. A white rabbit will survive in Arctic regions, while more conspicuous brown rabbits will be exterminated by foxes and wolves. Long-necked giraffes have survived, because in drought years they were able to reach a food supply at the tops of trees, while the short-necked giraffes starved. These favorable variations insured the survival of the fittest. In the course of many millenniums they led to the creation of essentially new species.

The law of tooth, fang, and claw, as it operates everywhere, was aptly dramatized by Darwin:

> We behold the face of nature bright with gladness, we often see superabundance of food; we do not see, or we forget, that the birds which are idly singing round us mostly live on insects or seeds, and are thus constantly destroying life; or we forget how largely these songsters, or their eggs, or their nestlings, are destroyed by birds and beasts of prey; we do not always bear in mind, that, though now food may be superabundant, it is not so at all seasons of each recurring year.

An important aspect of natural selection, Darwin pointed out, is sexual selection. "Generally, the most vigorous males, those which are best fitted for their places in nature, will leave most progeny. . . . A hornless stag or spurless cock would have a poor chance of leaving numerous offspring." Among birds, "the contest is often of a more peaceful character," as the males of different species seek to attract the females by beautiful singing, gorgeous plumage, or by performing strange antics.

Climate is also a major factor in natural selection, for "seasons of extreme cold or drought seem to be the most effective of all checks. . . . The action of climate seems at first sight to be quite independent of the struggle for existence; but in so far as climate chiefly acts in reducing food, it brings on the most severe struggle between the individuals, whether of the same or of distinct species, which subsist on the same kind of food." Most likely to survive are the vigorous individuals able to withstand heat or cold and most capable of obtaining food.

Darwin wrote:

Natural Selection is daily and hourly scrutinizing, throughout the world, the slightest variations; rejecting those that are bad, preserving and adding up all that are good; silently and insensibly working, *whenever and wherever opportunity offers,* at the improvement of each organic being in relation to its organic and inorganic conditions of life. We see nothing of these slow changes in progress until the hand of time has marked the lapse of ages, and then so imperfect is our view into long-past geological ages, that we see only that the forms of life are now different from what they formerly were.

In his final chapter, Darwin implied that the power of natural selection is virtually without limit, and suggested that one could "infer from analogy that probably all the organic beings which have ever lived on this earth have descended from some one primordial form, into which life was first breathed." All the complex forms of life, he believed, owed their existence to natural laws. He found the results of natural selection inspiring.

Thus from the war of Nature, from famine and death, the most exalted object which we are capable of conceiving, namely the production of the higher animals, directly follows. There is a grandeur in this view of life, with its several powers having been originally breathed by the Creator into a few forms or into one; and that, whilst this planet has gone circling on according to the fixed law of gravity, from so simple a beginning endless forms most beautiful and most wonderful have been, and are being, evolved.

In this fashion was the theory of unending evolution presented by the *Origin of Species.* Contrary to popular belief, however, Darwin did not originate the evolutionary theory. The idea is older than Aristotle and Lucretius. Such brilliant minds as Buffon, Goethe, Erasmus Darwin (Charles' grandfather), Lamarck, and Herbert Spencer had supported the doctrine. Charles Darwin's contribution was notable in two directions. First, he accumulated more indisputable evidence to show the *fact* of evolution than had ever been offered before. Secondly, he advanced his famous theory of natural selection as a reasonable explanation for the *method* of evolution.

The contemporary reception of the *Origin of Species* has been compared to "a conflagration like lightning in a full barn." If the revolutionary new theory were valid, the Biblical story of creation could no longer be accepted. The Church immediately viewed the Darwinian thesis as dangerous to religion, and roused a storm of opposition. Though Darwin had carefully omitted any application of his theory to mankind, the charge was spread that the author had represented men as having descended from monkeys.

Attempts were made to discredit Darwin by ridicule. An article in the *Quarterly Review* called him a "flighty person" attempting, in his book, "to prop up his utterly rotten fabric of guess and speculation," and whose "mode of dealing with nature" was "utterly dishonourable to science." The *Spectator* disliked the theory "because it utterly repudiates final causes and thereby indicates a demoralized understanding on the part of its advocates"; furthermore, Darwin was accused of collecting a mass of facts to substantiate a false principle, and "You cannot make a good rope out of a string of air bubbles." One reviewer asked if it were "credible that all favourable varieties of turnips are tending to become men." Since England had no Inquisition, the *Athenaeum,* in another scathing review, consigned Darwin "to the mercies of the Divinity Hall, the College, the Lecture Room, and the Museum." Darwin's comment on this was: "He would, on no account, burn me, but he would get the wood ready and tell the black beasts how to catch me."

At Darwin's alma mater, Whewell would not permit a copy of the *Origin of Species* to be placed in the Trinity College library at Cambridge.

From fellow-scientists, Darwin won strong support and met bitter opposition. The ultraconservative point of view was represented by such figures as Owen in England and Agassiz in America, both of whom held that the Darwinian ideas were scientific heresy and would soon be forgotten. The astronomer Sir John Herschel described Darwinism as "the law of higgledy-piggledy." Darwin's old geological professor at Cambridge, Sedgwick, held the theory to be "false and grievously mischievous," and wrote Darwin that he had "laughed till his sides ached" at his book, considering it was "machinery as wild as Bishop Wilkins's locomotive that was to sail with us to the moon."

But Darwin was not lacking in stalwart champions. Foremost among these were Charles Lyell, the geologist, Thomas Huxley, biologist, Joseph Hooker, botanist, and Asa Gray, the famous American botanist. Of them all, Darwin leaned most heavily on Huxley, whom he called his "agent general" and who referred to himself as "Darwin's bulldog." Darwin was not a controversialist, and never appeared in public to defend his theories. The brunt of the defense was carried by the able and aggressive Huxley.

It was Huxley who played one of the two leading roles in a dramatic conflict over Darwin's *Origin.* The stage was provided by a meeting of the British Association at Oxford in 1860. Darwinism was the conference theme. The big gun on the opposition side was Bishop Wilberforce of Oxford. At the conclusion of a forceful address which he believed had smashed Darwin's theory, the Bishop turned to Huxley, sitting on the platform. "I should like to ask Professor Huxley," he demanded sarcastically, "is it on his grandfather's or his grandmother's side that the ape ancestry comes in?" In an aside to a friend, Huxley exclaimed, "The Lord hath delivered him into my hands." Rising to reply, Huxley is reported to have said:

A man has no reason to be ashamed of having an ape for his grandfather. If there were an ancestor whom I should feel shame in recalling, it would be a man of restless and versatile intellect, who, not content with success in his own sphere of activity, plunges into scientific questions with which he has no real acquaintance, only to obscure them by an aimless rhetoric, and distract the attention of his hearers from the point at issue by eloquent digressions and skilled appeals to religious prejudice.

This was one of the first of innumerable clashes between church and science on the issue of Darwinism and evolution to rage in the succeeding years.

Darwin's own views on religion were modified as he grew older. As a young man, he had accepted the idea of special creation without question. In his *Life and Letters,* he expressed the belief that "man in the distant future will be a far more perfect creature than he is now."

Darwin added further:

Another source of conviction in the existence of God, connected with the reason, and not with the feelings, impresses me as having much more weight. This follows from the extreme difficulty or rather impossibility of conceiving this immense and wonderful universe, including man, with his capacity of looking far backward and far into futurity, as the result of blind chance or necessity. When thus reflecting I feel compelled to look to a First Cause, having an intelligent mind to some degree analogous to that of man; and I deserve to be called a Theist. This conclusion was strong in my mind about the time,

as far as I can remember, when I wrote the *Origin of
Species;* and it is since that time that it has very gradually, with many fluctuations, become weaker. But then
arises the doubt: Can the mind of man, which has, as I
fully believe, been developed from a mind as low as that
possessed by the lowest animals, be trusted when it draws
such grand conclusions?

Darwin threw up his hands at this point, and ended by
declaring:

I cannot pretend to throw the least light on such abstruse problems. The mystery of the beginning of all
things is insoluble by us; and I for one must be content to
remain an agnostic.

Following the *Origin of Species,* a stream of books flowed
from Darwin's active pen. They dealt with more specialized
topics, but all, in essence, were designed to elaborate, supplement, and substantiate the case for evolution by natural selection—presented comprehensively in the *Origin of Species.*
First came two little volumes entitled *On the Various Con-
trivances by Which Orchids Are Fertilized by Insects* and *The
Movements and Habits of Climbing Plants.* Next appeared
two major works: *The Variation of Animals and Plants under
Domestication* and *The Descent of Man and Selection in Relation to Sex.* Succeeding books were concerned with the expression of emotion in man and animals, insectivorous plants,
the effects of cross-fertilization, the power of movement in
plants, and the formation of vegetable mold.

In the *Origin of Species,* Darwin had intentionally soft-
pedaled any discussion of man's beginnings, because he
thought any emphasis on this phase of evolution would cause
his entire theory to be rejected. In the *Descent of Man,* however, a massive amount of evidence was advanced to demonstrate that the human race is also a product of evolution from
lower forms.

Viewed in retrospect, Darwin's impress on nearly all major
fields of learning was, and continues to be, profound. The doctrine of organic evolution has been accepted by biologists,
geologists, chemists, and physicists, by anthropologists, psy-
chologists, educators, philosophers, and sociologists, and even
by historians, political scientists, and philologists. Charles Ell-
wood declared:

When one reflects upon the immense influence which
Darwin's work has had on practically all lines of human

thought, and especially on the biological, psychological, and social sciences, one is forced to conclude that . . . Darwin must be given the seat of highest honor as the most fructifying thinker which the nineteenth century produced, not only in England, but in the whole world. And the social significance of Darwin's teachings is even yet only beginning to be apprehended.

West concurred, in writing of the *Origin of Species:* "The effect was truly tremendous. Almost by the mere statement of a new principle of approach, dynamic, not static, he revolutionized every department of study, from astronomy to history, from paleontology to psychology, from embryology to religion."

On the other hand, there have been applications of Darwin's theories of which he undoubtedly would have passionately disapproved. An example is fascism's use of the idea of natural selection, or survival of the fittest, to justify the liquidation of certain races. Similarly, wars between nations have been defended as a means of eliminating the weak and perpetuating the strong. Darwinism has been twisted further, by Marxists, to apply to the class struggle. And ruthless business corporations have justified methods of destroying smaller companies on the same grounds.

Because he was an extraordinarily acute observer and experimenter, Darwin's work has stood up well, for the most part, as scientific knowledge has expanded. Even though his theories have been modified by the findings of modern science, Darwin succeeded in foreshadowing in a remarkable fashion the ideas prevailing today in genetics, paleontology, and a variety of other fields.

A masterly summing-up of Darwin's place in the history of science has come from another great biologist, Julian Huxley, grandson of Darwin's coworker, defender, and friend:

> Darwin's work . . . put the world of life into the domain of natural law. It was no longer necessary or possible to imagine that every kind of animal or plant had been specially created, nor that the beautiful and ingenious devices by which they get their food or escape their enemies have been thought out by some supernatural power, or that there is any conscious purpose behind the evolutionary process. If the idea of natural selection holds good, then animals and plants and man himself have become what they are by natural causes, as blind and automatic as those which go to mould the shape

of a mountain, or make the earth and the other planets move in ellipses round the sun. The blind struggle for existence, the blind process of heredity, automatically result in the selection of the best adapted types, and a steady evolution of the stock in the direction of progress. . . .

Darwin's work has enabled us to see the position of man and of our present civilization in a truer light. Man is not a finished product incapable of further progress. He has a long history behind him, and it is a history not of a fall, but of an ascent. And he has the possibility of further progressive evolution before him. Further, in the light of evolution we learn to be more patient. The few thousand years of recorded history are nothing compared to the million years during which man has been on earth, and the thousand million years of life's progress. And we can afford to be patient when the astronomers assure us of at least another thousand million years ahead of us in which to carry evolution onwards to new heights.

15 | PSYCHOLOGIST OF THE UNCONSCIOUS

SIGMUND FREUD:

The Interpretation of Dreams

Of all branches of learning, it is generally conceded that psychology is most mystical and obscure, the least susceptible of scientific proof of any of the sciences. In the nature of things, the elusiveness and unpredictability are inescapable, because the psychologist is dealing with the most mysterious of natural phenomena: the mind of man. A theory in chemistry or physics can be verified or disproved by laboratory techniques, but the validity of a psychological theory may be impossible to demonstrate. Thus the storm of controversy that has raged around Sigmund Freud and psychoanalysis for over sixty years.

But whether demonstrable or not, Freudian theories have exerted an unrivaled influence on modern thought. Not even Einstein has touched the imaginations or permeated the lives of his contemporaries as has Freud. In exploring the unknown regions of the mind, Freud formulated ideas and terms that have now become part of our daily living. Virtually every field of knowledge—literature, art, religion, anthropology, education, law, sociology, criminology, history, biography, and other studies of society and the individual—has felt the effects of his teachings.

There is little, however, of sweetness and light in these teachings. A rather facetious critic has remarked:

> For laymen, as Freud's theories spread, he emerged as the greatest killjoy in the history of human thought, transforming man's jokes and gentle pleasures into dreary and mysterious repressions, discovering hatreds at the root of love, malice at the heart of tenderness, incest in filial affections, guilt in generosity, and the repressed hatred of one's father as a normal human inheritance.

Nevertheless, because of Freud, people think very differently about themselves today. They accept as commonplace such Freudian concepts as the influence of the subconscious on consciousness, the sexual basis of neuroses, the existence and importance of infantile sexuality, the function of dreams, the Oedipus complex, repression, resistance, and transference. Human foibles, like slips of the tongue, forgetting of names, and failure to remember social engagements take on new significance when viewed from a Freudian standpoint. It is now difficult to realize that the prejudices which Freud had to overcome to spread his doctrines were even more intense than those encountered by Copernicus and Darwin.

When Freud was born at Freiberg in Moravia, the *Origin of Species* had not yet appeared. The year was 1856. Like Karl Marx, Freud's ancestors included several rabbis; but unlike Marx, Freud said: "I have remained a Jew." He was taken to Vienna at the age of four, and spent practically all his adult life there. To his father, a wool merchant, he owed, according to his principal biographer, Ernest Jones, his "shrewd scepticism about the uncertain vicissitudes of life, his custom of pointing a moral by quoting a Jewish anecdote, his disbelief in matters of religion." Freud's mother lived to the age of ninety-five, a warm, lively personality. Sigmund was her first-born and favorite son. Later he wrote, "A man who has been the indisputable favorite of his mother keeps for life the feeling of a conqueror, that confidence of success that often induces real success."

In the early years, Freud was strongly attracted by Darwin's theories, for he felt that "they held out hopes of an extraordinary advance in our understanding of the world." Deciding to become a physician, he entered the University of Vienna to study medicine, receiving an M.D. in 1881. As a junior resident physician in the general hospital, he continued his studies in neurology and cerebral anatomy. A few years later came the turn in his fortunes that was eventually to establish his world-wide renown. A traveling fellowship took him to Paris to work under Jean Charcot, then a celebrated French pathologist and neurologist. Here he had his first-hand contact with Charcot's work on hysteria and his treatment of it by hypnotic suggestion. Charcot proved, to Freud's satisfaction, "the genuineness of hysterical phenomena, their frequent occurrence in men, the production of hysterical paralyses and contractures by hypnotic suggestion," and their close similarity in appearance to real attacks.

But back in Vienna, Freud was unable to convince his medical colleagues of any scientific basis for the treatment of nervous disorders by hypnotic methods. He was even punished for his radical ideas by being excluded from the cerebral anatomy laboratory. Henceforth, he was a lonely figure, withdrawn from academic life and ceasing to attend meetings of learned societies. In his private practice of medicine, he continued to experiment with hypnosis for several years, but gradually abandoned it because few people make good subjects and hypnosis sometimes has unfortunate effects on the personality. Instead, Freud began development of the technique termed "free association," ever since a standard psychoanalytic practice.

Freud is, without question, the founder of modern psychiatry. Prior to his time, psychiatry was concerned with such symptoms of insanity as schizophrenia and manic-depressive psychosis, requiring confinement in an institution. Beginning his clinical work with the treatment of repressions and conflicts of neurotics, Freud soon came to the conclusion that such conflicts were not peculiar to neurotics, but were also characteristic of well-adjusted persons. Further, neuroses were not diseases in the accepted sense, but psychological states of mind. The great problem was how to treat these widely prevalent mental disturbances. Upon his observations, experiments, and experience with many Viennese patients, around the turn of the century, Freud built the foundation of psychoanalysis.

Freud was one of the most prolific scientific writers of our time, and the variety of new concepts and psychological contributions which emanated from his pen cannot be found in any single book or paper. In his own eyes, probably the favorite was his earliest major work, *The Interpretation of Dreams,* issued in 1900, which contains nearly all of his fundamental observations and ideas. In an earlier work, *Studies in Hysteria*, 1895, he had indicated his belief that sexual disturbances were the *"essential* factor in the etiology of both neuroses and psychoneuroses"—one of the cornerstones of psychoanalytic theory. Within the next few years, Freud had also worked out his concepts of resistance, transference, childhood sexuality, relationship between unpleasant memories and fantasies, defense mechanisms, and repression.

A brief summary of its principal doctrines will reveal something of the complexity of psychoanalysis. In the first place, psychiatry and psychoanalysis are not synonymous. Psychoanalysis may be considered a subdivision of psychiatry, and is generally applied only to the most difficult cases of personality disturbances. Psychoanalysis, then, can be defined as a therapy in the treatment of nervous and psychic disorders. According to a recent report, a mere 300 of over 4,000 accredited psychiatrists in the United States are psychoanalyists.

Freud was interested only incidentally in individual therapy. The cases of maladjusted individuals, he regarded as but symptoms of the economic, social, and cultural derangements of the contemporary world. His aim was to attack the disease at its source.

Most critics would agree that Freud's claim to enduring fame rests on his discovery and exploration of the unconscious mind. Comparing the human mind to an iceberg, eight-ninths of which is submerged, he held that the mind is mainly hidden in the unconscious. Beneath the surface there are motives, feelings, and purposes which the individual conceals not only from others but even from himself. In Freudian psychology, the unconscious is supreme and conscious activity is reduced to a subordinate position. By coming to understand the profound and unknown depths of the unconscious, we learn the inner nature of man. Most of our thinking, declared Freud, is unconscious and only occasionally becomes conscious. The unconscious mind is the source of neuroses, because the individual tries to banish to that region his disagreeable memories and frustrated wishes, but only succeeds in storing them up for future trouble.

Freud classified mental activity in an individual as being carried on at three levels, which he named the Id, the Ego, and the Superego. Of first importance is the Id. "The domain of the Id," said Freud, "is the dark, inaccessible part of our personality; the little that we know of it we have learned through the study of dreams and of the formation of neurotic symptoms." The Id is the center of primitive instincts and impulses, reaching back to man's animal past, and is animal and sexual in nature. It is unconscious. The Id, continued Freud, "contains everything that is inherited, that is present at birth, that is fixed in the constitution." The Id is blind and ruthless, its sole purpose the gratification of desires and pleasures, without reckoning the consequences. In Thomas Mann's words, "It knows no values, no good or evil, no morality."

The new-born infant is the personification of the Id. Gradually, the Ego develops out of the Id as the child grows older. Instead of being guided entirely by the pleasure principle, the Ego is governed by the reality principle. The Ego is aware of the world around it, recognizing that the lawless tendencies of the Id must be curbed to prevent conflict with the rules of society. As Freud put it, the Ego is the mediator "between the reckless claims of the Id and the checks of the outer world." In effect, therefore, the Ego acts as censor of the Id's urges, adapting them to realistic situations, realizing that avoidance of punishment, or even self-preservation, may depend upon such repressions. Out of conflicts between the Ego and the Id, however, may develop neuroses seriously affecting the individual personality.

Finally, there is the third element in the mental process, the Superego, which may be broadly defined as conscience. The leading Freudian disciple in America, A. A. Brill, wrote:

> The Super-Ego is the highest mental evolution attainable by man, and consists of a precipitate of all prohibitions, all the rules of conduct which are impressed on the child by his parents and parental substitutes. The feeling of *conscience* depends altogether on the development of the Super-Ego.

Like the Id, the Superego is unconscious, and the two are in perpetual conflict, with the Ego acting as referee. Moral ideals and rules of behavior have the Superego as their home.

When the Id, Ego, and Superego are in reasonable harmony, the individual is well adjusted and happy. If the Ego permits the Id to break the rules, however, the Superego causes worry, feelings of guilt, and other manifestations of conscience.

Closely associated with the Id, is another concept originated by Freud: his theory of the *libido*. All the Id's impulses, he taught, are charged with a form of "psychic energy," termed *libido*, primarily sexual in character. The libido theory has been called "the essence of psychoanalytic doctrine." All man's cultural achievements, art, law, religion, etc., are regarded as developments of libido. While referred to as sexual energy, actually the word "sexual" is used in a very broad sense. In infants, it includes such activities as thumb-sucking, bottle-nursing, and excreting. In later years, the libido may be transferred to another person through marriage, take the form of sex perversion, or be expressed through artistic, literary, or musical creation—a process entitled "displacement." The sex instinct, in Freud's opinion, is the greatest source of creative work.

Under the influence of libido, Freud maintained, in perhaps the most controversial of all psychoanalytic theories, the child develops sexual feelings toward its parents. Beginning with its first sensual pleasures derived from feeding at the maternal breast, the infant forms a love attachment for its mother. As he matures, but at an early age, the male child develops strong sexual urges for the mother, while hating and fearing his father as a rival. The female child, on the other hand, may move away from the close relationship with her mother and fall in love with her father, with the mother becoming an object of dislike and rivalry. As applied to the male, this is called the Oedipus complex, named after the ancient Greek mythological figure, who killed his father and married his own mother. The Oedipus complex, Freud said, is a heritage from our primitive ancestors, who killed their fathers in jealous rages. As he reaches maturity, a normal person outgrows the Oedipus impulses. Weak individuals, on the other hand, may never succeed in breaking the parental attachment, and thus are led into a series of neuroses.

In fact, Freud declared, "The neuroses are without exception disturbances of the sexual function." Furthermore, neuroses cannot be blamed upon unsuccessful marriages or unfortunate adult love affairs, but all can be traced back to sex complexes of early childhood. Applying his theory to the field of anthropology, in his book *Totem and Taboo,* Freud concluded that nature and religious myths of primitive man are the product of father and mother complexes. Religion itself, he believed, is merely an expression of the father complex. After detailed analyses of hundreds of cases who came to him for treatment, Freud elevated sexual instinct and sexual desires to a pre-eminent role in the shaping of personality, as well as being the chief cause of neuroses. This is a judgment that has been rejected by some other prominent psychoanalysts, as will be indicated later.

Because he is forced by society to suppress many of his urges, the individual unconsciously accumulates many "repressions," to use Freud's term. Normally, one's consciousness succeeds in preventing the "dark unconscious forces" that have been repressed from again emerging. Neurotic persons, though, may go through periods of deep emotional disturbances because of such censorship. It is the task of psychoanalytic therapy, said Freud, to "uncover repressions and replace them by acts of judgment which might result either in the acceptance or in the rejection of what had formerly been repudiated." Because of the painful nature of the repressed material, the patient usually tries to prevent the uncovering of his repressions. Freud termed these efforts "resistances," which it is the physician's object to overcome.

The technique invented by Freud for dealing with repressions and resistances is the method now known as "free association"—stream-of-consciousness talk by a patient reclining on the psychoanalyst's couch, in a dimly lighted room. The patient is encouraged "to say whatever comes into his head, while ceasing to give any conscious direction to his thoughts." It was claimed by Freud that the method of free association is the only effective way of treating neurosis, and that it "achieved what was expected of it, namely the bringing into consciousness of the repressed material which was held back by resistances." As Brill described Freud's procedure with patients, "He persuaded them to give up all conscious reflection, abandon themselves to calm concentration, follow their spontaneous mental occurrences, and impart everything to him. In this way he finally obtained those *free associations* which lead to the origin of the symptoms." The forgotten material, dredged up by the subject out of his unconscious, after perhaps months of psychoanalytical treatment, usually represents something painful, disagreeable, frightening, or otherwise obnoxious out of his past, matters he dislikes to remember consciously.

Inevitably, in such a process, the rambling reminiscences produce a mass of diffuse, irrelevant, and apparently useless data. Everything, therefore, depends upon the ability of the physician to psychoanalyze his material, which, as various critics have pointed out, can be interpreted in an almost infinite number of ways. The intelligence and skill of the psychoanalyst, therefore, are of basic significance.

In the course of psychoanalytic treatment of patients, Freud discovered what he called "a factor of undreamt-of importance," an intense emotional relationship between the subject and the analyst. This is called "transference."

> The patient is not satisfied with regarding the analyst in the light of reality as a helper and adviser . . . on the contrary, the patient sees in his analyst the return—the reincarnation—of some important figure out of his child-

hood or past, and consequently transfers on to him feelings and reactions that undoubtedly applied to this model.

The transference "can vary between the extremes of a passionate, completely sensual love and the unbridled expression of an embittered defiance and hatred." In this situation, the analyst, "as a rule, is put in the place of one or other of the patient's parents, his father or his mother." The fact of transference, Freud regarded as "the best instrument of the analytic treatment," but "nevertheless its handling remains the most difficult as well as the most important part of the technique of analysis." The problem "is resolved," stated Freud, "by convincing the patient that he is re-experiencing emotional relations which had their origin in early childhood."

Another fruitful device for probing into inner conflicts and emotions developed by Freud was the analysis of dreams. Here again Freud was a pioneer. Before his time, dreams were regarded as without meaning or purpose. His *The Interpretation of Dreams* was the first attempt at a serious scientific study of the phenomenon. Thirty-one years after publication of the book, Freud remarked that "It contains, even according to my present-day judgment, the most valuable of all the discoveries it has been my good fortune to make." According to Freud, "We are justified in asserting that a dream is the disguised fulfillment of a repressed wish." Each dream represents a drama in the inner world. "Dreams are invariably the product of a conflict," stated Freud, and "The dream is the guardian of sleep." Its function is to aid rather than disturb sleep, releasing tensions that come from unattainable wishes.

The dream world, in the Freudian view, is dominated by the unconscious, by the Id, and dreams are important to the psychoanalyst because they lead him into the patient's unconscious. In the unconscious are all the primitive wishes and emotional desires suppressed from conscious life by the Ego and Superego. The animal desires are always present under the surface, and force themselves forward in dreams. Even in sleep, however, the Ego and Superego stand on guard as censors. For that reason, the meanings of dreams are not always clear, they are expressed in symbols, and require expert interpretation. As symbols, they cannot be taken literally, except perhaps in the simple dreams of children. *The Interpretation of Dreams* offers numerous examples of dreams psychoanalyzed by Freud.

Likewise indicative of the workings of the unconscious are misspellings, slips of the tongue, and odd tricks of absentmindedness. "In the same way that psychoanalysis makes use of dream-interpretation," said Freud, "it also profits by the numerous little slips and mistakes which people make—symptomatic actions, as they are called." The subject was investigated by Freud in 1904 in his *The Psychopathology of Everyday Life*. In this work, he maintained that "these phenomena are not accidental . . . they have a meaning and can be interpreted, and one is justified in inferring from them the presence of restrained or repressed impulses and intentions." To forget a name may mean that one dislikes the person with that name. If a man misses his train because of confusion over schedules, it may indicate he did not desire to catch it. A husband who loses or forgets his house key may be unhappy at home and not desire to return. A study of such blunders can lead the psychoanalyst into the mazes of the unconscious mind.

The same release is obtained with jokes, which Freud termed "the best safety valve modern man has evolved," for through them we are temporarily freed of repressions that polite society otherwise requires us to keep hidden.

Perhaps because of premonitions, increasing disillusionment, or extreme pessimism, toward the end of his life, Freud became preoccupied with the "death instinct." Eventually, he came to regard this conception as almost on a par in importance with the sexual instinct. Freud held that there is a death instinct driving all living matter to return to the inorganic state from which it came. According to this view, man is constantly torn between the urge to life, that is the sexual instinct, and a counter force, the urge to annihilation, or the death instinct. In the end, of course, the death instinct wins out. The instinct is responsible for war, and for such examples of sadism as prejudice against races and classes, the vicarious enjoyment of criminal trials, bullfighting, and lynching.

The foregoing, in brief, are the principal facets of Freudian theory. Present-day psychiatrists are split into two or more opposing camps, pro and anti Freud. Even his disciples have modified their full acceptance of the theories over the past fifty years. One of the early followers, Alfred Adler, seceded from the Freudian camp because he believed that Freud had overemphasized the sexual instincts. As an alternative doctrine, Adler taught that every man's desire to prove his superiority is the mainspring in human behavior. He developed the idea of an "inferiority complex" which impels the individual to strive for recognition in some activity. Another famous secessionist was Karl Jung, of Zurich, who also tried to minimize the role of sex. Jung divided mankind into two psychological types: extroverts and introverts, though he recognized that every individual is a mixture of the two. Unlike Freud, Jung emphasized hereditary factors in the development of personality. In general, Freud's critics part company with him on such issues as his insistence on the prime significance of childhood neuroses, his conviction that men are controlled by primeval, rigid instincts, and on his elevating the libido or sexual energy to a central place in the formation of personality. Some disagree with Freud also in his belief that free association is an infallible technique for exploring the unconscious, pointing out most particularly the difficulties in interpreting data produced by that method.

Nevertheless, as one psychiatrist observed:

> The changes and developments of sixty years have in no way diminished Freud's stature or influence. He opened up the realm of the unconscious. He showed how it helps to make us what we are and how to reach it. Many of his ideas and concepts have had to be modified by his successors in the light of further experience. You might say that they have been writing a New Testament for psychiatry. But Sigmund Freud wrote the Old Testament. His work will remain basic.

Much of our modern attitude toward insanity we owe to Freud. There is an increasing tendency to suggest that "Neurotics and psychotics are just like ourselves, only more so." Alexander Reid Martin stressed that "Whether acknowledged or not, all psychiatric and psychotherapeutic hospitals today utilize elements and fundamentals of Freudian psychology. What formerly was regarded as an unknown world, forbidding, grotesque, purposeless and meaningless, through Freud became enlightened and charged with meaning, attracting the interest and recognition not only of medicine, but of all the social sciences."

The impact of Freudian thought on literature and art has been equally noticeable. In fiction, poetry, drama, and other literary forms, Freudian motifs have flourished in recent years. Bernard De Voto has expressed the opinion that "no other scientist has ever had so strong and so widespread an influence on literature." The effect on painting, sculpture, and the world of art in general has been no less profound.

To sum up the manifold contribution of Freud's genius is difficult because of the breadth of his interests and the controversial nature of his findings. One attempt was made by an English writer, Robert Hamilton, whose conclusion was this:

Freud put psychology on the map. He was a great pioneer and much of his success was due to his originality and literary style. In spite of its nihilistic character, there has never been a system more interesting and original, nor, outside pure literature, a more attractive style. He made the world think psychologically—an essential need for our time; and he forced men to ask themselves questions vital to human welfare. Out of the thesis of the sterile academic psychology of the nineteenth century he brought the antithesis of psycho-analysis with its dark negations.

A noted American psychiatrist, Frederic Wertham, stated the case from another point of view:

One should make clear that, aside from the host of new clinical facts about patients that he observed, Freud brought about three fundamental changes in the approach to the study of personality and mental pathology. The first was to speak of psychological processes at all, and to think of them with the logic of natural science. This became possible only when Freud introduced the realistic concept of the unconscious and practical methods for its investigation. The second was his introduction of a new dimension into psychopathology: childhood. Before Freud, psychiatry was practiced as if every patient was Adam—who never was a child. The third was his inauguration of the genetic understanding of the sexual instinct. His real discovery here was not so much that children have a sex life, but that the sexual instinct has a childhood.

A similar judgment was expressed by A. G. Tansley, in an obituary prepared for the Royal Society of London:

The revolutionary nature of Freud's conclusions becomes intelligible when we remember that he was investigating an entirely unexplored field, a region of the human mind into which no one had penetrated before, and whose overt manifestations had been regarded as inexplicable or as degenerative aberrations, or had been ignored because they lay under the strongest human taboos. The very existence of this field was unrecognized. Freud was forced to assume the reality of an unconscious region of the mind, and then to attempt to explore it, by the apparent discontinuities in the chains of conscious mental events.

Finally, Winfred Overholser suggests that "There is every reason to think that one hundred years hence Freud will be classed with Copernicus and Newton as one of the men who opened up new vistas of thought. Certain it is that in our time no man has cast so much light upon the workings of the mind of man as Freud."

The last months of Freud's long lifetime were spent in exile. Following the Nazi occupation of Austria, he was forced to leave Vienna in 1938. England granted him asylum, but cancer of the mouth caused his death in September 1939, a little more than a year later.

16 GODFATHER OF THE ATOMIC AGE

ALBERT EINSTEIN:

Relativity, the Special and General Theories

Albert Einstein is one of the rare figures in history who succeeded in becoming a legend of heroic proportions during his own lifetime. The more incomprehensible to the lay public his ideas appeared, the more its curiosity was whetted, and the more it saw him as speaking from some remote Olympian height. As Bertrand Russell aptly remarked, "Everybody knows that Einstein has done something astonishing, but very few people know exactly what it is that he has done." To be told, though inaccurately, that there are scarely a dozen men in the entire world who fully grasp Einstein's theories of the universe, challenges and intrigues thousands, if not millions, who thereupon resolve to attempt to understand what the great mathematical wizard is saying.

Einstein's incomprehensibility stems from the extraordinarily complex nature of his field of operation. An unnamed English scientist, quoted by T. E. Bridges, stated the situation as follows:

> This [Einstein's] doctrine has to do with the relationship between physical and mathematical events and can therefore be explained only in mathematical terms. It is impossible to present it in any form which can be understood by those who have not a fairly advanced knowledge of algebra.

A similar point of view was expressed by George W. Gray:

Inasmuch as the theory of relativity is presented by its author in mathematical language, and in strictness of speaking cannot be expressed in any other, there is a certain presumption in every attempt to translate it into the vernacular. One might as well try to interpret Beethoven's Fifth Symphony on a saxophone.

Nevertheless, perhaps certain features of the Einstein cosmos can be suggested without resort to mathematical symbolism. And a fantastic world it is, extremely upsetting to ideas firmly established for centuries, "a strange pudding for the layman to digest." We are asked, for example, to accept such incredible conceptions as these: space is curved, the shortest distance between two points is not a straight line, the universe is finite but unbounded, parallel lines eventually meet, light rays are curved, time is relative and cannot be measured in exactly the same way everywhere, measurements of length vary with speed, the universe is cylindrical instead of spherical in shape, a body in motion will contract in size but increase in mass, and a fourth dimension—time—is added to the familiar three of height, length, and width.

Though Einstein's contributions to science have been innumerable, his fame rests primarily upon the theory of relativity, an achievement which, Banesh Hoffman concluded, "has a monumental quality that places its author among the truly great scientists of all time, in the select company of Isaac Newton and Archimedes. With its fascinating paradoxes and spectacular successes it fired the imagination of the public."

The Einstein revolution began in 1905, with the appearance in a German journal, *Annalen der Physik,* of a thirty-page paper carrying the unexciting title "On the Electrodynamics of Moving Bodies." At the time, Einstein was only twenty-six years of age, and serving as a minor official in the Swiss patent office. He had been born into a middle-class Jewish family at Ulm, Bavaria, in 1879. As a student, he was not precocious except in mathematics, a field in which he displayed early evidences of genius. Because of failure of the family fortune, Einstein was forced out on his own at fifteen. Emigrating to Switzerland, he was able to continue his scientific education at the Polytechnic Academy in Zurich, married a fellow student, and became a Swiss citizen. Denied his ambition for a university professorship, in order to earn a living he settled in a job making preliminary reports and rewriting inventors' applications for the patent office. His spare time was used for intensive study of the works of philosophers, scientists, and mathematicians. Soon he was ready to launch the first of a flood of original contributions to science, destined to have far-ranging repercussions.

In his 1905 paper, Einstein set forth the Special Theory of Relativity, challenging man's existing concepts of time and space, of matter and energy. The foundations for the theory were laid down in two basic assumptions. The first was the principle of relativity: all motion is relative. A familiar illustration of the principle is a moving train or ship. A person sitting in a train with darkened windows would have, if there was little commotion, no idea of speed or direction, or perhaps even that the train was moving at all. A man on a ship with portholes closed would be in a similar predicament. We conceive motion only in relative terms, that is in respect to other objects. On a vastly greater scale, the forward movement of the earth could not be detected if there were no heavenly bodies for comparisons.

Einstein's second major hypothesis was that the velocity of light is independent of the motion of its source. The speed of light, 186,000 miles a second, is always the same, anywhere in the universe, regardless of place, time or direction. Light travels in a moving train, for instance, at exactly the same speed as it does outside the train. No force can make it go faster or slower. Furthermore, nothing can exceed the velocity of light, though electrons closely approximate it. Light is, in fact, the only constant, unvarying factor in all of nature.

A famous experiment carried out by two American scientists, Michelson and Morley, in 1887, furnished the basis for Einstein's theory on light. To measure the speed of light with absolute exactness, an ingenious apparatus was built. Two pipes, each a mile in length, were placed at right angles to each other. One pipe was pointed in the direction of the earth's journey around the sun, and the second against the direction of the earth's motion. At the end of each pipe a mirror was placed and a beam of light shot into both pipes at exactly the same instant. If the theory then prevailing was true, that an invisible ether filled all space not occupied by solid objects, one ray of light would have been analogous to a swimmer crossing against the current, while the other was comparable to a swimmer going down stream. To the astonishment and mystification of the scientists, however, the two beams of light came back together, at the same identical moment. The experiment was considered a failure.

Einstein's paper in 1905 answered the question which had puzzled Michelson, Morley, and their fellow physicists. The existence of ether was rejected, and the experiment with the pipes had actually measured the speed of light correctly. The essential point deduced by Einstein was that light always travels at the same velocity no matter under what conditions it is measured, and the motion of the earth in regard to the sun has no influence upon the speed of light.

Differing with Newton's teachings, Einstein asserted that there is no such thing as absolute motion. The idea of absolute motion of a body in space is meaningless. Every body's movement is relative to that of another. Motion is the natural state of all things. Nowhere on earth or in the universe is there anything absolutely at rest. Throughout our restless cosmos, movement is constant, from the infinitesimally small atom to the largest celestial galaxies. For example, the earth is moving around the sun at the rate of twenty miles a second. In a universe where all is motion and fixed points of reference are lacking, there are no established standards for comparing velocities, length, size, mass, and time, except as they might be measured by relative motions. Only light is not relative, its velocity remaining changeless regardless of its source or the observer's position, as the Michelson-Morley experiment demonstrated.

Doubtless the most difficult of all Einsteinian concepts to comprehend and the most unsettling to traditional beliefs is the relativity of time. Einstein held that events at different places occurring at the same moment for one observer do not occur at the same moment for another observer moving relatively to the first. For example, two events judged as taking place at the same time by an observer on the ground are not simultaneous for an observer in a train or an airplane. Time is relative to the position and speed of the observer, and is not absolute. Applying the theory to the universe, an event on a distant star, say an explosion, witnessed by an earth dweller, did not occur on the star at the same time as it was seen on the earth. On the contrary, though light moves at 186,000 miles a second, an occurrence on a remote star may have taken place years before news of it reached our world. The star seen today is actually the star as it appeared long ago. Conceivably it may have even ceased to exist.

If it were possible to conceive of a human being attaining speed greater than the velocity of light, according to the theory of relativity, he could overtake his past and his birth would occur in the future. Every moving planet has its own system of time, varying from time schedules found elsewhere. A day on our planet is merely the period required for the earth to rotate on its axis. Since Jupiter takes more time in its revolution around the sun than does the earth, a year on Jupiter is longer than the earth's year. As speed increases, time slows down. We are accustomed to the thought that every physical object has three dimensions, but time, maintains Einstein, is also a dimension of space, and space is a dimension of time. Neither time nor space can exist without the other and they are, therefore, interdependent. Because movement and change are constant, we live in a four-dimensional universe, with time as the fourth dimension.

Thus the two basic premises of Einstein's theory, as first presented a half-century ago, were the relativity of all motions and the concept of light as the only unvarying quantity in the universe.

In developing the principle of relativity of motion, Einstein upset another firmly established belief. Previously, length and mass had been regarded as absolute and constant under every conceivable circumstance. Now, Einstein came along to state that the mass or weight of an object and its length depend on how fast the body is moving. As an example, he imagined a train one thousand feet long, traveling at four-fifths of the speed of light. To a stationary observer, watching it pass by, the length of the train would be reduced to only six hundred feet, though it would remain a thousand feet to a passenger on the train. Similarly, any material body traveling through space contracts according to velocity. A yardstick, if it could be shot through space at 161,000 miles per second would shrink to a half-yard. The rotation of the earth has the curious effect of diminishing its circumference by about three inches.

Mass, too is changeable. As velocity increases, the mass of an object becomes greater. Experiments have shown that particles of matter speeded up to eighty-six per cent of the speed of light weigh twice as much as they do when at rest. That fact had tremendous implications for the development of atomic energy.

Einstein's original statement of 1905 is known as the Special Theory of Relativity because its conclusions are limited to uniform motion in a straight line, and are not concerned with other kinds of motion. In our cosmos, however, stars, planets, and other celestial bodies seldom move uniformly in a straight line. Any theory, therefore, which fails to include every type of motion offers an incomplete description of the universe. Einstein's next step, accordingly, was the formulation of his General Theory of Relativity, a process which required ten years of intensive application. In the General Theory, Einstein studied the mysterious force that guides the movements

of the stars, comets, meteors, galaxies, and other bodies whirling around in the vast universe.

In his General Theory of Relativity, published in 1915,
Einstein advanced a new concept of gravitation, making fundamental changes in the ideas of gravity and light which had
been generally accepted since the time of Sir Isaac Newton.
Gravity had been regarded by Newton as a "force." Einstein
proved, however, that the space around a planet or other
celestial body is a gravitational field similar to the magnetic
field around a magnet. Tremendous bodies, such as the sun
or stars, are surrounded by enormous gravitational fields. The
earth's attraction for the moon is thus explained. The theory
also explained the erratic movements of Mercury, the planet
nearest the sun, a phenomenon that had puzzled astronomers
for centuries and had not been adequately covered by Newton's law of gravitation. So powerful are the great gravitational
fields that they even bend rays of light. In 1919, a few years
after the General Theory was first announced, photographs
taken of a complete eclipse of the sun conclusively demonstrated the validity of Einstein's theory that light rays passing
through the sun's gravitational field travel in curves rather
than in straight lines.

There followed from this premise a statement by Einstein
that space is curved. Revolving planets follow the shortest possible routes, influenced by the sun's presence, just as a river
flowing toward the sea follows the contour of the land, along
the easiest and most natural course. In our terrestrial scheme
of things, a ship or airplane crossing the ocean follows a
curved line, that is the arc of a circle, and not a straight line.
It is evident, therefore, that the shortest distance between
two points is a curve instead of a straight line. An identical
rule governs the movements of a planet or light ray.

If Einstein's theory of curved space is accepted, a logical
deduction is that space is finite. A light ray from a star, for
example, eventually returns, after hundreds of millions of
years, to the point from which it emanated, like a traveler who
circumnavigates the earth. The universe does not extend for-
ever into space, but has finite limitations, though no definite
boundaries can be established.

Of all the great scientific discoveries and findings coming
from Einstein, his contributions to atomic theory have had the
most direct and profound effect on the present-day world.
Shortly after his first paper on relativity was published in 1905,
in the *Annalen der Physik*, the same journal carried a short
article by Einstein projecting his theory further. It was entitled "Does the Inertia of a Body Depend on Its Energy?"

The use of atomic energy, declared Einstein, is possible—at least in principle. The release of this tremendous force could be achieved according to a formula which he offered, the most celebrated equation in history: $E = mc^2$. To interpret, energy equals mass multiplied by the speed of light and again by the speed of light. If all the energy in a half pound of any matter could be utilized, Einstein held, enough power would be released to equal the explosive force of seven million tons of TNT. Without Einstein's equation, as one commentator pointed out, "experimenters might still have stumbled upon the fission of uranium, but it is doubtful if they would have realized its significance in terms of energy, or of bombs."

In the famous equation $E = mc^2$, Einstein demonstrated that energy and mass are the same thing, differing only in state. Mass is actually concentrated energy. The formula, wrote Barnett in a brilliant evaluation, "provides the answer to many of the long-standing mysteries of physics. It explains how radioactive substances like radium and uranium are able to eject particles at enormous velocities and to go on doing so for millions of years. It explains how the sun and all the stars can go on radiating light and heat for billions of years, for if our sun were being consumed by ordinary processes of combustion the earth would have died in frozen darkness eons ago. It reveals the magnitude of the energy that slumbers in the nuclei of atoms, and forecasts how many grams of uranium must go into a bomb in order to destroy a city."

Einstein's equation remained a theory until 1939. By that time, its author had become a resident, and was shortly to become a citizen, of the United States, for he had been driven out of Europe by the Nazis. Learning that the Germans were engaged in importing uranium and were carrying on research on an atomic bomb, Einstein wrote President Roosevelt a highly confidential letter:

> Some recent work by E. Fermi and L. Szilard which has been communicated to me in manuscript, leads me to expect that the element uranium may be turned into a new and important source of energy in the immediate future. . . . This new phenomenon would also lead to the construction of bombs, and it is conceivable . . . that . . . a single bomb of this type, carried by boat and exploded in a port, might very well destroy the whole port together with some of the surrounding territory.

As an immediate result of Einstein's letter to Roosevelt, construction of the Manhattan atom-bomb project was started.

About five years later, the first bomb was exploded at the Almagordo Reservation in New Mexico, and shortly thereafter the dreadful destruction caused by a bomb dropped on Hiroshima was instrumental in bringing the war with Japan to a quick end.

Though the atomic bomb was the most spectacular of all practical applications of Einstein's theories, his fame was also established by another remarkable accomplishment. Almost simultaneously with his Special Theory of Relativity in 1905, there was developed Einstein's Photoelectric Law, explaining the mysterious photoelectric effect, paving the way for the coming of television, motion-picture sound tracks, and the "electric eye," with its varied uses. It was for this discovery that Einstein was awarded the Nobel Prize in physics in 1922.

In his later years, Einstein labored indefatigably on what is known as the Unified Field Theory, attempting to demonstrate the harmony and uniformity of nature. According to his view, physical laws for the minute atom should be equally applicable to immense celestial bodies. The Unified Field Theory would unite all physical phenomena into a single scheme. Gravitation, electricity, magnetism, and atomic energy are all forces that would be covered by the one theory. In 1950, after more than a generation of research, Einstein presented such a theory to the world. He expressed the belief that the theory holds the key to the universe, unifying in one concept the infinitesimal, whirling world of the atom and the vast reaches of star-filled space. Because of mathematical difficulties, the theory has not yet been fully checked against established facts in physics. Einstein had unshaken faith, however, that his Unified Field Theory would in time produce an explanation of the "atomic character of energy," and demonstrate the existence of a well-ordered universe.

The philosophy which inspired and guided Einstein through decades of intense intellectual effort, and the rewards thereof, were described by him in a lecture on the origins of the General Theory of Relativity, at the University of Glasgow in 1933.

The final results appear almost simple; any intelligent undergraduate can understand them without much trouble. But the years of searching in the dark for a truth that one feels, but cannot express; the intense desire and the alternations of confidence and misgiving, until one breaks through to clarity and understanding, are only known to him who has himself experienced them.

On another occasion, Einstein gave evidence of the deeply spiritual side of his nature by this statement:

> The most beautiful and most profound emotion we can experience is the sensation of the mystical. It is the sower of all true science. He to whom this emotion is a stranger, who can no longer wonder and stand rapt in awe, is as good as dead. To know that what is impenetrable to us really exists, manifesting itself as the highest wisdom and the most radiant beauty which our dull faculties can comprehend only in their most primitive forms—this knowledge, this feeling is at the center of true religiousness.

Innumerable scientists have paid tribute to Einstein. Quotations from two recent reviews of his career will illustrate his unique hold on the scientific world. Paul Oehser wrote:

> Influence is a weak word for the work of Albert Einstein. The theories he advanced were revolutionary. In them was born the Atomic Age, and where it leads mankind we know not. But we do know that here is the greatest scientist and philosopher of our century, who has become almost a saint in our eyes and whose achievement is a justification of our faith in the human mind, a symbol of man's eternal quest, his reaching for the stars.

Another scientist, Banesh Hoffman, concluded:

> The importance of Einstein's scientific ideas does not reside merely in their great success. Equally powerful has been their psychological effect. At a crucial epoch in the history of science Einstein demonstrated that long-accepted ideas were not in any way sacred. And it was this more than anything else that freed the imaginations of men like Bohr and de Broglie and inspired their daring triumphs in the realm of the quantum. Wherever we look, the physics of the 20th century bears the indelible imprint of Einstein's genius.

Bibliographical Notes

COPERNICUS, NICHOLAUS (1473-1543)

De Revolutionibus Orbium Coelestium. Nuremberg: 1543. 196 ff. The first accurate and complete edition was published in 1873, at Thorn (Torun), Poland, by the Copernicus-Verein für Wissenschaft und Kunst. What may be the only complete translation into English was reproduced from typewritten copy by the St. John's Bookstore, Annapolis, Maryland, 1939. Another basic document was issued by the Columbia University Press, in 1939, under the title *Three Copernican Treatises: The Commentariolus of Copernicus, the Letter Against Werner, the Narratio Prima of Rheticus.*

DARWIN, CHARLES (1809-1882)

On the Origin of Species By Means of Natural Selection, or, the Preservation of Favoured Races in the Struggle for Life. London: J. Murray, 1859. 502 pp.

EINSTEIN, ALBERT (1879-1955)

Relativity, the Special and General Theory. New York: Holt, 1920. 168 pp. Translated from the original German edition of 1916. The 15th edition, incorporating Einstein's more recent thought, was published in 1954.

FREUD, SIGMUND (1856-1939)

Die Traumdeutung. Leipzig: F. Deuticke, 1900. 375 pp. Translated by A. A. Brill as *The Interpretation of Dreams.* New York: Macmillan, 1913. Major complementary works by Freud include *Studies in Hysteria* (1895), *Psychopathology of Everyday Life* (1904), *Introductory Lectures on Psychoanalysis* (1909), *Totem and Taboo* (1913), *Wit and Its Relation to the Unconscious* (1916), and *Ego and the Id* (1923).

HARVEY, WILLIAM (1578-1657)

Exercitatio Anatomica de Motu Cordis et Sanguinis in Animalibus. Frankfort: 1628. 72 pp. First English translation, 1653. The best modern translation is by Chauncey D. Leake, 1928.

HITLER, ADOLF (1889-1945)

Mein Kampf. Munich: F. Eher, 1925-27. 2 vols. The English translation published by Houghton Mifflin in 1943 follows the first German edition.

MACHIAVELLI, NICCOLÓ (1469-1527)

Il Principe. Rome: Antonio Blado, 1532. 49 pp. The first English translation of *The Prince* was printed in London, 1640. Modern translations are numerous. The companion work, the *Discorsi,* was printed in 1531, also by Blado, and the first English version appeared in 1636.

MACKINDER, HALFORD JOHN (1861-1947)

"The Geographical Pivot of History," Proceedings of the Royal Geographical Society, 25 January 1904. *Geographical Journal,* vol. 23 (1904), pp. 421-37. Reprinted, together with the author's *The Scope and Methods of Geography*, London: Royal Geographical Society, 1951. 44 pp. The later, more definitive work, *Democratic Ideals and Reality*, was published in 1919, by Constable & Co. Ltd., London. 272 pp.

MAHAN, ALFRED THAYER (1840-1914)

The Influence of Sea Power Upon History, 1660-1783. Boston: Little, Brown, 1890. 557 pp. Supplementing this work were Mahan's *The Influence of Sea Power Upon the French Revolution and Empire, 1793-1812* (1892), and *Sea Power in Its Relation to the War of 1812* (1905).

MALTHUS, THOMAS ROBERT (1766-1834)

An Essay on the Principle of Population, as It Affects the Future Improvement of Society, with Remarks on the Speculations of Mr. Godwin, M. Condorcet, and Other Writers. London: Printed for J. Johnson, 1798. 396 pp. Other editions, revised and enlarged, printed in the author's lifetime were the 2nd (1803), 3rd (1806), 4th (1807), 5th (1817), and 6th (1826).

MARX, KARL (1818-1883)

Das Kapital; Kritik der Politischen Oekonomie. Hamburg: O. Meissner, 1867. Volume I. 784 pp. First translated into English, 1886. The second and third volumes, edited by Friedrich Engels, were published 1885-94, and a fourth, edited by Karl Kautsky, was issued 1905-10.

NEWTON, ISAAC (1642-1727)

Philosophiae Naturalis Principia Mathematica. London: 1687. 510 pp. First English translation, 1729, by Andrew Motte. Several modern translations.

PAINE, THOMAS (1737-1809)

Common Sense. Addressed to the Inhabitants of America. Philadelphia: Printed by R. Bell, 1776. 79 pp. Innumerable other contemporary and later editions.

SMITH, ADAM (1723-1790)

An Inquiry Into the Nature and Causes of the Wealth of Nations. London: W. Strahan and T. Cadell, 1776. 2 vols. Many subsequent editions.

STOWE, HARRIET BEECHER (1812-1896)

Uncle Tom's Cabin; or Life Among the Lowly, Boston: J. P. Jewett. 1852. 2 vols. First published serially in the *National Era*, June 5, 1851-April 1, 1852.

THOREAU, HENRY DAVID (1817-1862)

"Resistance to Civil Government." In: *Aesthetic Papers*, edited by Elizabeth P. Peabody (Boston, 1849), pp. 189-211. Later called "Civil Disobedience" and "On the Duty of Civil Disobedience." Reprinted frequently in separate form, e.g., New Haven: Rollins, 1828; London: Simple Life Press, 1903; and London: Peace Pledge Union, 1943.

Index